Lord Kames

Selected Writings

Edited and Introduced
By Andreas Rahmatian

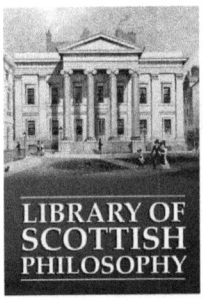

Copyright © Andreas Rahmatian, 2017

The moral rights of the author have been asserted.
No part of this publication may be reproduced in any form
without permission, except for the quotation of brief passages
in criticism and discussion.

Published in the UK by Imprint Academic
PO Box 200, Exeter EX5 5YX, UK

Distributed in the USA by
Ingram Book Company,
One Ingram Blvd., La Vergne, TN 37086, USA

ISBN 9781845409128

A CIP catalogue record for this book is available from the
British Library and US Library of Congress

Full series details:

www.imprint-academic.com/losp

Contents

Series Editor Note	v
Introduction	1
I. Aesthetics and Rhetoric	**14**
1. Definitions; Aesthetics	14
a) External and Internal Sense	14
b) Perception, Sensation and Conception	15
c) Emotions and Passions	16
d) Intrinsic and Relative Beauty	19
2. Rhetoric	21
a) External Signs of Emotions and Passions	21
b) Sentiments	31
c) Tropes and Figures	37
3. Standards of Taste	55
II. Philosophical History	**65**
1. Progress and Stage Theory of Human Society	65
a) Definition of Conjectural History	65
b) Examples of Conjectural History: General	66
c) Conjectural Progress of the Political System	71
d) Conjectural History in relation to Criminal Law	79
e) Conjectural History in relation to Contractual Obligations	82
f) Conjectural History in relation to Property	83
2. Origin of Men and Human Races	90
3. Development of Reasoning	102
4. Progress of Religion and Worshipping	111

III. Moral Philosophy and Legal Philosophy 119

    1. Reasoning: Principles 119
    2. Moral Sense, Duty and Justice 130
    3. Liberty and Necessity 140
    4. Causation 157
    5. Application of Moral Philosophy in the Law:
       Contract, Tort and Crime 161
    6. Legal History and Legal Science 173

IV. Property and Equity **177**

    1. Concept of Property 177
    2. Abolition of Feudalism 181
    3. Equity 191

V. Enlightened Improvement of Society **209**

    1. Progress of Commerce 209
    2. Progress of Flax-Husbandry in Scotland 225

Index of Names **241**

Series Editor's Note

Volumes in this series do not aim to provide scholars with accurate editions, but to make the writings of Scottish philosophers accessible to a new generation of modern readers in an attractively produced and competitively priced format. In accordance with this purpose, certain changes have been made to the original texts:
- Spelling and punctuation have been modernized.
- In some cases the selections have been given new titles.
- Some original footnotes and references have not been included.
- Some extracts have been shortened from their original length.
- Quotations from Greek have been transliterated, and passages in languages other than English translated, or omitted altogether.

Care has been taken to ensure that in no instance do these amendments truncate the argument or alter the meaning intended by the original author. For readers who want to consult the original texts, full bibliographical details are provided for each extract.

The first six volumes of *The Library of Scottish Philosophy* were published in 2004 and commissioned with financial support from the Carnegie Trust for the Universities of Scotland. Subsequent volumes have been published under the auspices of the Center for Scottish Philosophy at Princeton Theological Seminary. This volume of *Selections from Henry Home, Lord Kames* is the eighteenth volume in the series. Portions of the text were prepared for publication by

Christopher Choi, to whom a special debt of gratitude is owed.

The CSSP gratefully acknowledges financial support from the Carnegie Trust and Princeton Theological Seminary, the enthusiasm and excellent service of the publisher Imprint Academic, and the permission of the University of Aberdeen Special Collections and Libraries to use the engraving of the Faculty of Advocates (1829) as the logo for the series.

Gordon Graham,
Princeton, August 2016

Andreas Rahmatian

Introduction

1. Lord Kames's Life and Works

The judge, jurist and philosopher, Lord Kames, a central figure in the Scottish Enlightenment, was born as Henry Home[1] on the estate of Kames in Eccles (Berwickshire, Scottish Borders) in 1696. We know little about his earlier life; most information we have is what he told James Boswell as an old man. Henry Home was educated at home and did not attend university. This fact not only indicates his father's limited financial means, but also characterizes Kames's later career as an advocate and, especially, a man of letters. Since he was mostly self-taught, which was not unusual in the eighteenth century, it may explain why his interest in all disciplines—aesthetics, moral philosophy, law, legal history and theory, sociology, anthropology, agriculture, economics and even physics—never became more confined. He felt no need to specialize because he was, and wanted to be, a polymath. In contrast to our times, he regarded overspecialization as perilous, particularly for those who aim to serve their country in public offices. 'I venture to pronounce, that no man ever did, nor ever will, make a capital figure in the government of a state, whether as a judge, a general, or a minister, whose education is rigidly confined to one science.'[2] Kames cannot be said to have excelled in the various sub-disciplines he worked on, but his attempt at combining these to arrive at a universal understanding of the world and its appearances was outstanding, and among the jurists he is

---

[1] To be pronounced 'Hume'.
[2] *Sketches of the History of Man* (1788), Book 2, Sketch 9.

unique in seeing law not as a separate construction of fairly logical rules, but as an inextricably linked part of history, philosophy, anthropology, sociology and even aesthetics. Without these, law could not be properly understood. There are many shortcomings in his overarching philosophical scheme, but there is much to be learned from them. They stimulate creative thoughts in the reader and uncovering the mistakes sharpens the reader's mind. Kames made the law appear as a social and historical phenomenon and as a living body of mankind. With this interpretation of the law he is unrivalled up to the present day.

Kames's independent research and scholarship were not shaped by the orthodoxies of established institutions of learning, and this enabled him to maintain a sceptical attitude to authorities of all kind, no matter how illustrious. This scepticism, often well-argued, sometimes less so, runs through all his work, in combination with a somewhat caustic style and a markedly distrustful view about the 'good' nature of man. Kames had a strong sense of the absurd, and enjoyed exposing the many irrationalities in religions and manners as they developed towards a modern society based on reason. He was an ardent promoter of the Enlightenment cause, especially in Scotland, relentlessly pursuing improvement in the arts, manners, law, technology and the economy. But, as his works reveal, he was far more than that. His contemporary neglect arises from the fact that Kames is very little read today. Philosophers see him as too specialist and 'legal'. Lawyers regard him as out-dated (although occasionally Scottish courts still refer to Kames in their decisions). The general reader finds his books too extensive, discursive and disorganized. This selection from his writings aims to change all of these opinions.

It was only in his late thirties and into his forties that Kames became the promoter of Enlightenment ideas and the mentor of important younger thinkers. As a young man, Home obtained his legal education with a solicitor (Writer to the Signet) in Edinburgh. Being ambitious, he decided to train as an advocate, and he studied classics, French and Italian, literature and Roman law to prepare for the examination. He passed the examination and was admitted as an advocate in January 1723. Slowly and gradually his legal practice developed, which may have given him more time to study philosophy and to have intellectual exchanges with other men of letters, to publish his first work on law (*Essays upon Several Subjects in Law*, 1732), and to apply (unsuccessfully) for a chair of Civil (Roman) law at Edinburgh University. He married rather late, in 1741, and had a son and a daughter with his wife Agatha Drummond. About this time some of the figures who would later be included among the greatest representatives of the Scottish Enlightenment became his protégés and *élèves*. Many of them remained friends with him for the rest of his life — David Hume (with some reservations), Adam Smith, Thomas Reid, John Millar and others.

A domineering and authoritarian manner, combined with argumentativeness, a sharp wit, a certain honesty, both intellectually and in personal life, and the rumour that he had sympathies for the Jacobites, may have delayed Home's appointment as a judge. During the uprising in 1745 he wrote his first major work on law and legal history — *Essays upon several Subjects concerning British Antiquities* (published in 1747). It contains no endorsement of the Jacobite cause, but an interesting discussion of the constitutional position of Parliament and the king as a magistrate subjected to the law.[3] In 1751 Home published the first of his major works, the *Essays on the Principles of Morality and Natural Religion*. This was an important contribution to the developing 'Common Sense' philosophy of the Scottish Enlightenment. It sets out the basis of Kames's thought and is the philosophical framework for all the disciplines he would later be concerned with — moral philosophy, aesthetics, law and legal history, philosophical history and sociology/anthropology. The *Essays* offer a critical reply to David Hume's occasionalist idea of causation, his concept of justice as not a natural, but artificial (conventionalist, utilitarian) virtue, and his conventional (contractual) idea of property.[4]

In 1752 Henry Home was finally elevated to the Bench as Lord Ordinary of the Scottish Court of Session, and he took

---

[3] Selection II.1.c).
[4] Selections III.2–4.

the title Lord Kames after his estate. In his early years as a judge he was subjected to intense criticism by the conservative branch of the Church of Scotland and came close to excommunication in 1755, because his *Essays on the Principles of Morality* put forward the idea that in a world determined entirely by natural laws our sense of free will is God's benevolent deceit.[5] From the 1750s onwards, Kames published his other principal works: *Historical Law-Tracts* (1758), *Principles of Equity* (1760), *Elements of Criticism* (1762), *Sketches of the History of Man* (1774), and *Elucidations respecting the Common and Statute Law of Scotland* (1777). In his role as 'improver' Kames also wrote *The Gentleman Farmer* (1776), 'an attempt to improve Agriculture, by subjecting it to the test of Rational Principles', and the pamphlet *Progress of Flax-Husbandry in Scotland* (1766).[6] As an educator, Kames published the *Introduction to the Art of Thinking* (1761) and *Loose Hints on Education, Chiefly Concerning the Culture of the Heart* (1781). The most comprehensive of these works are the *Sketches of the History of Man*, a philosophical history of the progress of man which incorporates large sections from some of his earlier works. The sketches discuss the development of all aspects of human endeavour, and of human society: 'Progress of Men independent of Society', 'Progress of Men in Society' and 'Progress of Sciences'. They deal with the development of languages and cultures, property,[7] commerce,[8] manners, luxury, the origin of men and human societies,[9] forms of government, patriotism, finances and taxation, the progress of reason,[10] morality and theology.[11] The *Essays on the Principles of Morality*, the *Elements of Criticism* and the *Sketches* were widely known in Europe and in North America and were translated into German.

---

[5] Selections III.3.ii–iii.
[6] Selection V.2.
[7] The selection is taken from the *Historical Law-Tracts* in particular, see selections II.1.f), IV.1.
[8] Selection V.1.
[9] Selection II.2.
[10] Selections II.3 and III.1.
[11] Selection II.4.

Kames took on many social commitments and offices to further the improvement of the Scottish economy and society in accordance with his Enlightenment principles. He was a founder member of the Edinburgh Philosophical Society, as well as a member of the Board of Trustees for Encouraging the Fisheries, Arts and Manufactures of Scotland. In 1763 Kames was appointed judge to the Scottish Criminal Court (High Court of Justiciary), and in 1766 his wife unexpectedly inherited the family estate. For the first time in his life Kames was wealthy, and this allowed him to move to a new estate in Blair Drummond (Perthshire). He served as a judge until the end of his long life, and died in Edinburgh in 1782 at the age of eighty-six.

In the second half of the eighteenth century, Kames was one of the most renowned men of letters of his time. He was well-known in France—and fiercely attacked by Voltaire for his theories on aesthetics. In Germany his writings on aesthetics, rhetoric and moral philosophy exercised a considerable influence, at least initially, on Kant, Moses Mendelssohn, Herder and others. His philosophy of history in relation to human society and its progress, and with particular reference to law, made an important intellectual contribution. His writings on legal history, legal sociology, property theory and the philosophical concept of equity in the law proved very attractive to some of the younger lawyers and politicians in colonial America who would later become founders of the United States. The young John Adams was much impressed by Kames's theory of property and his rejection of feudalism in the *Historical Law-Tracts*, while Thomas Jefferson held Kames's *Essays on the Principles of Morality* and the *Principles of Equity* in high regard throughout his life.

From the early 1800s onwards, Kames's works were gradually eclipsed by the works of some of his brilliant students. It is difficult to assess the interest in his works at present. While new editions have appeared, specialization, distrust of Enlightenment ideas of 'progress' and a more inward looking nationalism in Scotland count against it.

2. Kames's System of Moral and Legal Philosophy

The *Essays on the Principles of Morality* set out Kames's moral philosophy, centred around the innate *moral sense*, a legacy from Hutcheson and Shaftesbury, with some significant variations.[12] The moral sense is source of the concept of moral beauty. Beauty for Kames (influenced particularly by Hutcheson) is intrinsic beauty, a quality of visible objects, and relative beauty, a quality of the relation between objects. Relative beauty relates to some good end or purpose, it is a beauty of utility, a higher degree of beauty.[13] Beauty is an emotion which derives from the perception of an object, and creates an agitation of the mind. In addition to pleasant emotions, there are disagreeable or painful emotions. Where the emotion leads to desire, it is a passion.[14] Emotions and passions can also be imaginary. In this case they have to be stimulated by stylistic means in literature and the arts. The thoughts which the passions prompt are sentiments.[15] The purpose of literary and art criticism is to study, in literature, in plays, in poems, in the arts, both appropriate and inadequate forms of expression for the stimulation of desired passions and sentiments. These techniques are revealed by the study of style and rhetoric.[16] The foundation for developing, and being educated in, a standard of taste that is supposedly common to mankind lies in understanding these sentiments and the proper application of rhetoric and stylistic forms and figures in literature and the arts.[17]

The standard of taste is an application of a more general principle—the ability, innate in all human beings in more or less the same manner, to distinguish between what is right (aesthetically pleasing) and what is wrong, and what individuals ought to do to conform to it. The moral quality of beauty in Kames's aesthetics leads to morality proper. Moral beauty enables man to distinguish right from wrong, and to

---

[12] Selection III.2.
[13] Selection I.1.d).
[14] Selection I.1.c).
[15] Selection I.2.b).
[16] Selection I.2.
[17] Selection I.3.

disapprove of or to punish transgressions. This is the structure of Kames's legal philosophy. Justice originates from the innate moral sense that enables people to distinguish between beautiful and ugly, and to realize that what is beautiful may also be useful. Such awareness is not confined to an object, but can also refer to a human action. Human actions may be agreeable or disagreeable ('beautiful or deformed') and they are also useful or otherwise ('fit/unfit and meet/unmeet to be done'). Thus human actions are *morally beautiful* or *morally deformed*. Justice is a primary virtue, that is, a virtue that is essential for the functioning of society. So acting in conformity with moral beauty is not only a moral duty, but an obligation that may be enforced by the law.[18] This is also the basis for property rights ('the sense of property')[19] and for delictual liability and criminal offences.[20]

Benevolence is only a morally desirable and commendable virtue, and thus a secondary virtue. It cannot be enforced by law, unless there is a special connection between human beings (covenants, relationship between parents and children, persons in distress). In this case benevolent actions are exceptionally enforceable by the law. This is the area of equity, as Kames explains at length in his *Principles of Equity*.[21] Equity is designed to remedy the shortcomings and injustices of the common law, so that the petitioner may obtain redress at the court's discretion where the common law denies him a right, especially because of reasons of legal formality. This, it is generally agreed, reflects the historical development of the body of the law of equity in England (in Scotland the position of equity is more complicated). Kames builds this historical fact into his system of moral philosophy by declaring equity to be the secondary virtue of benevolence, one that is legally enforceable only as an exception.

Legal institutions, such as property or equity, passed through phases of historical development which refined

---

[18] Selection III.2.
[19] Selection IV.1.
[20] Selection III.5.
[21] Selection IV.3.

them and led to higher and more sophisticated stages of progress of human society. It is the purpose of legal history to detect and explain these developments, to obtain a proper understanding of the present law.[22]

3. Kames's Idea of Progress of Human Society: Philosophical and Anthropological History

The last point hints at one of the best-known features of the Scottish Enlightenment—the stadial theory of the natural history of society. It is the notion that human societies developed in several (commonly four) relatively distinct stages based on modes of subsistence: the ages of hunting, herding (age of shepherds), farming (age of agriculture) and, finally, the age of commerce. Within this framework, the thinkers of the Scottish Enlightenment presented and explained the course of human progress in social history. These stages of socio-economic and (implicitly) moral improvement lead to the currently most advanced stage, the age of commerce. They apply universally, and there is a certain determinism to the progression of socio-historical events. Kames was one of the inventors of this Scottish version of stadial theory or periodization in the progress of society. He established this evolutionary concept of history mostly with regard to legal institutions, especially property, where it is most persuasive and for which it had probably been developed,[23] and criminal law,[24] where the theory is less plausible. The stadial theory of human development appears often in Kames's works, and in different contexts, initially in relation to the law, as for example in the explanation of the development of obligations,[25] but also in the context of human reasoning and the sciences,[26] or religion.[27]

The stadial theory of the 'natural' history of human society is an application of the Scottish concept of theoretical

---

[22] Selection III.6.
[23] Selection II.1.f).
[24] Selection II.1.d).
[25] Selection II.1.e).
[26] Selection II.3.
[27] Selection II.4.

(philosophical) or *conjectural history*[28] and is its most important example. Conjectural history is a form of interpretation whereby a few known and established facts are connected by hypotheses ('conjectures') that fill in, with some probability, the missing facts, and thereby reconstruct the 'likely' historical development of a social or legal institution. These hypotheses are technically inductive arguments, founded on known historical facts or other circumstances that are postulated as empirically ascertainable, such as 'the known principles of human nature'. The Scottish Enlightenment considered conjectural history as a suitable method for political and social history,[29] for law, modes of government, but also for the history of the sciences, mathematics, or the arts. The narrative often appears persuasive. It is indeed cogent when Kames argues that there was not much understanding of property rights among hunters and gatherers, so that for them property did not mean more than possession as a mere fact. The idea of a proprietary relationship between a man and a thing developed first only with regard to moveable property, among shepherds in relation to their cattle.[30] Property rights in relation to land evolved with the stage of agriculture. It was especially the fourth and highest stage of social development, the age of commerce, that advanced and presupposed the right to transfer property (alienation). Persuasive though this account may be, it is nevertheless conjectural and speculative, and whether modern anthropological and historical research can prove it, and for which parts of the world, is a very different matter. Nevertheless, one of Kames's lasting contributions is his historical, legal and anthropological property theory. His desire for progress towards the highest societal stage of commerce explains his continuing, severe and uncompromising criticism of the feudal system, particularly the entail, in Scotland,[31] because the entail prevents free alienation of land.

---

[28] Selection II.1.a).
[29] Selection II.1.b).
[30] The word chattel derives from cattle which itself comes from the medieval Latin word 'capitale', (moveable) property.
[31] Selection IV.3.

Kames the anthropologist is something of a curiosity. As a child of his time, his account of the supposed origin and development of the human races (Kames was a polygenist) and societies is full of alarming oversimplifications, stereotypes and prejudices.[32] But it also shows the intrinsic conflict between the supposed differences of the human races and the Enlightenment ideal of the uniform and equal nature of man—all men—worldwide. Kames upholds this ideal and consequently concludes that black peoples are not necessarily intellectually inferior but would develop in the same way as white peoples if they were exposed to the same enlightened education. At work here is the idea that different intellectual faculties may still be qualitatively equal. That is difficult for the majority of people to understand even today, so one should not censure Kames too much *ex post facto*.

While Kames ceaselessly promoted the improvement of society in all aspects, he also held that economic progress leads to wealth and riches and so to luxury, which encourages the intellectual and moral degeneration of a society, its decline and its retrograde development towards an earlier stage of social progress. Thus Kames's understanding of social evolution was, at least in part, cyclical. He did not believe that the world is the best of all worlds, but he did believe that it could be better than it is.

4. Bibliography

Primary Sources

This list only contains works by Kames from which selections are included in this anthology:

Henry Home (later: Lord Kames) (1732), *Essays Upon Several Subjects in Law*, Edinburgh: R. Fleming & Company.
Henry Home (later: Lord Kames) (1749), *Essays Upon Several Subjects Concerning British Antiquities*, 2nd ed., London: M. Cooper.
Henry Home, Lord Kames (1766), *Progress of Flax-Husbandry in Scotland*, Edinburgh: Sands, Murray and Cochran.
Henry Home, Lord Kames (1777), *Elucidations Respecting the Common and Statute Law of Scotland*, Edinburgh: W. Creech, T. Cadell.

---

[32] Selection II.2.

Henry Home, Lord Kames (1778), *Principles of Equity*, Vols. 1 and 2, 3rd ed., Edinburgh: J. Bell, W. Creech, T. Cadell.

Henry Home, Lord Kames (1779), *Essays on the Principles of Morality and Natural Religion*, 3rd ed., Edinburgh: John Bell and John Murray in London (some extracts from the 1st ed. of 1751).

Henry Home, Lord Kames (1785), *Elements of Criticism*, Vols. 1 and 2, 6th ed., Edinburgh: John Bell and William Creech (some extracts from the 1st ed. of 1762.)

Henry Home, Lord Kames (1788), *Sketches of the History of Man, Books I, II, III* (in 4 volumes), 3rd ed., Edinburgh: A. Strahan, T. Cadell, W. Creech.

Henry Home, Lord Kames (1792), *Historical Law-Tracts*, 4th ed., Edinburgh: Cadell, Bell & Bradfute, Creech.

Select Bibliography of Secondary Sources

Berry, Christopher J. (1997), *Social Theory of the Scottish Enlightenment*, Edinburgh: Edinburgh University Press.

Lehmann, William C. (1971), *Henry Home, Lord Kames, and the Scottish Enlightenment: A Study in National Character and the History of Ideas*, The Hague: Martinus Nijhoff.

Lieberman, David (1983), 'The Legal Needs of a Commercial Society: the Jurisprudence of Lord Kames', in: Istvan Hont and Michael Ignatieff (eds), *Wealth and Virtue: The Shaping of Political Economy in the Scottish Enlightenment*, Cambridge: Cambridge University Press, pp. 203-234.

Lobban, Michael (2004), 'The Ambition of Lord Kames's Equity', in: Andrew Lewis and Michael Lobban (eds), *Law and History (Current Legal Issues 2003, vol. 6)*, Oxford: Oxford University Press, pp. 97-121.

Rahmatian, Andreas (2006), 'The Property Theory of Lord Kames (Henry Home)', 2(2) *International Journal of Law in Context*, 177-205.

Rahmatian, Andreas (2015), *Lord Kames: Legal and Social Theorist*, Edinburgh: Edinburgh University Press.

Randall, Helen Whitcomb (1944), *The Critical Theory of Lord Kames*, Northampton, MA: Department of Modern Languages of Smith College (Smith College Studies in Modern Languages, vol. 22, nos. 1-4, 1940-41).

Ross, Ian Simpson (1972), *Lord Kames and the Scotland of his Day*, Oxford: Clarendon Press.

Stein, Peter (1988), 'The Four Stage Theory of the Development of Societies', in: Peter Stein, *The Character and Influence of the Roman Civil Law. Historical Essays*, London and Ronceverte: The Hambledon Press, pp. 395-409.

5. Editor's Notes

Unlike other anthologies of the Library of Scottish Philosophy, this reader rarely contains a complete work or a complete chapter from Lord Kames's works. The texts are rather shortened considerably and arranged thematically. This is because several works discuss more or less the same subject, so that the best version has been chosen for this anthology. Furthermore, Kames often indulges in an abundance of examples to prove the same argument, goes off on a tangent, engages in a prolix discussion of side issues, or does not structure parts of his work in a too lucid way. Sometimes Kames discusses associated aspects of the same argument in different places, even in different books. All that obscures the organization of his thought and the underlying line of argument. Therefore it was necessary to shorten some of the texts repeatedly, especially with regard to the *Elements of Criticism* and the *Sketches of the History of Man*, and to group them together under thematic headings, also when they come from different works.

The omitted passages of text are indicated by '[...]'. The reference to the original source of the selections is indicated at the beginning of each extract to allow the reader to find easily the original text in full length. All texts by Kames are available in the form of scanned eighteenth-century editions, either on the internet or on specialist databases. In addition, Kames's major works have appeared in modern editions by the Liberty Fund (Indianapolis) since 2005. Editorial changes have been kept to a minimum, but ancient spellings and archaic forms have been replaced (hath—has; doth—does; 'tis—it is; pronounceth—pronounces; tho'—though; passeth—passes; produceth—produces; etc.). All italicized words and passages are Kames's. The headings of the selections are not original but the editor's. Footnotes have generally been omitted, but there are some essential, and usually long, footnotes by Kames which have been reproduced (indicated at the beginning as '[Footnote by Kames]'). Explanatory footnotes by the editor are indicated by square brackets.

I would like to thank the series editor Gordon Graham for including this anthology of Kames's works in the Library of Scottish Philosophy, and to Christopher Choi for typing up the last selection in chapter five from the facsimile of the original text. I am also grateful to Graham Horswell and the staff at Imprint Academic for producing this book which aims at making Kames's works and thought more accessible to the modern reader.

One

Aesthetics and Rhetoric

1. Definitions; Aesthetics

a) *External and Internal Sense*

From: *Elements of Criticism*, 6th ed. (1785), vol. 2, Appendix, p. 505

That act of the mind which makes known to me an external object, is termed *perception*. That act of the mind which makes known to me an internal object, is termed *consciousness*. The power or faculty from which consciousness proceeds, is termed an *internal sense*. The power or faculty from which perception proceeds, is termed an *external sense*. This distinction refers to the objects of our knowledge; for the senses, whether external or internal, are all of them powers or faculties of the mind.[1]

---

[1] [Footnote by Kames] I have complied with all who have gone before me in describing the senses internal and external to be powers or faculties; and yet, after much attention, I have not discovered any thing active in their operations to entitle them to that character. The following chain of thought has led me to hesitate. One being operates on another: the first is active, the other passive. If the first act, it must have a power to act: if an effect be produced on the other, it must have a capacity to have that effect produced upon it. Fire melts wax: *ergo* fire has a power to produce that effect; and wax must be capable to have that effect produced in it. Now as to the senses. A tree in flourish makes an impression on me, and by that means I see the tree. But in this operation I do not find that the mind is active: seeing the tree is only an effect produced on it by intervention of the rays of light. What seems to have led us into an error

b) Perception, Sensation and Conception

i) From: *Elements of Criticism*, 6th ed. (1785), vol. 2, Appendix, pp. 508–509

Perception and sensation are commonly reckoned synonymous terms, signifying that internal act by which external objects are made known to us. But they ought to be distinguished. *Perceiving* is a general term for hearing, seeing, tasting, touching, smelling; and therefore *perception* signifies every internal act by which we are made acquainted with external objects: thus we are said to perceive a certain animal, a certain colour, sound, taste, smell, etc. *Sensation* properly signifies that internal act by which we are made conscious of pleasure or pain felt at the organ of sense: thus we have a sensation of the pleasure arising from warmth, from a fragrant smell, from a sweet taste; and of the pain arising from a wound, from a fetid smell, from a disagreeable taste. In perception, my attention is directed to the external object: in sensation, it is directed to the pleasure or pain I feel.

The terms *perception* and *sensation* are sometimes employed to signify the objects of perception and sensation. Perception in that sense is a general term for every external thing we perceive; and sensation a general term for every pleasure and pain felt at the organ of sense.

Conception is different from perception. The latter includes a conviction of the reality of its object: the former does not; for I can conceive the most extravagant stories told in a romance, without having any conviction of their reality. Conception differs also from imagination. By the power of fancy I can imagine a golden mountain, or an ebony ship with sails and ropes of silk. When I describe a picture of that

---

is the word *seeing*, which, under the form of an active verb, has a passive signification. *I feel* is a similar example; for to feel is certainly not to act, but the effect of being acted upon: the feeling pleasure is the effect produced in my mind when a beautiful object is presented. Perception accordingly is not an action, but an effect produced in the mind. Sensation is another effect: it is the pleasure I feel upon perceiving what is agreeable.

kind to another, the idea he forms of it is termed a *conception*. Imagination is active, conception is passive.

ii) From: *Elements of Criticism*, 1st ed. (1762), vol. 3, Appendix, p. 379

Conception ought to be distinguished from perception. External things and their attributes are objects of perception: relations among things are objects of conception. I see two men, James and John: the consciousness I have of them is a perception: but the consciousness I have of their relation as father and son, is termed a *conception*. Again, perception relates to objects really existing: conception to fictitious objects, or to those framed by the imagination.

c) *Emotions and Passions*

From: *Elements of Criticism*, 6th ed. (1785), vol. 1, chapter 2, pp. 35–42

It is a fact universally admitted, that no emotion or passion ever starts up in the mind, without a cause: if I love a person, it is for good qualities or good offices: if I have resentment against a man, it must be for some injury he has done me: and I cannot pity any one who is under no distress of body nor of mind. [...]

Such is our nature, that upon perceiving certain external objects, we are instantaneously conscious of pleasure or pain: a gently-flowing river, a smooth extended plain, a spreading oak, a towering hill, are objects of sight that raise pleasant emotions: a barren heath, a dirty marsh, a rotten carcass, raise painful emotions. Of the emotions thus produced, we enquire for no other cause but merely the presence of the object. [...]

If external properties be agreeable, we have reason to expect the same from those which are internal; and accordingly power, discernment, wit, mildness, sympathy, courage, benevolence, are agreeable in a high degree: upon perceiving these qualities in others, we instantaneously feel pleasant emotions, without the slightest act of reflection, or of attention to consequences. It is almost unnecessary to add, that certain qualities opposite to the former, such as dullness, peevishness, inhumanity, cowardice, occasion in the same manner painful emotions.

Sensible beings affect us remarkably by their actions. Some actions raise pleasant emotions in the spectator, without the least reflection; such as graceful motion and genteel behaviour. But as *intention*, a capital circumstance in human actions, is not visible, it requires reflection to discover their true character: I see one delivering a purse of money to another, but I can make nothing of that action, till I learn with what intention the money is given: if it be given to discharge a debt, the action pleases me in a slight degree; if it be a grateful return, I feel a stronger emotion; and the pleasant emotion rises to a great height, when it is the intention of the giver to relieve a virtuous family from want. Thus actions are qualified by intention: but they are not qualified by the event; for an action well intended gives pleasure, whatever the event be. Further, human actions are perceived to be *right* or *wrong*; and that perception qualifies the pleasure or pain that results from them.[2] [...]

---

[2] [Footnote by Kames] In tracing our emotions and passions to their origin, my first thought was, that qualities and actions are the primary causes of emotions; and that these emotions are afterward expanded upon the being to which these qualities and actions belong. But I am now convinced that this opinion is erroneous. An attribute is not, even in imagination, separable from the being to which it belongs; and for that reason, cannot of itself be the cause of any emotion. We have, it is true, no knowledge of any being or substance but by means of its attributes; and therefore no being can be agreeable to us otherwise than by their means. But still, when an emotion is raised, it is the being itself, as we apprehend the matter, that raises the emotion; and it raises it by means of one or other of its attributes. If it be urged, that we can in idea abstract a quality from the thing to which it belongs; it might be answered, that such abstraction may serve the purposes of reasoning, but is too faint to produce any sort of emotion. But it is sufficient for the present purpose to answer, that the eye never abstracts: by that organ we perceive things as they really exist, and never perceive a quality as separated from the subject. Hence it must be evident, that emotions are raised, not by qualities abstractly considered, but by the substance or body so and so qualified. Thus a spreading oak raises a pleasant emotion, by means of its colour, figure, umbrage, etc.: it is not the colour, strictly speaking, that produces the emotion, but the tree coloured: it is not the figure abstractly considered that produces the emotion, but the tree of a certain figure. And hence by the way it

Having explained the nature of an emotion, and mentioned several causes by which it is produced, we proceed to an observation of considerable importance in the science of human nature, which is, that desire follows some emotions, and not others. The emotion raised by a beautiful garden, a magnificent building, or a number of fine faces in a crowded assembly, is seldom accompanied with desire. Other emotions are accompanied with desire; emotions, for example, raised by human actions and qualities: a virtuous action raises in every spectator a pleasant emotion, which is commonly attended with desire to reward the author of the action: a vicious action, on the contrary, produces a painful emotion, attended with desire to punish the delinquent. [...]

It is a truth verified by induction, that every passion is accompanied with desire; and if an emotion be sometimes accompanied with desire, sometimes not, it comes to be a material enquiry, in what respect a passion differs from an emotion. Is passion in its nature or feeling distinguishable from emotion? [...] Are *passion* and *emotion* synonymous terms? That cannot be averred; because no feeling nor agitation of the mind void of desire, is termed a passion; and we have discovered, that there are many emotions which pass away without raising desire of any kind. How is the difficulty to be solved? There appears to me but one solution, which I relish the more, as it renders the doctrine of the passions and emotions simple and perspicuous. The solution follows. An internal motion or agitation of the mind, when it passes away without desire, is denominated *an emotion*: when desire follows, the motion or agitation is denominated *a passion*. A fine face, for example, raises in me a pleasant feeling: if that feeling vanish without producing any effect, it is in proper language an emotion; but if the feeling, by reiterated views of the object, become sufficiently strong to occasion desire, it loses its name of emotion, and acquires that of passion. The same holds in all the other passions: the painful feeling raised in a spectator by a slight injury done to

---

appears, that the beauty of such an object is complex, resolvable into several beauties more simple.

a stranger, being accompanied with no desire of revenge, is termed an emotion; but that injury raises in the stranger a stronger emotion, which being accompanied with desire of revenge, is a passion: external expressions of distress produce in the spectator a painful feeling, which being sometimes so slight as to pass away without any effect, is an emotion; but if the feeling be so strong as to prompt desire of affording relief, it is a passion, and is termed *pity*: envy is emulation in excess; if the exaltation of a competitor be barely disagreeable, the painful feeling is an emotion; if it produce desire to depress him, it is a passion.

d) Intrinsic and Relative Beauty

From: *Elements of Criticism*, 6th ed. (1785), vol. 1, chapter 3, pp. 196-199

The term *beauty*, in its native signification, is appropriated to objects of sight: objects of the other senses may be agreeable, such as the sounds of musical instruments, the smoothness and softness of some surfaces; but the agreeableness denominated *beauty* belongs to objects of sight.

Of all the objects of external sense, an object of sight is the most complex: in the very simplest, colour is perceived, figure, and length, breadth, and thickness. A tree is composed of a trunk, branches, and leaves; it has colour, figure, size, and sometimes motion: by means of each of these particulars, separately considered, it appears beautiful; how much more so, when they are all united together? The beauty of the human figure is extraordinary, being a composition of numberless beauties arising from the parts and qualities of the object, various colours, various motions, figures, size, etc.; all united in one complex object, and striking the eye with combined force. Hence it is, that beauty, a quality so remarkable in visible objects, lends its name to express every thing that is eminently agreeable: thus, by a figure of speech, we say a beautiful sound, a beautiful thought or expression, a beautiful theorem, a beautiful event, a beautiful discovery in art or science. […]

Considering attentively the beauty of visible objects, we discover two kinds.[3] The first may be termed *intrinsic* beauty, because it is discovered in a single object viewed apart without relation to any other: the examples above given are of that kind. The other may be termed *relative* beauty, being founded on the relation of objects. [...] Intrinsic beauty is an object of sense merely: to perceive the beauty of a spreading oak or of a flowing river, no more is required but singly an act of vision. The perception of relative beauty is accompanied with an act of understanding and reflection; for of a fine instrument or engine, we perceive not the relative beauty, until we be made acquainted with its use and destination. In a word, intrinsic beauty is ultimate: relative beauty is that of means relating to some good end or purpose. These different beauties agree in one capital circumstance, that both are equally perceived as belonging to the object. This is evident with respect to intrinsic beauty; but will not be so readily admitted with respect to the other: the utility of the plough, for example, may make it an object of admiration or of desire; but why should utility make it appear beautiful? A natural propensity [...] will explain that doubt: the beauty of the effect, by an easy transition of ideas, is transferred to the cause; and is perceived as one of the qualities of the cause. Thus a subject void of intrinsic beauty, appears beautiful from its utility; an old Gothic tower, that has no beauty in itself, appears beautiful, considered as proper to defend against an enemy; a dwelling-house void of all regularity, is however beautiful in the view of convenience; and the want of form or symmetry in a tree, will not prevent its appearing beautiful, if it be known to produce good fruit.

When these two beauties coincide in any object, it appears delightful: every member of the human body possesses both in a high degree: the fine proportions and

---

[3] [Kames is here significantly influenced by Francis Hutcheson's (1696–1746), *An Inquiry into the Original of our Ideas of Beauty and Virtue* (1725), and his categories of original/absolute and relative/comparative beauty, and beauty with useful or beautiful effects, in Treatise 1, sect. 2, 1, sect. 4, 1, sect. 5, 17. However, Kames does not follow Hutcheson, but develops his own systematization.]

slender make of a horse destined for running, please every eye; partly from symmetry, and partly from utility.

The beauty of utility, being proportioned accurately to the degree of utility, requires no illustration; but intrinsic beauty, so complex as I have said, cannot be handled distinctly without being analysed into its constituent parts. If a tree be beautiful by means of its colour, its figure, its size, its motion, it is in reality possessed of so many different beauties, which ought to be examined separately, in order to have a clear notion of them when combined. The beauty of colour is too familiar to need explanation. Do not the bright and cheerful colours of gold and silver contribute to preserve these metals in high estimation? The beauty of figure, arising from various circumstances and different views, is more complex: for example, viewing any body as a whole, the beauty of its figure arises from regularity and simplicity; viewing the parts with relation to each other, uniformity, proportion, and order, contribute to its beauty.

2. Rhetoric

a) *External Signs of Emotions and Passions*

From: *Elements of Criticism*, 6th ed. (1785), vol. 1, chapter 15, pp. 426–448

So intimately connected are the soul and body, that every agitation in the former, produces a visible effect upon the latter. There is, at the same time, a wonderful uniformity in that operation; each class of emotions and passions being invariably attended with an external appearance peculiar to itself.[4] These external appearances or signs, may not improperly be considered as a natural language, expressing to all beholders emotions and passions as they arise in the heart. Hope, fear, joy, grief, are displayed externally: the character of a man can be read in his face; and beauty, which makes so

---

[4] [Footnote by Kames] Omnis enim motus animi, suum quemdam a natura habet vultum et sonum et gestum. *Cicero, l. 3. De oratore.* [Book 3, 57, 216: 'For nature has assigned to every emotion a particular look and tone of voice and bearing of its own' (trans. H. Rackham).]

deep an impression, is known to result, not so much from regular features and a fine complexion, as from good nature, good sense, sprightliness, sweetness, or other mental quality, expressed upon the countenance. Though perfect skill in that language be rare, yet what is generally known is sufficient for the ordinary purposes of life. But by what means we come to understand the language, is a point of some intricacy: it cannot be by sight merely; for upon the most attentive inspection of the human face, all that can be discerned, are figure, colour, and motion, which singly or combined, never can represent a passion, nor a sentiment: the external sign is indeed visible; but to understand its meaning we must be able to connect it with the passion that causes it, an operation far beyond the reach of eye-sight. Where then is the instructor to be found that can unveil this secret connection? If we apply to experience, it is yielded, that from long and diligent observation, we may gather, in some measure, in what manner those we are acquainted with express their passions externally: but with respect to strangers, we are left in the dark; and yet we are not puzzled about the meaning of these external expressions in a stranger, more than in a bosom-companion. Further, had we no other means but experience for understanding the external signs of passion, we could not expect any degree of skill in the bulk of individuals: yet matters are so much better ordered, that the external expressions of passion form a language understood by all, by the young as well as the old, by the ignorant as well as the learned: I talk of the plain and legible characters of that language: for undoubtedly we are much indebted to experience, in deciphering the dark and more delicate expressions. Where then shall we apply for a solution of this intricate problem, which seems to penetrate deep into human nature? In my mind it will be convenient to suspend the enquiry, till we are better acquainted with the nature of external signs, and with their operations. These articles therefore shall be premised.

The external signs of passion are of two kinds, voluntary and involuntary. The voluntary signs are also of two kinds: some are arbitrary, some natural. Words are obviously voluntary signs: and they are also arbitrary; excepting a few simple sounds expressive of certain internal emotions, which sounds being the same in all languages, must be the work of nature: thus the unpremeditated tones of admiration are the same in all men; as also of compassion, resentment, and despair. Dramatic writers ought to be well acquainted with this natural language of passion: the chief talent of such a writer, is a ready command of the expressions that nature dictates to every person, when any vivid emotion struggles for utterance; and the chief talent of a fine reader, is a ready command of tones suited to these expressions.

The other kind of voluntary signs, comprehends certain attitudes and gestures that naturally accompany certain emotions with a surprising uniformity; excessive joy is expressed by leaping, dancing, or some elevation of the body: excessive grief, by sinking or depressing it: and prostration and kneeling have been employed by all nations and in all ages to signify profound veneration. Another circumstance, still more than uniformity, demonstrates these gestures to be natural, viz. their remarkable conformity or resemblance to the passions that produce them. Joy, which is a cheerful elevation of mind, is expressed by an elevation of body: pride, magnanimity, courage, and the whole tribe of elevating passions, are expressed by external gestures that are the same as to the circumstance of elevation, however distinguishable in other respects; and hence an erect posture is a sign or expression of dignity:

> Two of far nobler shape, erect and tall,
> Godlike erect, with native honour clad,
> In naked majesty, seem'd lords of all.[5]

Grief, on the other hand, as well as respect, which depress the mind, cannot for that reason be expressed more significantly than by a similar depression of the body; and hence, to be cast down, is a common phrase, signifying to be grieved or dispirited. [...]

The foregoing signs, though in a strict sense voluntary, cannot however be restrained but with the utmost difficulty when prompted by passion. We scarce need a stronger proof than the gestures of a keen player at bowls: observe only

---

[5] [John Milton, *Paradise Lost*, book 4, lines 288–290.]

how he writhes his body, in order to restore a stray bowl to the right track. It is one article of good breeding, to suppress, as much as possible, these external signs of passion, that we may not in company appear too warm, or too interested. The same observation holds in speech: a passion, it is true, when in extreme, is silent; but when less violent it must be vented in words, which have a peculiar force not to be equalled in a sedate composition. The ease and security we have in a confident, may encourage us to talk of ourselves and of our feelings: but the cause is more general; for it operates when we are alone as well as in company. Passion is the cause; for in many instances it is no slight gratification, to vent a passion externally by words as well as by gestures. [...]

The natural signs of emotions, voluntary and involuntary, being nearly the same in all men, form a universal language; which no distance of place, no difference of tribe, no diversity of tongue, can darken or render doubtful: even education, though of mighty influence, has not power to vary nor sophisticate, far less to destroy, their signification. This is a wise appointment of providence: for if these signs were, like words, arbitrary and variable, the thoughts and volitions of strangers would be entirely hid from us; which would prove a great or rather invincible obstruction to the formation of societies: but as matters are ordered, the external appearances of joy, grief, anger, fear, shame, and of the other passions, forming a universal language, open a direct avenue to the heart. As the arbitrary signs vary in every country, there could be no communication of thoughts among different nations, were it not for the natural signs, in which all agree: and as the discovering passions instantly at their birth, is essential to our well-being, and often necessary for self-preservation, the author of our nature, attentive to our wants, has provided a passage to the heart, which never can be obstructed while eye-sight remains. [...]

Emotions indeed properly so called, which are quiescent, produce no remarkable signs externally. Nor is it necessary that the more deliberate passions should, because the operation of such passions is neither sudden nor violent: these however remain not altogether in obscurity; for being more frequent than violent passion, the bulk of our actions are directed by them. Actions therefore display, with sufficient evidence, the more deliberate passions; and complete the admirable system of external signs, by which we become skilful in human nature.

What comes next in order is, to examine the effects produced upon a spectator by external signs of passion. None of these signs are beheld with indifference; they are productive of various emotions, tending all of them to ends wise and good. This curious subject makes a capital branch of human nature: it is peculiarly useful to writers who deal in the pathetic; and to history-painters it is indispensable.

[...] Each passion, or class of passions, has its peculiar signs; and with respect to the present subject it must be added, that these invariably make certain impressions on a spectator: the external signs of joy, for example, produce a cheerful emotion; the external signs of grief produce pity; and the external signs of rage, produce a sort of terror even in those who are not aimed at.

Secondly, it is natural to think, that pleasant passions should express themselves externally by signs that to a spectator appear agreeable, and painful passions by signs that to him appear disagreeable. This conjecture, which nature suggests, is confirmed by experience. Pride possibly may be thought an exception, the external signs of which are disagreeable, though it be commonly reckoned a pleasant passion: but pride is not an exception, being in reality a mixed passion, partly pleasant partly painful; for when a proud man confines his thoughts to himself, and to his own dignity or importance, the passion is pleasant, and its external signs agreeable; but as pride chiefly consists in undervaluing or contemning others, it is so far painful, and its external signs disagreeable.

Thirdly, it is laid down above, that an agreeable object produces always a pleasant emotion, and a disagreeable object one that is painful. According to this law, the external signs of a pleasant passion, being agreeable, must produce in the spectator a pleasant emotion: and the external signs of a painful passion, being disagreeable, must produce in him a painful emotion.

Fourthly, in the present chapter it is observed, that pleasant passions are, for the most part, expressed externally in one uniform manner; but that all the painful passions are distinguishable from each other by their external expressions. The emotions accordingly raised in a spectator by external signs of pleasant passions, have little variety: these emotions are pleasant or cheerful, and we have not words to reach a more particular description. But the external signs of painful passions produce in the spectator emotions of different kinds: the emotions, for example, raised by external signs of grief, of remorse, of anger, of envy, of malice, are clearly distinguishable from each other.

Fifthly, external signs of painful passions, are some of them *attractive*, some *repulsive*. Of every painful passion that is also disagreeable the external signs are repulsive, repelling the spectator from the object: and the passion raised by such external signs may be also considered as repulsive. Painful passions that are agreeable produce an opposite effect: their external signs are attractive, drawing the spectator to them, and producing in him benevolence to the person upon whom these signs appear; witness distress painted on the countenance, which instantaneously inspires the spectator with pity, and impels him to afford relief. And the passion raised by such external signs may also be considered as attractive. [...]

We may then venture to pronounce, with some degree of assurance, that man is provided by nature with a sense or faculty that lays open to him every passion by means of its external expressions. And we cannot entertain any reasonable doubt of this, when we reflect, that the meaning of external signs is not hid even from infants: an infant is remarkably affected with the passions of its nurse expressed on her countenance; a smile cheers it, a frown makes it afraid: but fear cannot be without apprehending danger; and what danger can the infant apprehend, unless it be sensible that its nurse is angry? We must therefore admit, that a child can read anger in its nurse's face; of which it must be sensible intuitively, for it has no other mean of knowledge. I do not affirm, that these particulars are clearly apprehended by the child; for to produce clear and distinct perceptions, reflection and experience are requisite: but that even an infant, when afraid, must have some notion of its being in danger, is evident.

That we should be conscious intuitively of a passion from its external expressions, is conformable to the analogy of nature: the knowledge of that language is of too great importance to be left upon experience; because a foundation so uncertain and precarious, would prove a great obstacle to the formation of societies. Wisely therefore is it ordered and agreeably to the system of providence, that we should have nature for our instructor. [...]

Passion, strictly speaking, is not an object of external sense: but its external signs are; and by means of these signs, passions may be appealed to with tolerable accuracy: thus the words that denote our passions, next to those that denote external objects, have the most distinct meaning. Words signifying internal action and the more delicate feelings, are less distinct. This defect with regard to internal action, is what chiefly occasions the intricacy of logic: the terms of that science are far from being sufficiently ascertained, even after much care and labour bestowed by an eminent writer;[6] to whom however the world is greatly indebted, for removing a mountain of rubbish, and moulding the subject into a rational and correct form. The same defect is remarkable in criticism, which has for its object the more delicate feelings; the terms that denote these feelings being not more distinct than those of logic. To reduce the science of criticism to any regular form, has never once been attempted: however rich the ore may be, no critical chymist[7] has been found, to analyse its constituent parts, and to distinguish each by its own name.

In the second place, society among individuals is greatly promoted by that universal language. Looks and gestures give direct access to the heart; and lead us to select, with tolerable accuracy, the persons who are worthy of our confidence. It is surprising how quickly, and for the most part how correctly, we judge of character from external appearance.

---

[6] [Footnote by Kames] Locke.

[7] [Kames's use of the word 'chymist' should not just be read as 'chemist', for it reflects the transition from alchemy to modern chemistry ('... to analyse its constituent parts ...') during this time.]

Thirdly, after social intercourse is commenced, these external signs, which diffuse through a whole assembly the feelings of each individual, contribute above all other means to improve the social affections. Language no doubt is the most comprehensive vehicle for communicating emotions: but in expedition, as well as in power of conviction, it falls short of the signs under consideration; the involuntary signs especially, which are incapable of deceit. Where the countenance, the tones, the gestures, the actions, join with the words in communicating emotions, these united have a force irresistible: thus all the pleasant emotions of the human heart, with all the social and virtuous affections, are, by means of these external signs, not only perceived but felt. By this admirable contrivance, conversation becomes that lively and animating amusement, without which life would at best be insipid: one joyful countenance spreads cheerfulness instantaneously through a multitude of spectators.

Fourthly, dissocial passions, being hurtful by prompting violence and mischief, are noted by the most conspicuous external signs, in order to put us upon our guard: thus anger and revenge, especially when sudden, display themselves on the countenance in legible character.[8] The external signs again of every passion that threatens danger raise in us the passion of fear: which frequently operating without reason

---

[8] [Footnote by Kames] Rough and blunt manners are allied to anger, by an internal feeling, as well as by external expressions resembling in a faint degree those of anger: therefore such manners are easily heightened into anger; and savages for that reason are prone to anger. Thus rough and blunt manners are unhappy in two respects: first, they are readily converted into anger; and next, the change being imperceptible because of the similitude of their external signs, the person against whom the anger is directed is not put upon his guard. It is for these reasons a great object in society, to correct such manners, and to bring on a habit of sweetness and calmness. This temper has two opposite good effects. First, it is not easily provoked to wrath. Next, the interval being great between it and real anger, a person of that temper who receives an affront, has many changes to go through before his anger be inflamed; these changes have each of them their external sign; and the offending party is put upon his guard, to retire, or to endeavour a reconciliation.

or reflection, moves us by a sudden impulse to avoid the impending danger.

In the fifth place, these external signs are remarkably subservient to morality. A painful passion, being accompanied with disagreeable external signs, must produce in every spectator a painful emotion: but then if the passion be social, the emotion it produces is attractive, and connects the spectator with the person who suffers. Dissocial passions only, are productive of repulsive emotions, involving the spectator's aversion, and frequently his indignation. This beautiful contrivance makes us cling to the virtuous, and abhor the wicked.

Sixthly, of all the external signs of passion, those of affliction or distress are the most illustrious with respect to a final cause. They are illustrious by the singularity of their contrivance; and also by inspiring sympathy, a passion to which human society is indebted for its greatest blessing, that of providing relief for the distressed. A subject so interesting, deserves a leisurely and attentive examination. The conformity of the nature of man to his external circumstances, is in every particular wonderful: his nature makes him prone to society; and society is necessary to his well-being, because in a solitary state he is a helpless being, destitute of support, and in his manifold distresses destitute of relief: but mutual support, the shining attribute of society, is of too great moment to be left dependent upon cool reason; it is ordered more wisely, and with greater conformity to the analogy of nature, that it should be enforced even instinctively by the passion of sympathy. Here sympathy makes a capital figure; and contributes, more than any other means, to make life easy and comfortable. But however essential the sympathy of others may be to our well-being, one beforehand would not readily conceive how it could be raised by external signs of distress: for considering the analogy of nature, if these signs be agreeable, they must give birth to a pleasant emotion leading every beholder to be pleased with human woes; if disagreeable, as they undoubtedly are, ought they not naturally to repel the spectator from them, in order to be relieved from pain? Such would be the reasoning beforehand; and such would be the effect were man purely a selfish being. But the benevolence of our nature gives a very different direction to the painful passion of sympathy, and to the desire involved in it: instead of avoiding distress, we fly to it in order to afford relief; and our sympathy cannot be otherwise gratified but by giving all the succour in our power. Thus external signs of distress, though disagreeable, are attractive: and the sympathy they inspire is a powerful cause, impelling us to afford relief even to a stranger as if he were our friend or relation.[9]

The effects produced in all beholders by external signs of passion, tend so visibly to advance the social state, that I must indulge my heart with a more narrow inspection of this admirable branch of the human constitution. These external signs, being all of them resolvable into colour, figure, and motion, should not naturally make any deep impression on a spectator: and supposing them qualified for making deep impressions, we have seen above, that the effects they produce are not such as might be expected. We cannot therefore account otherwise for the operation of these external signs, but by ascribing it to the original constitution of human nature: to improve the social state, by making us instinctively rejoice with the glad of heart, weep with the mourner, and shun those who threaten danger, is a contrivance no less illustrious for its wisdom than for its benevolence. [...]

---

[9] [Footnote by Kames] It is a noted observation, that the deepest tragedies are the most crowded; which in a slight view will be thought an unaccountable bias in human nature. Love of novelty, desire of occupation, beauty of action, make us fond of theatrical representations; and when once engaged, we must follow the story to the conclusion, whatever distress it may create. But we generally become wise by experience; and when we foresee what pain we shall suffer during the course of the representation, is it not surprising that persons of reflection do not avoid such spectacles altogether? And yet one who has scarce recovered from the distress of a deep tragedy, resolves coolly and deliberately to go to the very next, without the slightest obstruction from self-love. The whole mystery is explained by a single observation, that sympathy, though painful, is attractive, and attaches us to an object in distress, the opposition of self-love notwithstanding, which would prompt us to fly from it. And by this curious mechanism it is that persons of any degree of sensibility are attracted by affliction still more than by joy.

b) Sentiments

From: *Elements of Criticism*, 6th ed. (1785), vol. 1, chapter 16, pp. 451–493

Every thought prompted by passion, is termed a *sentiment*. To have a general notion of the different passions, will not alone enable an artist to make a just representation of any passion: he ought, over and above, to know the various appearances of the same passion in different persons. Passions receive a tincture from every peculiarity of character; and for that reason it rarely happens, that a passion, in the different circumstances of feeling, of sentiment, and of expression, is precisely the same in any two persons. Hence the following rule concerning dramatic and epic compositions, that a passion be adjusted to the character, the sentiments to the passion, and the language to the sentiments. If nature be not faithfully copied in each of these, a defect in execution is perceived: there may appear some resemblance; but the picture upon the whole will be insipid, through want of grace and delicacy. A painter, in order to represent the various attitudes of the body, ought to be intimately acquainted with muscular motion: no less intimately acquainted with emotions and characters ought a writer to be, in order to represent the various attitudes of the mind. A general notion of the passions, in their grosser differences of strong and weak, elevated and humble, severe and gay, is far from being sufficient: pictures formed so superficially have little resemblance, and no expression; yet it will appear by and by, that in many instances our artists are deficient even in that superficial knowledge.

In handling the present subject, it would be endless to trace even the ordinary passions through their nice and minute differences. Mine shall be a humbler task; which is, to select from the best writers instances of faulty sentiments, after paving the way by some general observations.

To talk in the language of music, each passion has a certain tone, to which every sentiment proceeding from it ought to be tuned with the greatest accuracy: which is no easy work, especially where such harmony ought to be supported during the course of a long theatrical representation. In order to reach such delicacy of execution, it is necessary that a writer assume the precise character and passion of the personage represented; which requires an uncommon genius. But it is the only difficulty; for the writer, who, annihilating himself, can thus become another person, need be in no pain about the sentiments that belong to the assumed character: these will flow without the least study, or even preconception; and will frequently be as delightfully new to himself as to his reader. But if a lively picture even of a single emotion, require an effort of genius, how much greater the effort to compose a passionate dialogue with as many different tones of passion as there are speakers? With what ductility of feeling must that writer be endued, who approaches perfection in such a work; when it is necessary to assume different and even opposite characters and passions, in the quickest succession? Yet this work, difficult as it is, yields to that of composing a dialogue in genteel comedy, exhibiting characters without passion. The reason is, that the different tones of character are more delicate and less in sight, than those of passion; and, accordingly, many writers who have no genius for drawing characters, make a shift to represent, tolerably well, an ordinary passion in its simple movements. But of all works of this kind, what is truly the most difficult, is a characteristical dialogue upon any philosophical subject: to interweave characters with reasoning, by suiting to the character of each speaker, a peculiarity not only of thought, but of expression, requires the perfection of genius, taste, and judgement.

How nice dialogue-writing is, will be evident, even without reasoning, from the miserable compositions of that kind found without number in all languages. The art of mimicking any singularity in gesture or in voice, is a rare talent, though directed by sight and hearing, the acutest and most lively of our external senses: how much more rare must the talent be, of imitating characters and internal emotions, tracing all their different tints, and representing them in a lively manner by natural sentiments properly expressed? The truth is, such execution is too delicate for an ordinary genius; and for that reason, the bulk of writers, instead of expressing a passion as one does who feels it, content themselves with describing it in the language of a spectator. To awake passion by an internal effort merely, without any external cause, requires great sensibility: and yet that operation is necessary, no less to the writer than to the actor; because none but those who actually feel a passion, can represent it to the life. The writer's part is the more complicated: he must add composition to passion; and must, in the quickest succession, adopt every different character. But a very humble flight of imagination, may serve to convert a writer into a spectator; so as to figure, in some obscure manner, an action as passing in his sight and hearing. In that figured situation, being led naturally to write like a spectator, he entertains his readers with his own reflections, with cool description, and florid declamation; instead of making them eye-witnesses, as it were, to a real event, and to every movement of genuine passion. Thus most of our plays appear to be cast in the same mould; personages without character, the mere outlines of passion, a tiresome monotony, and a pompous declamatory style.

This descriptive manner of representing passion, is a very cold entertainment: our sympathy is not raised by description; we must first be lulled into a dream of reality, and every thing must appear as passing in our sight. Unhappy is the player of genius who acts a capital part in what may be termed a *descriptive tragedy*: after assuming the very passion that is to be represented, how is he cramped in action, when he must utter, not the sentiments of the passion he feels, but a cold description in the language of a bystander? It is that imperfection, I am persuaded, in the bulk of our plays, which confines our stage almost entirely to Shakespeare, notwithstanding his many irregularities. In our late English tragedies, we sometimes find sentiments tolerably well adapted to a plain passion: but we must not, in any of them, expect a sentiment expressive of character; and, upon that very account, our late performances of the dramatic kind are for the most part intolerably insipid.

Looking back upon what is said, I am in some apprehension of not being perfectly understood; for it is not easy to avoid obscurity in handling a matter so complicated: but I promise to set it in the clearest light, by adding example to precept. The first examples shall be of sentiments that appear the legitimate offspring of passion; to which shall be opposed what are descriptive only, and illegitimate: and in making this comparison, I borrow my instances from Shakespeare and Corneille,[10] who for genius in dramatic composition stand uppermost in the rolls of fame.

Shakespeare shall furnish the first example, being of sentiments dictated by a violent and perturbed passion: [Kames quotes from Shakespeare's *King Lear*, Act 3, Scene 4, lines 14–36, and from *Othello*, Act 5, Scene 2, lines 263–284] [...]

The sentiments here displayed flow so naturally from the passions represented, that we cannot conceive any imitation more perfect.

With regard to the French author, truth obliges me to acknowledge, that he describes in the style of a spectator, instead of expressing passion like one who feels it; which naturally betrays him into a tiresome monotony, and a pompous declamatory style.[11] It is scarce necessary to give examples, for he never varies from that tone. I shall however take two passages at a venture, in order to be confronted with those transcribed above. In the tragedy of *Cinna*,[12] Aemilia, after the conspiracy was discovered, having nothing in view but racks and death to herself and her lover, receives a pardon from Augustus, attended with the brightest circumstances of magnanimity and tenderness. This is a lucky situation for representing the passions of surprise and gratitude in their different stages, which seem naturally to be what follow. These passions, raised at once to the utmost pitch, and being at first too big for utterance, must, for some moments, be expressed by violent gestures only: as soon as there is vent for words, the first expressions are broken and

---

[10] [Pierre Corneille (1606–1684), playwright of tragedies and one of the three great French seventeenth-century playwrights, together with Molière and Racine.]

[11] [Footnote by Kames] This criticism reaches the French dramatic writers in general, with very few exceptions: their tragedies, excepting those of Racine, are mostly, if not totally, descriptive. Corneille led the way; and later writers, imitating his manner, have accustomed the French ear to a style, formal, pompous, declamatory, which suits not with any passion. Hence to burlesque a French tragedy, is not more difficult than to burlesque a stiff solemn fop. [...]

[12] [*Cinna ou la Clémence d'Auguste*, by Pierre Corneille, 1639.]

interrupted: at last we ought to expect a tide of intermingled sentiments, occasioned by the fluctuation of the mind between the two passions. Aemilia is made to behave in a very different manner: with extreme coolness she describes her own situation, as if she were merely a spectator; or rather the poet takes the task off her hands: [Kames quotes from Corneille's *Cinna*, Act 5, Scene 3, lines 1715–1728] [...]

The different stages of a passion, and its different directions, from birth to extinction, must be carefully represented in their order; because otherwise the sentiments, by being misplaced, will appear forced and unnatural. Resentment, for example, when provoked by an atrocious injury, discharges itself first upon the author: sentiments therefore of revenge come always first, and must in some measure be exhausted before the person injured think of grieving for himself. In the *Cid* of Corneille,[13] Don Diègue having been affronted in a cruel manner, expresses scarce any sentiment of revenge, but is totally occupied in contemplating the low situation to which he is reduced by the affront: [Kames quotes from Corneille's *Le Cid*, Act 1, Scene 4, lines 237–260] [...]

These sentiments are certainly not the first that are suggested by the passion of resentment. As the first movements of resentment are always directed to its object, the very same is the case of grief. Yet with relation to the sudden and severe distemper that seized Alexander bathing in the river Cydnus, Quintus Curtius[14] describes the first emotions of the army as directed to themselves, lamenting that they were left without a leader, far from home, and had scarce any hopes of returning in safety: their King's distress, which must naturally have been their first concern, occupies them but in the second place according to that author. [...]

A person sometimes is agitated at once by different passions; and the mind in that case, vibrating like a

---

[13] [*Le Cid*, by Pierre Corneille, 1637.]
[14] [Quintus Curtius Rufus, Roman rhetorician and historian in the first century A.D. Kames refers here to book 10 of the *History of Alexander The Great*, a work, partially missing, that scholars generally regard as historically unreliable.]

pendulum, vents itself in sentiments that partake of the same vibration. This I give as a third observation: [Kames quotes from Shakespeare's Henry VIII, Act 3, Scene 1, lines 144–151] [...]

Another observation is, that nature, which gave us passions, and made them extremely beneficial when moderate, intended undoubtedly that they should be subjected to the government of reason and conscience. It is therefore against the order of nature, that passion in any case should take the lead in contradiction to reason and conscience: such a state of mind is a sort of anarchy, which every one is ashamed of, and endeavours to hide or dissemble. Even love, however laudable, is attended with a conscious shame when it becomes immoderate: it is covered from the world, and disclosed only to the beloved object [...]. Hence a capital rule in the representation of immoderate passions, that they ought to be hid or dissembled as much as possible. And this holds in an especial manner with respect to criminal passions: one never counsels the commission of a crime in plain terms: guilt must not appear in its native colours, even in thought: the proposal must be made by hints, and by representing the action in some favourable light. Of the propriety of sentiment upon such an occasion, Shakespeare, in the *Tempest*, has given us a beautiful example, in a speech by the usurping Duke of Milan, advising Sebastian to murder his brother the King of Naples: [Kames quotes from Shakespeare's *Tempest*, Act 2, Scene 1, lines 205–210] [...]

Fanciful or finical sentiments. Sentiments that degenerate into point or conceit, however they may amuse in an idle hour, can never be the offspring of any serious or important passion. In the *Jerusalem* of Tasso,[15] Tancred, after a single combat, spent with fatigue and loss of blood, falls into a swoon; in which situation, understood to be dead, he is discovered by Erminia, who was in love with him to distraction. A more happy situation cannot be imagined, to raise grief in an instant to its height; and yet, in venting her sorrow, she descends most abominably into antithesis and

---

[15] [Torquato Tasso (1544–1595), Italian poet of the late Renaissance.]

conceit, even of the lowest kind: [Kames quotes from Tasso's *Jerusalem Delivered*, Canto 19, stan. 105] [...]

Corneille, in his *Examen of the Cid*, answering an objection, that his sentiments are sometimes too much refined for persons in deep distress, observes, that if poets did not indulge sentiments more ingenious or refined than are prompted by passion, their performances would often be low, and extreme grief would never suggest but exclamations merely. This is in plain language to assert, that forced thoughts are more agreeable than those that are natural, and ought to be preferred. [...]

The last class comprehends sentiments that are unnatural, as being suited to no character nor passion. These may be subdivided into three branches: first, sentiments unsuitable to the constitution of man, and to the laws of his nature; second, inconsistent sentiments; third, sentiments that are pure rant and extravagance.

When the fable is of human affairs, every event, every incident, and every circumstance, ought to be natural, otherwise the imitation is imperfect. [...]

So much upon sentiments: the language proper for expressing them, comes next in order.

c) *Tropes and Figures*

From: *Elements of Criticism*, 6th ed. (1785), vol. 2, chapter 20, pp. 227–305

The endless variety of expressions brought under the head of tropes and figures by ancient critics and grammarians, makes it evident, that they had no precise criterion for distinguishing tropes and figures from plain language. It was accordingly my opinion, that little could be made of them in the way of rational criticism; till discovering, by a sort of accident, that many of them depend on principles formerly explained, I gladly embrace the opportunity to show the influence of these principles where it would be the least expected. Confining myself therefore to such figures, I am luckily freed from much trash; without dropping, as far as I remember, any trope or figure that merits a proper name. And I begin with Prosopopoeia or personification, which is justly entitled to the first place.

SECTION I: *Personification.*

The bestowing sensibility and voluntary motion upon things inanimate, is so bold a figure, as to require, one should imagine, very peculiar circumstances for operating the delusion: and yet, in the language of poetry, we find variety of expressions, which, though commonly reduced to that figure, are used without ceremony, or any sort of preparation; as, for example, *thirsty* ground, *hungry* church-yard, *furious* dart, *angry* ocean. These epithets, in their proper meaning, are attributes of sensible beings: what is their meaning, when applied to things inanimate? Do they make us conceive the ground, the church-yard, the dart, the ocean, to be endued with animal functions? This is a curious inquiry; and whether so or not, it cannot be declined in handling the present subject.

The mind, agitated by certain passions, is prone to bestow sensibility upon things inanimate. This is an additional instance of the influence of passion upon our opinions and belief. I give examples. Antony, mourning over the body of Caesar murdered in the senate-house, vents his passion in the following words:

> *Antony.*
> O pardon me, thou bleeding piece of earth,
> That I am meek and gentle with these butchers.
> Thou art the ruins of the noblest man
> That ever lived in the tide of times.[16]

Here Antony must have been impressed with a notion, that the body of Caesar was listening to him, without which the speech would be foolish and absurd. Nor will it appear strange, [...] that passion should have such power over the mind of man.

[...] In all the foregoing examples, the personification, if I mistake not, is so complete as to afford conviction, momentary indeed, of life and intelligence. But it is evident from numberless instances, that personification is not always so complete: it is a common figure in descriptive poetry, understood to be the language of the writer, and not of the persons

---

[16] [Shakespeare, *Julius Caesar*, Act 3, Scene 1, lines 254–257.]

he describes: in this case, it seldom or never comes up to conviction, even momentary, of life and intelligence. I give the following examples.

> First in *his* east the glorious lamp was seen,
> Regent of day, and all th' horizon round
> Invested with bright rays; jocund to run
> His longitude through heav'n's high road: the gray
> Dawn and the Pleiades before *him* danc'd,
> Shedding sweet influence. Less bright, the moon,
> But opposite, in levell'd west was set
> *His* mirror, with full face borrowing *her* light
> From *him*; for other light *she* needed none.[17]

> Night's candles are burnt out, and jocund day
> Stands tiptoe on the misty mountain-tops.[18]

> But look, the morn, in russet mantle clad,
> Walks o'er the dew of yon high eastward hill.[19]

It may, I presume, be taken for granted, that, in the foregoing instances, the personification, either with the poet or his reader, amounts not to a conviction of intelligence: that the sun, the moon, the day, the morn, are not here understood to be sensible beings. What then is the nature of this personification? I think it must be referred to the imagination: the inanimate object is imagined to be a sensible being, but without any conviction, even for a moment, that it really is so. Ideas or fictions of imagination have power to raise emotions in the mind; and when any thing inanimate is, in imagination, supposed to be a sensible being, it makes by that means a greater figure than when an idea is formed of it according to truth. This sort of personification, however, is far inferior to the other in elevation. Thus personification is of two kinds. The first, being more noble, may be termed *passionate personification*: the other, more humble, *descriptive personification*;

---

[17] [John Milton, *Paradise Lost*, book 7, lines 370–378. The emphasis is by Kames.]
[18] [Shakespeare, *Romeo and Juliet*, Act 3, Scene 5, lines 9–10.]
[19] [Shakespeare, *Hamlet*, Act 1, Scene 1, lines 166–167.]

because seldom or never is personification in a description carried to conviction.

The imagination is so lively and active, that its images are raised with very little effort; and this justifies the frequent use of descriptive personification. [...]

Abstract and general terms, as well as particular objects, are often necessary in poetry. Such terms however are not well adapted to poetry, because they suggest not any image: I can readily form an image of Alexander or Achilles in wrath; but I cannot form an image of wrath in the abstract, or of wrath independent of a person. Upon that account, in works addressed to the imagination, abstract terms are frequently personified: but such personification rests upon imagination merely, not upon conviction. [...]

Hitherto success has attended our steps: but whether we shall complete our progress with equal success, seems doubtful; for when we look back to the expressions mentioned in the beginning, *thirsty* ground, *furious* dart, and such like, it seems no less difficult than at first, to say whether there be in them any sort of personification. Such expressions evidently raise not the slightest conviction of sensibility: nor do I think they amount to descriptive personification; because, in them, we do not even figure the ground or the dart to be animated. If so, they cannot at all come under the present subject. To show which, I shall endeavour to trace the effect that such expressions have in the mind. Does not the expression *angry ocean*, for example, tacitly compare the ocean in a storm to a man in wrath? By this tacit comparison, the ocean is elevated above its rank in nature; and yet personification is excluded, because, by the very nature of comparison, the things compared are kept distinct, and the native appearance of each is preserved. It will be shown afterward, that expressions of this kind belong to another figure, which I term a *figure of speech* [...].

Though thus in general we can distinguish descriptive personification from what is merely a figure of speech, it is, however, often difficult to say, with respect to some expressions, whether they are of the one kind or of the other. [...]

SECTION II: Apostrophe.

This figure and the former are derived from the same principle. If, to humour a plaintive passion, we can bestow a momentary sensibility upon an inanimate object, it is not more difficult to bestow a momentary presence upon a sensible being who is absent:

> Hinc Drepani me portus et illaetabilis ora
> Accipit. Hic, pelagi tot tempestatibus actus,
> Heu! genitorem, omnis curae casusque levamen,
> Amitto Anchisen: *hic me pater optime, fessum*
> *Deseris*, heu! tantis nequicquam erepte periclis.
> Nec vates Helenus, cum multa horrenda moneret,
> Hos mihi praedixit luctus; non dira Celaeno.[20]

[...] This figure is sometimes joined with the former: things inanimate, to qualify them for listening to a passionate expostulation, are not only personified, but also conceived to be present [...].

SECTION III: Hyperbole.

In this figure, by which an object is magnified or diminished beyond truth, we have another effect of the foregoing principle. An object of an uncommon size, either very great of its kind or very little, strikes us with surprise; and this emotion produces a momentary conviction that the object is greater or less than it is in reality: the same effect, precisely, attends figurative grandeur or littleness; and hence the hyperbole, which expresses that momentary conviction. A writer, taking advantage of this natural delusion, warms his description greatly by the hyperbole: and the reader, even in his coolest moments, relishes the figure, being sensible that it is the operation of nature upon a glowing fancy.

---

[20] [Virgil, *Aeneid*, Book iii, lines 707–713: 'Next the harbour of Drepanum and its joyless shore receive me. Here I, who have been driven by so many ocean-storms, lose, alas! my father Anchises, solace of every care and chance; here, best of fathers, thou leavest me in weariness, snatched, alas! from such mighty perils all for naught. Nor did seer Helenus, though he warned me of many horrors, nor grim Celaeno foretell me this grief' (trans. H. Rushton Fairclough).]

It cannot have escaped observation, that a writer is commonly more successful in magnifying by a hyperbole than in diminishing. The reason is, that a minute object contracts the mind, and fetters its power of imagination; but that the mind, dilated and inflamed with a grand object, moulds objects for its gratification with great facility. Longinus,[21] with respect to a diminishing hyperbole, quotes the following ludicrous thought from a comic poet: 'He was owner of a bit of ground no larger than a Lacedemonian letter.'[22] But, for the reason now given, the hyperbole has by far the greater force in magnifying objects; of which take the following examples:

> For all the land which thou seest, to thee will I give it, and to thy seed for ever. And I will make thy seed as the dust of the earth: so that if a man can number the dust of the earth, then shall thy seed also be numbered.[23]

> Illa vel intactae segetis per summa volaret
> Gramina: nec teneras cursu laesisset aristas.[24]

> —Atque imo barathri ter gurgite vastos
> Sorbet in abruptum fluctus, rursusque sub auras
> Erigit alternos, et sidera verberat undâ.[25]

> —Horificis juxta tonat Aetna ruinis,
> Interdumque atram prorumpit ad aethera nubem,

---

[21] [Longinus, usual name for the author of *On the Sublime* (his real name is unknown), Greek teacher of rhetoric and writer, perhaps in the first century AD.]

[22] [Footnote by Kames] Chap. 31 of his Treatise on the Sublime. ['Lacedemonian letter' refers to the Greek iota, the smallest letter in the Greek alphabet, or a very short letter.]

[23] [Genesis 13, 15–16.]

[24] [Virgil, *Aeneid*, Book vii, lines 808–809: 'She might have flown o'er the topmost blades of unmown corn, nor in her course bruised the tender ears' (trans. H. Rushton Fairclough).]

[25] [Virgil, *Aeneid*, Book iii, lines 421–423: 'And at the bottom of her seething chasm thrice she sucks the vast waves into the abyss, and again in turn casts them upwards, lashing the stars with spray' (trans. H. Rushton Fairclough).]

Turbine fumantem piceo et candente favilla,
Attollitque globos flammarum, et sidera lambit.[26]

[...]

Quintilian[27] is sensible that this figure is natural: 'For,' says he, 'not contented with truth, we naturally incline to augment or diminish beyond it; and for that reason the hyperbole is familiar even among the vulgar and illiterate': and he adds, very justly, 'That the hyperbole is then proper, when the subject of itself exceeds the common measure.' From these premisses, one would not expect the following inference, the only reason he can find for justifying this figure of speech, 'Conceditur enim amplius dicere, quia dici quantum est, non potest: meliusque ultra quam citra stat oratio.' (We are indulged to say more than enough, because we cannot say enough; and it is better to be above than under.) In the name of wonder, why this childish reasoning, after observing that the hyperbole is founded on human nature? I could not resist this personal stroke of criticism; intended not against our author, for no human creature is exempt from error, but against the blind veneration that is paid to the ancient classic writers, without distinguishing their blemishes from their beauties.

Having examined the nature of this figure, and the principle on which it is erected, I proceed, as in the first section, to the rules by which it ought to be governed. And, in the first place, it is a capital fault, to introduce an hyperbole in the description of any thing ordinary or familiar; for in such a case, it is altogether unnatural, being destitute of surprise, its only foundation. Take the following instance, where the subject is extremely familiar, viz. swimming to gain the shore after a shipwreck.

---

[26] [Virgil, *Aeneid*, Book iii, lines 571–574: 'Near at hand Aetna thunders with terrifying crashes, and now hurls forth to the sky a black cloud, and uplifts balls of flame and licks the stars' (trans. H. Rushton Fairclough).]

[27] [Footnote by Kames] Quintilian [Marcus Fabius Quintilianus (around 35-96 AD), Roman teacher of rhetoric and author of the *Institutio oratoria*, most influential between the 16th-18th centuries], L. 8, cap. 6 in fin [book 8, chapter 6, para. 75].

> I saw him beat the surges under him,
> And ride upon their backs; he trode the water;
> Whose enmity he flung aside, and breasted
> The surge most swoln that met him: his bold head
> 'Bove the contentious waves he kept, and oar'd
> Himself with his good arms, in lusty strokes
> To th' *shore*, that o'er his wave-borne basis bow'd,
> As stooping to relieve him.[28]

[...] A writer, if he wish to succeed, ought always to have the reader in his eye: he ought in particular never to venture a bold thought or expression, till the reader be warmed and prepared. For that reason, an hyperbole in the beginning of a work can never be in its place. Example:

> Jam pauca aratro jugera regiae
> Moles relinquent.[29]

The nicest point of all, is to ascertain the natural limits of an hyperbole, beyond which being overstrained it has a bad effect. Longinus, in the above-cited chapter, with great propriety of thought, enters a caveat against an hyperbole of this kind: he compares it to a bow-string, which relaxes by overstraining, and produces an effect directly opposite to what is intended. To ascertain any precise boundary, would be difficult, if not impracticable. [...]

Lastly, an hyperbole, after it is introduced with all advantages, ought to be comprehended within the fewest words possible: as it cannot be relished but in the hurry and swelling of the mind, a leisurely view dissolves the charm, and discovers the description to be extravagant at least, and perhaps also ridiculous. [...]

SECTION IV: *The Means or Instrument conceived to be the Agent.*

When we survey a number of connected objects, that which makes the greatest figure employs chiefly our attention; and the emotion it raises, if lively, prompts us even to exceed

---

[28] [Shakespeare, *Tempest*, Act 2, Scene 1, lines 113–120.]
[29] [Horace, *Carmina*, Book 2, Ode 15: 'A short time and our princely piles will leave but few acres to the plough' (trans. C.E. Bennett).]

nature in the conception we form of it. Take the following examples.

For Neleus' son Alcides' *rage* had slain.

A broken rock the *force* of Pirus threw.

In these instances, the rage of Hercules and the force of Pirus, being the capital circumstances, are so far exalted as to be conceived the agents that produce the effects. [...]

SECTION V: *A Figure, which, among related Objects, extends the Properties of one to another.*

This figure is not dignified with a proper name, because it has been overlooked by writers. It merits, however, a place in this work; and must be distinguished from those formerly handled, as depending on a different principle. *Giddy brink, jovial wine, daring wound,* are examples of this figure. Here are adjectives that cannot be made to signify any quality of the substantives to which they are joined: a *brink*, for example, cannot be termed *giddy* in a sense, either proper or figurative, that can signify any of its qualities or attributes. When we examine attentively the expression, we discover, that a *brink* is termed *giddy* from producing that effect in those who stand on it. In the same manner a wound is said to be *daring*, not with respect to itself, but with respect to the boldness of the person who inflicts it: and wine is said to be *jovial*, as inspiring mirth and jollity. Thus the attributes of one subject are extended to another with which it is connected; and the expression of such a thought must be considered as a figure, because the attribute is not applicable to the subject in any proper sense.

How are we to account for this figure, which we see lies in the thought, and to what principle shall we refer it? Have poets a privilege to alter the nature of things, and at pleasure to bestow attributes upon a subject to which they do not belong? We have had often occasion to inculcate, that the mind passes easily and sweetly along a train of connected objects; and, where the objects are intimately connected, that it is disposed to carry along the good or bad properties of one to another; especially when it is in any degree inflamed with these properties. From this principle is derived the figure under consideration. Language, invented for the communication of thought, would be imperfect, if it were not expressive even of the slighter propensities and more delicate feelings: but language cannot remain so imperfect among a people who have received any polish; because language is regulated by internal feeling, and is gradually improved to express whatever passes in the mind. Thus, for example, when a sword in the hand of a coward, is termed *a coward sword*, the expression is significative of an internal operation; for the mind, in passing from the agent to its instrument, is disposed to extend to the latter the properties of the former. Governed by the same principle, we say *listening* fear, by extending the attribute *listening* of the man who listens, to the passion with which he is moved. In the expression, *bold deed*, or *audax facinus*, we extend to the effect what properly belongs to the cause. But not to waste time by making a commentary upon every expression of this kind, the best way to give a complete view of the subject, is to exhibit a table of the different relations that may give occasion to this figure. And in viewing the table, it will be observed, that the figure can never have any grace but where the relations are of the most intimate kind.

1. An attribute of the cause expressed as an attribute of the effect.

Audax facinus.

Of yonder fleet a *bold* discovery make.

An impious mortal gave the *daring* wound.

—To my *advent'rous* song,
That with no middle flight intends to soar.[30]

2. An attribute of the effect expressed as an attribute of the cause.

Quos periisse ambos *misera* censebam in mari.[31]

---

[30] [John Milton, *Paradise Lost*, Book 1, lines 13-14.]
[31] [Plautus, *Rudens*, Act 2, Scene 4, 'I thought that each of them has perished in the miserable sea.']

No wonder, fall'n such a *pernicious* height.[32]

3. An effect expressed as an attribute of the cause.

Jovial wine, Giddy brink, Drowsy night, Musing midnight, Panting height, Astonish'd thought, Mournful gloom.

Casting a dim *religious* light.[33] […]

4. An attribute of a subject bestowed upon one of its parts or members.

Longing arms.

It was the nightingale, and not the lark,
That pierc'd the *fearful* hollow of thine ear.[34] […]

5. A quality of the agent given to the instrument with which it operates.

Why peep your coward swords half out their shells!

6. An attribute of the agent given to the subject upon which it operates.

High-climbing hill.[35]

7. A quality of one subject given to another.

Icci, *beatis* nunc Arabum invides
Gazis.[36]

When sapless age, and weak unable limbs,
Should bring thy father to his *drooping* chair.[37] […]

8. A circumstance connected with a subject, expressed as a quality of the subject.

Breezy summit.

---

[32] [John Milton, *Paradise Lost*, Book 1, line 282.]
[33] [John Milton, *Il Penseroso*.]
[34] [Shakespeare, *Romeo and Juliet*, Act 3, Scene 5, lines 2–3.]
[35] [Reference given by Kames] Milton. [*Paradise Lost*, Book 3, line 546.]
[36] [Horace, *Carmina*, Book 1, Ode 29, 'Iccius, art thou looking now with envious eye at the rich treasures of the Arabians' (trans. C.E. Bennett).]
[37] [Shakespeare, *Henry VI*, Part 1, Act 4, Scene 5, lines 4–5.]

> 'Tis ours the chance of *fighting* fields to try.[38]
>
> Oh! had I dy'd before that *well-fought* wall.[39]

From this table it appears, that the adorning a cause with an attribute of the effect, is not so agreeable as the opposite expression. The progress from cause to effect is natural and easy: the opposite progress resembles retrograde motion; and therefore *panting height, astonish'd thought*, are strained and uncouth expressions, which a writer of taste will avoid. [...]

SECTION VI: *Metaphor and Allegory.*

A metaphor differs from a simile, in form only, not in substance: in a simile, the two subjects are kept distinct in the expression, as well as in the thought; in a metaphor, the two subjects are kept distinct in the thought only, not in the expression. A hero resembles a lion, and upon that resemblance many similes have been raised by Homer and other poets. But instead of resembling a lion, let us take the aid of the imagination, and feign or figure the hero to be a lion: by that variation the simile is converted into a metaphor; which is carried on by describing all the qualities of a lion that resemble those of the hero. The fundamental pleasure here, that of resemblance, belongs to the thought. An additional pleasure arises from the expression: the poet, by figuring his hero to be a lion, goes on to describe the lion in appearance, but in reality the hero; and his description is peculiarly beautiful, by expressing the virtues and qualities of the hero in new terms, which, properly speaking, belong not to him, but to the lion. This will better be understood by examples. A family connected with a common parent, resembles a tree, the trunk and branches of which are connected with a common root: but let us suppose, that a family is figured, not barely to be like a tree, but to be a tree; and then the simile will be converted into a metaphor, in the following manner:

---

[38] [Homer, *Iliad* I, 301.]
[39] [Homer, *Odyssey* V, 395.]

> Edward's sev'n sons, whereof thyself art one,
> Were sev'n fair branches, springing from one root:
> Some of these branches by the dest'nies cut:
> But Thomas, my dear lord, my life, my Glo'ster,
> One flourishing branch of his most royal root,
> Is hack'd down, and his summer-leaves all faded,
> By Envy's hand and Murder's bloody axe.[40] [...]

I am aware that the term *metaphor* has been used in a more extensive sense than I give it; but I thought it of consequence, in a disquisition of some intricacy, to confine the term to its proper sense, and to separate from it things that are distinguished by different names. An allegory differs from a metaphor; and what I would choose to call *a figure of speech*, differs from both. I proceed to explain these differences. A metaphor is defined above to be an act of the imagination, figuring one thing to be another. An allegory requires no such operation, nor is one thing figured to be another: it consists in choosing a subject having properties or circumstances resembling those of the principal subject; and the former is described in such a manner as to represent the latter: the subject thus represented is kept out of view; we are left to discover it by reflection; and we are pleased with the discovery, because it is our own work. Quintilian[41] gives the following instance of an allegory,

> O navis, referent in mare te novi
> Fluctus. O quid agis? fortiter occupa portum.[42]

and explains it elegantly in the following words: 'Totusque ille Horatii locus, quo navim pro republica, fluctuum tempestates pro bellis civilibus, portum pro pace atque concordia, dicit.'[43] [...]

---

[40] [Shakespeare, *Richard II*, Act 1, Scene 2, lines 11–21.]
[41] [Footnote by Kames] L. 8, cap. 6, sec. 2 [correctly: Book 8, chapter 6, section 44].
[42] [Horace, *Carmina*, Book 1, Ode 14: 'O ship, new billows threaten to bear thee out to sea again. Beware! Haste valiantly to reach the haven!' (trans. C.E. Bennett).]
[43] [Quintilian: 'And the rest of the ode, in which Horace represents the state under the semblance of a ship, the civil wars as tempests, and peace and good-will as the haven' (trans. H.E. Butler).]

In a word, an allegory is in every respect similar to an hieroglyphical painting, excepting only that words are used instead of colours. Their effects are precisely the same: a hieroglyphic raises two images in the mind; one seen, which represents one not seen: an allegory does the same; the representative subject is described; and resemblance leads us to apply the description to the subject represented. In a figure of speech, there is no fiction of the imagination employed, as in a metaphor, nor a representative subject introduced, as in an allegory. This figure, as its name implies, regards the expression only, not the thought; and it may be defined, the using a word in a sense different from what is proper to it. Thus youth, or the beginning of life, is expressed figuratively by *morning of life*: morning is the beginning of the day; and in that view it is employed to signify the beginning of any other series, life especially, the progress of which is reckoned by days. [...]

The rules that govern metaphors and allegories, are of two kinds: the construction of these figures comes under the first kind: the propriety or impropriety of introduction comes under the other. I begin with rules of the first kind; some of which coincide with those already given for similes; some are peculiar to metaphors and allegories.

And, in the first place, it has been observed, that a simile cannot be agreeable where the resemblance is either too strong or too faint. This holds equally in metaphor and allegory; and the reason is the same in all. In the following instances, the resemblance is too faint to be agreeable.

> *Malcolm.*
> —But there's no bottom, none,
> In my voluptuousness: your wives, your daughters,
> Your matrons, and your maids, could not fill up
> The cistern of my lust.[44]

The best way to judge of this metaphor, is to convert it into a simile; which would be bad, because there is scarce any resemblance between lust and a cistern, or betwixt enormous lust and a large cistern.

---

[44] [Shakespeare, *Macbeth*, Act 4, Scene 3, lines 60–63.]

Again:

> He cannot buckle his distemper'd cause
> Within the belt of rule.[45]

There is no resemblance between a distempered cause and any body that can be confined within a belt.

[...] The comparison carried on in a simile, being in a metaphor sunk by imagining the principal subject to be that very thing which it only resembles; an opportunity is furnished to describe it in terms taken strictly or literally with respect to its imagined nature. This suggests another rule, that in constructing a metaphor, the writer ought to make use of such words only as are applicable literally to the imagined nature of his subject: figurative words ought carefully to be avoided; for such complicated figures, instead of setting the principal subject in a strong light, involve it in a cloud; and it is well if the reader, without rejecting by the lump, endeavour patiently to gather the plain meaning regardless of the figures.

[...] It is unpleasant to join different metaphors in the same period, even where they are preserved distinct: for when the subject is imagined to be first one thing and then another in the same period without interval, the mind is distracted by the rapid transition; and when the imagination is put on such hard duty, its images are too faint to produce any good effect:

> At regina gravi jamdudum saucia cura,
> Vulnus alit venis, et caeco carpitur igni.[46]

> — Est mollis flamma medullas
> Interea, et tacitum vivit sub pectore volnus.[47]

---

[45] [Shakespeare, *Macbeth*, Act 5, Scene 2, lines 15-16.]
[46] [Virgil, *Aeneid*, Book iv, lines 1-2: 'But the queen, long since smitten with a grievous love-pang, feeds the wound with her life-blood, and is wasted with fire unseen' (trans. H. Rushton Fairclough).]
[47] [Virgil, *Aeneid*, Book iv, lines 66-67: 'All the while the flame devours her tender heart-strings, and deep in her breast lives the silent wound' (trans. H. Rushton Fairclough).]

[...] It is still worse to jumble together metaphorical and natural expression, so as that the period must be understood in part metaphorically in part literally; for the imagination cannot follow with sufficient ease changes so sudden and unprepared: a metaphor begun and not carried on, has no beauty; and instead of light there is nothing but obscurity and confusion. Instances of such incorrect composition are without number. I shall, for a specimen, select a few from different authors.

Speaking of Britain,

> This precious stone set in the silver sea,
> Which serves it in the office of a wall,
> Or as a moat defensive to a house
> Against the envy of less happier lands.[48]

In the first line Britain is figured to be a precious stone: in the following lines, Britain, divested of her metaphorical dress, is presented to the reader in her natural appearance. [...]

A few words more upon allegory. Nothing gives greater pleasure than this figure, when the representative subject bears a strong analogy, in all its circumstances, to that which is represented: but the choice is seldom so lucky; the analogy being generally so faint and obscure, as to puzzle and not please. An allegory is still more difficult in painting than in poetry: the former can show no resemblance but what appears to the eye; the latter has many other resources for showing the resemblance. And therefore, with respect to what the Abbé du Bos[49] terms mixed allegorical compositions, these may do in poetry; because, in writing, the allegory can easily be distinguished from the historical part: no person, for example, mistakes Virgil's Fame for a real being. But such a mixture in a picture is intolerable; because in a picture the objects must appear all of the same kind, wholly real or wholly emblematical. For this reason, the history of Mary de Medicis, in the palace of Luxembourg,

---

[48] [Shakespeare, *Richard II*, Act 2, Scene 1, lines 46–49.]
[49] [Footnote by Kames] [Abbé du Bos, Jean-Baptiste Dubos (1670–1742)], Reflections sur la Poésie [*Réflexions critiques sur la poésie et la peinture*, 1719], vol. 1, sect. 24.

painted by Rubens, is unpleasant by a perpetual jumble of real and allegorical personages, which produce a discordance of parts, and an obscurity upon the whole: witness, in particular, the tablature representing the arrival of Mary de Medicis at Marseilles; where, together with the real personages, the Nereids and Tritons appear sounding their shells: such a mixture of fiction and reality in the same group, is strangely absurd. [...]

In an allegory as well as in a metaphor, terms ought to be chosen that properly and literally are applicable to the representative subject: nor ought any circumstance to be added that is not proper to the representative subject, however justly it may be applicable properly or figuratively to the principal. [...]

SECTION VII: *Figure of Speech.*

In the section immediately foregoing, a figure of speech is defined, 'The using a word in a sense different from what is proper to it'; and the new or uncommon sense of the word is termed *the figurative sense*. The figurative sense must have a relation to that which is proper; and the more intimate the relation is, the figure is the more happy. How ornamental this figure is to language, will not be readily imagined by any one who has not given peculiar attention; and therefore I shall endeavour to unfold its capital beauties and advantages. In the first place, a word used figuratively or in a new sense, suggests at the same time the sense it commonly bears: and thus it has the effect to present two objects; one signified by the figurative sense, which may be termed *the principal object*; and one signified by the proper sense, which may be termed *accessory*: the principal makes a part of the thought; the accessory is merely ornamental. In this respect, a figure of speech is precisely similar to concordant sounds in music, which, without contributing to the melody, make it harmonious. I explain myself by examples. *Youth*, by a figure of speech, is termed *the morning of life*. This expression signifies *youth*, the principal object, which enters into the thought: it suggests, at the same time, the proper sense of *morning*; and this accessory object, being in itself beautiful, and connected by resemblance to the principal object, is not a little ornamental. *Imperious ocean* is an example of a different kind, where an attribute is expressed figuratively: together with *stormy*, the figurative meaning of the epithet *imperious*, there is suggested its proper meaning, *viz.* the stern authority of a despotic prince; and these two are strongly connected by resemblance. [...]

Not only subjects, but qualities, actions, effects, may be expressed figuratively. Thus, as to subjects, the *gates of breath* for the lips, the *watery kingdom* for the ocean. As to qualities, *fierce* for stormy, in the expression *Fierce winter*: *Altus* for *profundus*; *Altus puteus*, *Altum mare*: *Breathing* for *perspiring*; *Breathing plants*. Again, as to actions, the sea *rages*, time will *melt* her frozen thoughts, time kills grief. An effect is put for the cause, as *lux* for the sun; and a cause for the effect, as *boum labores* for corn. The relation of resemblance is one plentiful source of figures of speech; and nothing is more common than to apply to one object the name of another that resembles it in any respect: height, size, and worldly greatness, resemble not each other; but the emotions they produce resemble each other, and prompted by this resemblance, we naturally express worldly greatness by height or size: one feels a certain uneasiness in seeing a great depth; and hence depth is made to express any thing disagreeable by excess, as *depth* of grief, *depth* of despair: again, height of place, and time long past, produce similar feelings [...].

Many words, originally figurative, having, by long and constant use, lost their figurative power, are degraded to the inferior rank of proper terms. Thus the words that express the operations of the mind, have in all languages been originally figurative: the reason holds in all, that when these operations came first under consideration, there was no other way of describing them but by what they resembled: it was not practicable to give them proper names, as may be done to objects that can be ascertained by sight and touch. A *soft* nature, *jarring* tempers, *weight* of wo, *pompous* phrase, *beget* compassion, *assuage* grief, *break* a vow, *bend* the eye downward, *shower* down curses, *drowned* in tears, *wrapt* in joy, *warmed* with eloquence, *loaded* with spoils, and a thousand other expressions of the like nature, have lost their figurative sense. Some terms there are, that cannot be said to be either altogether figurative or altogether proper: originally figurative, they are tending to simplicity, without having lost altogether their figurative power.

3. Standard of Taste

From: *Elements of Criticism*, 6th ed. (1785), vol. 2, chapter 25, pp. 487–504

'That there is no disputing about taste,' meaning taste in its figurative as well as proper sense, is a saying so generally received as to have become a proverb. One thing even at first view is evident, that if the proverb hold true with respect to taste in its proper meaning, it must hold equally true with respect to our other external senses: if the pleasures of the palate disdain a comparative trial, and reject all criticism, the pleasures of touch, of smell, of sound, and even of sight, must be equally privileged. At that rate, a man is not within the reach of censure, even where he prefers the Saracen's head upon a signpost before the best tablature of Raphael, or a rude Gothic tower before the finest Grecian building; or where he prefers the smell of a rotten carcass before that of the most odoriferous flower, or discords before the most exquisite harmony.

But we cannot stop here. If the pleasures of external sense be exempted from criticism, why not every one of our pleasures, from whatever source derived? If taste in its proper sense cannot be disputed, there is little room for disputing it in its figurative sense. The proverb accordingly comprehends both; and in that large sense may be resolved into the following general proposition, that with respect to the perceptions of sense, by which some objects appear agreeable some disagreeable, there is not such a thing as a *good* or a *bad*, a *right* or a *wrong*; that every man's taste is to himself an ultimate standard without appeal; and consequently that there is no ground of censure against any one, if such a one there be, who prefers Blackmore before Homer, selfishness before benevolence, or cowardice before magnanimity.

The proverb in the foregoing examples is indeed carried very far: it seems difficult, however, to sap its foundation, or with success to attack it from any quarter: for is not every man equally a judge of what ought to be agreeable or disagreeable to himself? Does it not seem whimsical, and perhaps absurd, to assert, that a man *ought not* to be pleased when he is, or that he *ought* to be pleased when he is not?

This reasoning may perplex, but will never afford conviction: every one of taste will reject it as false, however unqualified to detect the fallacy. At the same time, though no man of taste will assent to the proverb as holding true in every case, no man will affirm that it holds true in no case: objects there are, undoubtedly, that we may like or dislike indifferently, without any imputation upon our taste. Were a philosopher to make a scale for human pleasures, he would not think of making divisions without end; but would rank together many pleasures arising perhaps from different objects, either as equally conducing to happiness, or differing so imperceptibly as to make a separation unnecessary. Nature has taken this course, at least it appears so to the generality of mankind. There may be subdivisions without end; but we are only sensible of the grosser divisions, comprehending each of them various pleasures equally affecting: to these the proverb is applicable in the strictest sense; for with respect to pleasures of the same rank, what ground can there be for preferring one before another? If a preference in fact be given by any individual, it cannot proceed from taste, but from custom, imitation, or some peculiarity of mind. [...]

The proverb will hold true as to the particulars now explained; but when applied in general to every subject of taste, the difficulties to be encountered are insuperable. We need only to mention the difficulty that arises from human nature itself; do we not talk of a good and a bad taste? of a right and a wrong taste? And upon that supposition, do we not, with great confidence, censure writers, painters, architects, and every one who deals in the fine arts? Are such criticisms absurd, and void of common sense? Have the foregoing expressions, familiar in all languages and among all people, no sort of meaning? This can hardly be; for what is universal, must have a foundation in nature. If we can reach that foundation, the standard of taste will no longer be a secret.

We have a sense or conviction of a common nature, not only in our own species, but in every species of animals: and our conviction is verified by experience; for there appears a remarkable uniformity among creatures of the same kind, and a deformity no less remarkable among creatures of different kinds. This common nature is conceived to be a model or standard for each individual that belongs to the kind. Hence it is a wonder to find an individual deviating from the common nature of the species, whether in its internal or external construction: a child born with aversion to its mother's milk, is a wonder, no less than if born without a mouth, or with more than one. This conviction of a common nature in every species, paves the way finely for distributing things into *genera* and *species*; to which we are extremely prone, not only with regard to animals and vegetables, where nature has led the way; but also with regard to many other things, where there is no ground for such distribution, but fancy merely.

With respect to the common nature of man in particular, we have a conviction that it is invariable not less than universal; that it will be the same hereafter as at present, and as it was in time past; the same among all nations and in all corners of the earth. Nor are we deceived; because, giving allowance for the difference of culture and gradual refinement of manners, the fact corresponds to our conviction.

We are so constituted, as to conceive this common nature, to be not only invariable, but also *perfect* or *right*; and consequently that individuals *ought* to be made conformable to it. Every remarkable deviation from the standard, makes accordingly an impression upon us of imperfection, irregularity, or disorder: it is disagreeable, and raises in us a painful emotion: monstrous births, exciting the curiosity of a philosopher, fail not at the same time to excite a sort of horror.

This conviction of a common nature or standard and of its perfection, accounts clearly for that remarkable conception we have, of a right and a wrong sense or taste in morals. It accounts not less clearly for the conception we have of a right and a wrong sense or taste in the fine arts. A man who, avoiding objects generally agreeable, delights in objects generally disagreeable, is condemned as a monster: we disapprove his taste as bad or wrong, because we have a clear conception that he deviates from the common standard. If man were so framed as not to have any notion of a common standard, the proverb mentioned in the beginning would hold universally, not only in the fine arts, but in morals: upon that supposition, the taste of every man, with respect to both, would to himself be an ultimate standard. But as the conviction of a common standard is universal and a branch of our nature, we intuitively conceive a taste to be right or good if conformable to the common standard, and wrong or bad if disconformable.

No particular in human nature is more universal, than the uneasiness a man feels when in matters of importance his opinions are rejected by others: why should difference in opinion create uneasiness, more than difference in stature, in countenance, or in dress? The conviction of a common standard explains the mystery: every man, generally speaking, taking it for granted that his opinions agree with the common sense of mankind, is therefore disgusted with those who think differently, not as differing from him, but as differing from the common standard: hence in all disputes, we find the parties, each of them equally, appealing constantly to the common sense of mankind as the ultimate rule or standard. With respect to points arbitrary or indifferent, which are not supposed to be regulated by any standard, individuals are permitted to think for themselves with impunity: the same liberty is not indulged with respect to points that are reckoned of moment; for what reason, other than that the standard by which these are regulated, ought, as we judge, to produce a uniformity of opinion in all men? In a word, to this conviction of a common standard must be wholly attributed, the pleasure we take in those who espouse the same principles and opinions with ourselves, as well as the aversion we have at those who differ from us. In matters left indifferent by the standard, we find nothing of the same pleasure or pain: a bookish man, unless swayed by convenience, relishes not the contemplative man more than the active; his friends and companions are chosen indifferently out of either class: a painter consorts with a poet or musician, as readily as with those of his own art; and one is not the more agreeable to me for loving beef, as I do, nor the less agreeable for preferring mutton.

I have ventured to say, that my disgust is raised, not by differing from me, but by differing from what I judge to be the common standard. This point, being of importance, ought to be firmly established. Men, it is true, are prone to flatter themselves, by taking it for granted that their opinions and their taste are in all respects conformable to the common standard; but there may be exceptions, and experience shows there are some: there are instances without number, of persons who are addicted to the grosser amusements of gaming, eating, drinking, without having any relish for more elegant pleasures, such, for example, as are afforded by the fine arts; yet these very persons, talking the same language with the rest of mankind, pronounce in favour of the more elegant pleasures, and they invariably approve those who have a more refined taste, being ashamed of their own as low and sensual. It is in vain to think of giving a reason for this singular impartiality, other than the authority of the common standard with respect to the dignity of human nature: and from the instances now given we discover, that the authority of that standard, even upon the most grovelling souls, is so vigorous, as to prevail over self-partiality, and to make them despise their own taste compared with the more elevated taste of others.

Uniformity of taste and sentiment resulting from our conviction of a common standard, leads to two important final causes; the one respecting our duty, the other our pastime. Barely to mention the first shall be sufficient, because it does not properly belong to the present undertaking. Unhappy it would be for us did not uniformity prevail in morals: that our actions should uniformly be directed to what is good and against what is ill, is the greatest blessing in society; and in order to uniformity of action, uniformity of opinion and sentiment is indispensable.

With respect to pastime in general, and the fine arts in particular, the final cause of uniformity is illustrious. Uniformity of taste gives opportunity for sumptuous and elegant buildings, for fine gardens, and extensive embellishments, which please universally: and the reason is, that without uniformity of taste, there could not be any suitable reward, either of profit or honour, to encourage men of genius to labour in such works, and to advance them toward perfection. The same uniformity of taste is equally necessary to perfect the art of music, sculpture, and painting, and to support the expense they require after they are brought to perfection. Nature is in every particular consistent with herself: we are framed by Nature to have a high relish for the fine arts, which are a great source of happiness, and friendly in a high degree to virtue: we are, at the same time, framed with uniformity of taste, to furnish proper objects for that high relish; and if uniformity did not prevail, the fine arts could never have made any figure.

And this suggests another final cause no less illustrious. The separation of men into different classes, by birth, office, or occupation, however necessary, tends to relax the connection that ought to be among members of the same state; which bad effect is in some measure prevented by the access all ranks of people have to public spectacles, and to amusements that are best enjoyed in company. Such meetings, where every one partakes of the same pleasures in common, are no slight support to the social affections.

Thus, upon a conviction common to the species, is erected a standard of taste, which without hesitation is applied to the taste of every individual. That standard, ascertaining what actions are right what wrong, what proper what improper, has enabled moralists to establish rules for our conduct, from which no person is permitted to swerve. We have the same standard for ascertaining in all the fine arts, what is beautiful or ugly, high or low, proper or improper, proportioned or disproportioned: and here, as in morals, we justly condemn every taste that deviates from what is thus ascertained by the common standard.

That there exists a rule or standard in nature for trying the taste of individuals, in the fine arts as well as in morals, is a discovery; but is not sufficient to complete the task undertaken. A branch still more important remains upon hand; which is, to ascertain what is truly the standard of nature, that we may not lie open to have a false standard imposed on us. But what means shall be employed for bringing to light this natural standard? This is not obvious: for when we have recourse to general opinion and general practice, we are betrayed into endless perplexities. History informs us, that nothing is more variable than taste in the fine arts: judging by numbers, the Gothic taste of architecture must be preferred before that of Greece, and the Chinese taste probably before either.

[…] A standard for morals has been ascertained with a good deal of accuracy, and is daily applied by able judges with general satisfaction. The standard of taste in the fine arts, is not yet brought to such perfection; and we can account for its slower progress: the sense of right and wrong in actions is vivid and distinct, because its objects are clearly distinguishable from each other; whereas the sense of right and wrong in the fine arts is faint and wavering, because its objects are commonly not so clearly distinguishable from each other. And there appears to me a striking final cause in thus distinguishing the moral sense from the sense of right and wrong in the fine arts. The former, as a rule of conduct, and as a law we ought to obey, must be clear and authoritative. The latter is not entitled to the same privilege, because it contributes to our pleasure and amusement only: were it strong and lively, it would usurp upon our duty, and call off the attention from matters of greater moment: were it clear and authoritative, it would banish all difference of taste, leaving no distinction between a refined taste and one that is not so; which would put an end to rivalship, and consequently to all improvement.

But to return to our subject. However languid and cloudy the common sense of mankind may be as to the fine arts, it is notwithstanding the only standard in these as well as in morals. True it is indeed, that in gathering the common sense of mankind, more circumspection is requisite with respect to the fine arts than with respect to morals: upon the latter, any person may be consulted; but in the former, a wary choice is necessary, for to collect votes indifferently would certainly mislead us. Those who depend for food on bodily labour, are totally void of taste; of such a taste at least as can be of use in the fine arts. This consideration bars the greater part of mankind; and of the remaining part, many by a corrupted taste are unqualified for voting. The common sense of mankind must then be confined to the few that fall not under these exceptions. But as such selection seems to throw matters again into uncertainty, we must be more explicit upon this branch of our subject.

Nothing tends more than voluptuousness to corrupt the whole internal frame, and to vitiate our taste, not only in the fine arts, but even in morals: Voluptuousness never fails, in course of time, to extinguish all the sympathetic affections, and to bring on a beastly selfishness, which leaves nothing of man but the shape: about excluding such persons there will be no dispute. Let us next bring under trial, the opulent who delight in expense: the appetite for superiority and respect, inflamed by riches, is vented upon costly furniture, numerous attendants, a princely dwelling, sumptuous feasts, every thing superb and gorgeous, to amaze and humble all beholders: simplicity, elegance, propriety, and things natural, sweet, or amiable, are despised or neglected; for these are not appropriated to the rich, nor make a figure in the public eye: in a word, nothing is relished, but what serves to gratify pride, by an imaginary exaltation of the possessor above those who surround him. Such sentiments contract the heart, and make every principle give way to self-love: benevolence and public spirit, with all their refined emotions, are little felt, and less regarded; and if these be excluded, there can be no place for the faint and delicate emotions of the fine arts.

The exclusion of classes so many and numerous, reduces within a narrow compass those who are qualified to be judges in the fine arts. Many circumstances are necessary to form such a judge: there must be a good natural taste; that is, a taste approaching, at least in some degree, to the delicacy of taste above described: that taste must be improved by education, reflection, and experience:[50] it must be preserved

---

[50] [Footnote by Kames] That these particulars are useful, it may be said necessary, for acquiring a discerning taste in the fine arts, will appear from the following facts, which show the influence of experience singly. Those who live in the world and in good company, are quick-sighted with respect to every defect or irregularity in behaviour: the every slightest singularity in motion, in speech, or in dress, which to a peasant would be invisible, escapes not their observation. The most minute differences in the human countenance, so minute as to be far beyond the reach of words, are distinctly perceived by the plainest person; while, at the same time, the generality have very little discernment in the faces of other animals to which they are less accustomed: Sheep, for example, appear to

in vigour by living regularly, by using the goods of fortune with moderation, and by following the dictates of improved nature, which give welcome to every rational pleasure without indulging any excess. This is the tenor of life which of all contributes the most to refinement of taste; and the same tenor of life contributes the most to happiness in general.

If there appear much uncertainty in a standard that requires so painful and intricate a selection, we may possibly be reconciled to it by the following consideration, that, with respect to the fine arts, there is less difference of taste than is commonly imagined. Nature has marked all her works with indelible characters of high or low, plain or elegant, strong or weak: these, if at all perceived, are seldom misapprehended; and the same marks are equally perceptible in works of art. A defective taste is incurable; and it hurts none but the possessor, because it carries no authority to impose upon others. I know not if there be such a thing as a taste naturally bad or wrong; a taste, for example, that prefers a grovelling pleasure before one that is high and elegant: grovelling pleasures are never preferred; they are only made welcome by those who know no better. Differences about objects of taste, it is true, are endless; but they generally concern trifles, or possibly matters of equal rank, where preference may be given either way with impunity: if, on any occasion, persons differ where they ought not, a depraved taste will readily be discovered on one or other side, occasioned by imitation, custom, or corrupted manners, such as are described above. And considering that every individual partakes of a common nature, what is there that should occasion any wide difference in taste or sentiment? By the principles that constitute the sensative part of our nature, a wonderful uniformity is preserved in the emotions and feelings of the different races of men; the same object making upon every person the same impression, the same in kind, if not in degree. [...]

I know but of one other means for ascertaining the common sense of mankind; which I mention, not in despair,

---

have all the same face, except to the shepherd, who knows every individual in his flock as he does his relations and neighbours. [...]

but in great confidence of success. As the taste of every individual ought to be governed by the principles above mentioned, an appeal to these principles must necessarily be decisive of every controversy that can arise upon matters of taste. In general, every doubt with relation to the common sense of man, or standard of taste, may be cleared by the same appeal; and to unfold these principles is the declared purpose of the present undertaking.

Two

Philosophical History

1. Progress and Stage Theory of Human Society

a) *Definition of Conjectural History*
From: *Historical Law-Tracts*, 4th ed. (1792), Tract I: Criminal Law, pp. 25–26

In tracing the history of law through dark ages, unprovided with records, or so slenderly provided as not to afford any regular historical chain, we must endeavour to supply the broken links, by hints from poets and historians, by collateral facts, and by cautious conjectures drawn from the nature of the government, of the people, and of the times. If we use all the light that is afforded, and if the conjectural facts correspond with the few facts that are distinctly vouched, and join all in one regular chain, more cannot be expected from human endeavours. Evidence must afford conviction, if it be the best of the kind. This apology is necessary with regard to the subject under consideration. In tracing the history of the criminal law, we must not hope that all its steps and changes can be drawn from the archives of any one nation. In fact, many steps were taken and many changes made, before archives were kept, and even before writing was a common art. We must be satisfied with collecting the facts and circumstances as they may be gathered from the laws of different countries: and if these put together make a regular chain of causes and effects, we may rationally conclude, that the progress has been the same among all nations, in the capital circumstances at least; for accidents, or the singular nature of a people, or of a government, will always produce some peculiarities.

b) Examples of Conjectural History: General

From: *Essays upon Several Subjects concerning British Antiquities*, 2nd ed. (1749): Essay I, 'Of the Introduction of the Feudal Law into Scotland', pp. 1–21

The introduction of the feudal law into *Scotland* is an event, which makes not such a figure in our history as it ought to do: it is mentioned indeed by most of our historians, but dryly and cursorily, as if it were an ordinary incident. And yet, as the story is told, it appears to be a very singular revolution, for which no adequate cause is assigned. If credit can be given to history or tradition, we were once a free people; nay, we are reported to have been fierce and untamed, our nobles of great power, and generally too mighty for the sovereign. Now, as it is the plan of the feudal law, to bestow the whole land property upon the king, and to subject the bulk of the people to him in quality of servants and vassals; a constitution so contradictory to all the principles which govern mankind can never be brought about, one should imagine, without violence, whether conquest from without, or military force from within: Yet neither of these causes is assigned by our authors, nor will the history of *Scotland* admit of such suppositions; for no period can be assigned, during which the feudal law might have been introduced, where there are any traces of conquest, or of military power, sufficient to enforce so unnatural a constitution.

All our historians are agreed, that this revolution happened in the reign of *Malcolm II*,[1] and they are also pretty much agreed upon the circumstances which brought it about. This king had been engaged in fierce wars with the *Danes*, which, after various fortune, ended in driving the invaders out of this part of the island. Many of his nobles had done him notable service; and, to reward their fidelity, (it is said) he divided all the Crown lands amongst them. And so circumstantiate is the story, that it is averred he retained no lands to himself, but the *Mute-hill* in the Town of *Scoon*. A very extensive and unprecedented piece of

---

[1] [Scottish king (1005–34).]

liberality. But what follows is still more difficult to be believed; that the Lords, to testify their gratitude, gave and granted to their sovereign, and to his heirs for ever, the ward and relief of their lands with the marriage of their heirs. This is a short way of expressing a thing, which bears this obvious meaning, that all the lands in Scotland were surrendered to the king as his property; that all the great men came under personal obligations to be his servants and vassals, holding only the possession of the lands which they had surrendered, for sustenance of themselves and their people, ready upon all occasions to fight his battles. There are few examples of so warm returns of gratitude among individuals; but, in a whole nation, altogether incredible. I should be stunned with such liberty of fiction in a romance. Therefore, laying aside this account of the matter, as utterly improbable, the design of this essay is to bring together some circumstances whence probable conjectures may be formed, at what time, and after what manner, the feudal law was introduced into Scotland. I shall first endeavour to settle the time of introduction, as it may give light to the other branch of the disquisition; and I must confess, that, notwithstanding the concurring testimonies of all our historians, I entertain some doubts whether the feudal law was introduced into Scotland so early as in the reign of *Malcolm II*. What to me brought this matter first under suspicion, is a fact that can be made extremely evident. When one dives into the antiquities of Scotland and England, it will appear that we borrowed all our laws and customs from the English. No sooner is a statute enacted in England, but, upon the first opportunity, it is introduced into Scotland; so that our oldest statutes are mere copies of theirs. Let the *Magna Charta*[2] be put into the Hands of any Scotsman, without giving its history, and he will have no doubt that that he is reading a collection of Scots statutes or regulations. Now it is a point settled among the best English

---

2 [Settlement between King John and a group of rebel barons on 15 June 1215 in Runnymede (Windsor). The *Magna Carta* became a powerful symbol of English rights and liberties in general, especially from the seventeenth century onwards, well beyond the historical reality and the original purpose of this agreement.]

antiquaries, that the feudal law was introduced into England by *William* the Conqueror. I need not spend time upon this topic, after what is said by the accurate *Spelman*,[3] and by our countryman *Craig*.[4] Joining these two things together, a strong presumption arises, that the feudal law made its progress from England to this country, as all the English statutes, making improvements and alterations upon it, certainly did. But this presumption receives additional force, when it is considered, that if we had the feudal law before it came into England, it must have been taken from some other people than the *Normans*, with whom we had no intercourse. Upon that supposition, we must expect to find the feudal customs in Scotland, after the days of *William* the Conqueror, somewhat different from what they were in England, as the feudal customs were very different in different nations. What we had in Scotland must have been formed upon the plan of those of the country from which we borrowed them, perhaps a little varied in our practice. Yet, upon inquiry, we find no such disparity as we ought to expect from the supposition. On the contrary, I think it may with assurance be pronounced, that the feudal customs in England and Scotland were precisely the same, for a century or two after the days of *William* the Conqueror. This congruity betwixt the laws of the different countries affords evidence, as high as probability can go, either that we borrowed the feudal law from England, or, that they borrowed it from us. The latter is not maintained by any author; nor is there any foundation for the assertion, it being as well vouched as any point can be, of that antiquity, that *William* the Conqueror brought the feudal customs along with him from Normandy: And it is certain, he had no intercourse with Scotland unless in the shape of enmity and war.

In fair reasoning it must be yielded, that the circumstance now mentioned ought to create a suspicion, that the feudal law is not of such antiquity in Scotland as is generally

---

[3] [Sir Henry Spelman (1564?–1641), *Posthumous Works relating to the Laws and Antiquities of England* (1695).]

[4] [Scottish institutional writer of feudal law, author of *Jus Feudale* (1655).]

believed. But it will be said, that doubts and suspicions, however great, must yield to positive evidence; and that we have not only the authority of all our historians for the fact above mentioned, but still a more convincing evidence, the laws of *Malcolm II* still extant [...]

These authorities appear to be of weight, and shall be handled deliberately. Supposing the above mentioned laws to be those of *Malcolm II* the dispute is at an end, and the evidence complete [...] because in these laws frequent mention is made of feudal customs, such as the Office of Chancery, charters, sasines,[5] barons holding of the king, knights holding of barons, and others holding of knights, etc. But when I weigh this evidence of the antiquity of the feudal law in Scotland, I perceive one circumstance wanting to make it complete. That these are the laws of king *Malcolm* cannot be denied; they have in all ages been reckoned authentic, and king *Malcolm* is mentioned in the body of the work: But it may be controverted, whether these are the laws of *Malcolm II*. We had four kings of the name of *Malcolm;* and we have no authority, but from the title, to ascribe these laws to the second of that name: But at what time, or upon what evidence this title was added, we are altogether uncertain. The title in the printed copy is obviously a *post facto* work [...] This title proves only, that *Skeen* the publisher believed these to be *Malcolm II*'s laws: Upon what evidence he does not say, nor can it well be gathered, if it be not what arises from the title given to the manuscript copies, which in all probability had no better foundation than a vague tradition.

But I choose not to rest upon negative arguments. There is evidence the most convincing, that *Malcolm II* was not the author of these laws: This evidence is drawn from the work itself, wherein frequent mention is made of earls and barons, of the Chancellor and his court, coroner, etc. none of which names, in all probability, had a being in the time of *Malcolm II*. The Court of Chancery was not known in England before *William* the Conqueror; and it is not probable we had it before his time. But more positively, it is a fact agreed upon

---

[5]   [*Sasine* is the symbolic giving of possession in the Scottish feudal system.]

by all writers, that it was *Malcolm III* who created the first barons and earls. [...]

The argument drawn from the authority of the historians will be easily got over. We have no author who wrote in the days of *Malcolm Canmore*,⁶ nor for many ages after: therefore, as our histories rest upon no better authority than tradition, it is not surprising, that an event which happened in the reign of one king, should be ascribed to a predecessor of the same name, there being a prevailing bias in most nations to carry back their antiquities as far as possible. But the matter does not rest here, the error of these historians may be detected from their own writings. [...]

The *Regiam Majestatem*,⁷ the oldest institute we have of our laws, is generally believed to have been compiled in the reign, and by the authority of *David I*. And, as it contains a full and accurate system of our feudal customs, a probable argument may be suggested from it, that the feudal law had a beginning in Scotland before the days of *Malcolm Canmore*. For, if the feudal law was introduced by that king, there is no probability it should make so sudden a progress, as to be ripe for a regular institute in the days of his son *David*. This is not agreeable to the natural course of things, and therefore not readily to be credited. Law is but of slow growth, especially among a rude people, more addicted to the arts of war than of peace. And yet, whatever be the era of the *Regiam Majestatem*, it appears from it, that the feudal law was brought to a considerable degree of perfection in Scotland at that time. The argument is weighty; and we must either give the feudal law a more early date in Scotland than the reign of *Malcolm Canmore*, or the *Regiam Majestatem* a later date than the reign of *David I*. With regard to this matter one thing is certain, that the *Regiam Majestatem* was compiled in the reign of one of our *Davids*. [...]

---

6   [Malcolm III Canmore ('Bighead'), Scottish king (1057–93).]
7   [*Regiam Majestatem* is the first treatise on Scots law and derived from the treaty by Ranulf de Glanvill (late twelfth century), itself a principal source for medieval English legal history. According to modern scholarship, *Regiam Majestatem* has probably been composed in the reign of Robert I (1306–29).]

I cannot readily bring myself to believe, that *Malcolm Canmore* gave away the whole Crown lands, as is related. And on the other hand, I can as little bring myself to believe, that by any means less than absolute force, could the bulk of the nation be brought to submit to an act so visibly prejudicial to them, that of surrendering their whole lands to the king, and their persons also, reserving only the usufruct,[8] in name of wages, for services to be performed by them.

In a matter so dark and intricate, I dare venture no further, than to suggest a few conjectures. Before the feudal law was known in Scotland, I take it for granted, that our people held their lands without writ,[9] and that possession was the circumstance which determined the property of lands, as at this day it does of moveables. Some traces of this we have remaining in the Orkney islands, where the feudal law is scarce yet fully established. If instead of introducing the feudal law, all at once over the whole kingdom, it shall be supposed, that *Malcolm Canmore* did no more but lay the foundation of a building, which was finished by his successors, the thing will be easily credited.

c) *Conjectural Progress of the Political System*

i) From: *Essays upon Several Subjects concerning British Antiquities*, 2nd ed. (1749): Essay II, 'Constitution of Parliament', pp. 28–48

The idea of a king, where the feudal law took place, is not that of a chief magistrate or governor, but that of a paramount superior, having the whole land property of the nation vested in him, having his vassals attached to him by homage and fealty,[10] and supported by him out of the produce of his lands: which makes a very strict connection and union betwixt them. The idea of a Parliament, [...] is that of a court where all the king's vassals are obliged to attend

---

[8] [Proprietary right to use and enjoy the property of another.]
[9] [In this context, an instrument under seal containing an entitlement granted by the sovereign.]
[10] [The personal feudal bond between superior and vassal was created by the act of homage (usually a ceremony in which the kneeling vassal is placing his clasped hands between the hands of his lord) and the oath of fealty. There were many variants in reality.]

for administrating of justice, and for making regulations to bind the whole society.

It was one effect of the feudal law to withdraw land from commerce. Land being allotted for the maintenance of servants or vassals, ready to obey their masters' commands in war and peace, the superior could not sell, because the whole profits arising from the subject[11] belonged to the vassal, and the vassal could not sell because he was not proprietor. This was an unnatural constitution, which could not subsist long in peaceable times. The severity of the feudal law gave place by degrees to milder and more natural regulations. Land the most desirable acquisition came to be *in commercio*,[12] and the crown vassals originally few in number, and possessing large territories were greatly multiplied. Purchasers were willing to hold of the king rather than of a subject; and the King was willing to encourage this commerce, as it lessened the power of the great barons. In time the obliging so many small vassals to an expensive attendance in Parliament, was considered as a grievance. In England this grievance was remedied, probably in the days of *John* or *Henry III*[13] for the record of that transaction is lost. The remedy was introduced with us later, and we have the record entire. By the Act 101, *Parl*. 1427, the attendance of small barons and freeholders is dispensed with, provided they send to Parliament, from every shire, two or more of their number to represent them.

We followed the English so close in all their regulations concerning law and policy, that I am persuaded our Statute 1427 has been copied from some English statute enacted by King *John*, or in the beginning of the reign of *Henry III* which is now lost with many other statutes of that period. [...]

As our *James I* was perfectly well acquainted with the English constitution, by his long residence in England, it appears to have been his plan to introduce into his own kingdom many of the laws and customs of that country. What we have at present to take notice of, are contained in the above-

---

[11] [Here: property, estate.]
[12] [An object of commercial dealings.]
[13] [English kings: King John (1199–1216), Henry III (1216–1272).]

mentioned Statute, Act 101 *Parl.* 1427, 1st, exempting the small barons and freeholders from attendance in Parliament, upon condition of sending representatives; 2nd, making these representatives, perhaps with the representatives from the burrows, a separate body, which appears from the regulation appointing a president to be chosen, called the common Speaker of the Parliament; 3rd, enacting that the Prelates and Peers should be called to Parliament *nominatim*[14] by special precepts. [...] The Prelates and great Lords, in whom the power of the Parliament centred after this regulation, had no interest to enforce it. The king indeed had an interest, in order to balance the exorbitant power of the nobles; but in these rude times this was overlooked, insomuch that a statute was obtained in the reign of *James II* [...], relieving all freeholders from attendance, whose yearly rent did not amount to £20 without a word of their being obliged to send representatives. Matters continued upon this footing till the days of *James VI* save that [...] all were exempted from attendance whose rent was within one hundred Merks. The Reformation greatly increased the power of the nobility, as it almost extinguished the Prelates. The Abbacies were totally demolished; and but few of the bishops frequented the Parliament. By this means the nobility had all in their power: They oppressed the burrows, and were too strong for the king. Thus the government became purely aristocratical, and stood in need of some regulation to bring it to its former poise. Had the Act of *James I* been followed out, in the same manner as the like regulation was followed out in England, this evil would have been prevented: and now the only remedy was to revive that Act. The surprise is, that a majority was found among the nobility, to countenance a regulation, which behoved remarkably to abridge their authority. It appears from [a] statute [...] that great opposition was made. The attendance of the small barons in Parliament was so thoroughly in disuse, that they could not now think of resuming as a privilege, what they had so long been exempted from, considered as a service. But it had all along been understood to be the prerogative of the Crown,

---

[14] [Called by name.]

acknowledged in every statute relating to the Parliament, that the king might call, by special writ, any of his vassals to attend the Parliament, notwithstanding of their exemption. Probably this has been the instrument made use of by the king's ministers, to gain the end proposed: The nobles would be told, that if they voted against the regulation, the king would use his privilege of calling to Parliament a number of his small vassals, sufficient to over-balance the nobility. As this is but mere conjecture, it is submitted to the judgment of others. One thing is certain, that the Act 1427 was revived, and the small barons sent representatives to Parliament from that period downwards. [...]

It was a part of the plan of *James I* to divide his Parliament into two bodies, as in England. This was not followed by *James VI* for our Parliament continued one body to the end. It is left to conjecture, whether this was of design, or by accident; for our historians are extremely defective upon our civil transactions. We have no occasion to go further than to England, to learn what influence it has upon the constitution to divide a Parliament into two Houses; and as it was a politic age, this of *James VI*, I am apt to believe, it was not without design, that the Parliament of this kingdom was continued upon its old footing. This is a curious subject, and deserves to be attended to. It is pretty obvious, that the king's negative against a regulation agreed to by both Houses is not a very valuable privilege. The opinion of the two Houses, being understood to be the sense of the nation, has rather too great force to be resisted by the *veto* of any single man, the king not excepted. His refusing an assent in such a case, is virtually declaring himself against the interest of his people. But an English monarch is seldom brought under this dilemma. If he can but get a majority in either House on his side, the work is done. He may appear to be neuter. Thus, taking the Parliament complexly, a great majority may be against the king, bent, we may suppose, to fetter him by new limitations; and yet he may ward the blow, by procuring a scrimp majority in either House for him. This cannot happen where the Parliament makes but one body, as in Scotland. So far the advantage lies on the king's side, where the Parliament is composed of two bodies. But to balance this, the same advantage lies on the side of the people, where the king's views are to enlarge his prerogative by authority of Parliament; for a scrimp majority in either House, interposing a veto, frustrates his design. In a word, a single body gives great opportunities of making encroachments on either side; whereas, supposing the constitution to be found and entire, it is best preserved so, by a Parliament composed of two bodies.

ii) From: *Essays upon Several Subjects concerning British Antiquities*, 2nd ed. (1749): 'Appendix: The Hereditary and Indefeasible Right of Kings', pp. 192-202

When we consider man, abstracted from all positive engagements, we find nothing in his nature, or in his situation, to subject him to the power of any, his creator, and his parents excepted. The parental power is at an end, when children are grown up, and can provide for themselves. At any rate the parental power cannot subsist longer than the life of the parents; for it is not a matter of property to be transmitted by succession, since it depends upon personal circumstances. And supposing it a subject to be taken by succession, it must descend to all the children equally, at least to all the sons equally; for primogeniture,[15] it is certain, is not a privilege of the law of nature, but only of the feudal law. Hence it is a principle embraced by the gravest writers, that all mankind are born free, and independent of one another.

Man indeed is fitted for society. His wants prompt him to it, and his inclinations render it agreeable. Accordingly we find mankind almost everywhere parcelled out into societies, which have been originally formed by accidental circumstances, more or less extensive. A society of any extent cannot be without government. The members must have laws to determine their differences, and they must have rulers to put their laws in execution. At the same time, we find the constitutions of different states, with regard to government, almost as various, as are the sentiments of men concerning it: So that though government be necessary to the well-being of society, yet from this circumstance alone, were

---

[15] [The right of the first-born son to inherit the family estate, thus ousting the daughters and younger sons.]

we to look no further back, we may conclude no particular form to be necessary, but that all are the effect of choice, or perhaps in some measure of accident.

Let us trace this matter further, because it is of importance. Man is a shy animal, and in his original state, rather averse to society. In that state his wants were few, and easily supplied; therefore we may readily conclude, that while acorns were the food of man, and water his drink, there was neither use nor appetite for society. Accordingly we find mankind originally in every corner of the earth living in scattered habitations, with little intercourse, except among the members of the same family. The culture of corn laid the foundation of a more extensive intercourse, because thereby mutual assistance became necessary. When arts were invented, and industry increased, it was found convenient to herd together in towns and villages. From this closer connection one evil sprung, opposition of interests, formerly rare; which at first was the occasion of quarrels and bloodshed, and afterwards of frequent appeals to men of weight and probity. In time the necessity of fixed judges to determine differences being discovered, the election of these judges, which could not otherwise be than popular, was the first step to government. The chief magistrate therefore was originally no more but the chief judge, whose powers were gradually extended, as cases occurred, which required the interposition of a superior or governor. War introduced slavery, as it subjected those taken in battle to the arbitrary will of their conquerors; and absolute power was too desirable an acquisition, to be confined to private persons. The chief magistrate, however repugnant it is to the nature of his office, did often grasp at it: And history informs us, that the chief magistrate, in different societies, has been often but too successful. In a word, absolute independence and absolute power are the two extremes; and the latter, at least so far as concerns sovereignty, could never have been introduced, but by passing through all the intermediate degrees.

Government therefore is one of the arts which necessity has suggested, which time and experience have ripened, and which must be perpetually susceptible of further improvements. For government, like all other arts, being invented for the good of mankind, it must be the privilege of every society to improve upon it, as well as upon manufactures or husbandry. No particular form therefore can be necessary, as no particular form is preferable to another, unless so far as it has a greater tendency to promote its end, the good of the society. Comparing democracy, aristocracy and monarchy together, this is their common standard.

There is a people inhabiting the earth, who are not left to the choice of their governors, but are by nature subjected to monarchy. In every society there is a royal family, of a different species from the other members. Every monarch is born with marks of royalty, of a peculiar shape, and with superior beauty. We may suppose, that the excellences of the mind are not inferior to those of the body; and no wonder when this is the case, that perfect obedience is given through all the state, and that their monarch's will is their only law. Here the parts are justly distributed, the sovereign framed for command, as the subjects for obedience, each in their several capacities equally contributing to the only end of government, the well-being of the society. In this community there can be no stretching of prerogative on the one hand, no resistance nor even murmurs on the other. The monarch taught by nature, that the sovereign power is a trust which ought not to be abused, has no desire but to promote the public welfare. The people taught by nature, that passive obedience and non-resistance are the means to promote their happiness, implicitly submit themselves to their monarch's will.

Were mankind so framed, for of insects we have been speaking, these gentlemen would have reason on their side, who declare so strongly for indefeasible-hereditary right, and the reciprocal duty of passive obedience and non-resistance: Were our royal family, like that of the bees, distinguished from the mass of the people by superior excellences, whether of the mind or body, were they unerringly prompted by nature to exercise their power for the welfare of the society, blind obedience to their will would be a virtue. But when we trust with sovereign power one of the common stamp of mankind, who has by nature no marks of royalty, and who perhaps by nature is not fitted for command, the absurdity is great, to maintain, that this person ought to be under no control, and that we ought to continue to trust him, after repeated instances of his betraying the trust reposed in him.

I have no occasion to consider whether conquest be a good title by the law of nature, to acquire the absolute dominion of a state, as in Turkey, where the Grand Seignior is supposed to be the Lord of the Manor, and all the people his slaves. This is not government, the characteristic of which is, trust reposed in one for the good of the whole. It is like a private estate, which may be disposed of by the proprietor without control, and applied for his own purposes. It cannot be pretended that the king of Britain has his right by conquest; and therefore no support can be brought to the argument from this quarter.

The scheme, it must be yielded, is so far consistent, that if we suppose the king's right to be indefeasible, and that he cannot be deprived of his authority, however much his measures swerve from the rules of good government, it must follow, that the people are tied to passive obedience and nonresistance, as there is no *medium* betwixt resistance and obedience. But where is the foundation of the indefeasible right of the king, more than of any other officer of the state? Does it lie in the name? One should scarce think so, when the name is indifferently applied to governors who have very little power, as well as to those whose power is the most extensive. It cannot lie in the nature of the office, which being a trust, is undoubtedly forfeitable upon maladministration. It will perhaps be said to lie in the constitution of our government. So far from it, that no man is bound to obey the king's commands, unless delivered in a certain form prescribed by law. And even in France, supposing it an absolute monarchy, without any constitutional check upon the king's actions, the king's power is notwithstanding limited. There cannot be such a thing in nature, as for a people voluntarily to surrender their liberties to the arbitrary will of any man. The act would be void as inconsistent with the great law of nature, *salus populi suprema lex*.[16]

---

[16] [Actually '*ollis salus populi suprema lex esto*', 'The good/safety of the people should be the highest law', reference to Cicero's *Laws* (*De Legibus*), book 3, 3, 8.]

But the favourers of this doctrine, when beat out of these entrenchments, have a retreat, which they suppose impregnable. They allow at last that the king may do wrong, by betraying the trust reposed in him. But then they maintain, that a king having no superior on earth, can have no proper judge of his actions but God alone, from whom his power flows; and therefore is accountable to the Almighty only. This is a fortress built upon sand. All power no doubt is from God, natural and legal; for he is the creator and upholder of all things. But it follows from this, instead of being contradictory to it, that every sort of power is limited by the opposition of other powers, natural or legal, which are equally from God with the power resisted. Perhaps they mean that every king has his commission from the Almighty, and not from the people. History alone may suffice to inform us, that this cannot be, when there have existed so many kings unworthy of command. But supposing the fact, it does not follow, that this commission is unlimited. On the contrary, it must be limited; for who can patronise so impious a doctrine as that God should give a direct commission to any being to plague and persecute mankind, unless for their sins? The voice of nature is the voice of God; and it is a fixed principle in the law of nature, that where there is no common judge to appeal to, the party injured may do himself justice. The laws are superior to the king, and these he must be judged by. And supposing an absolute government in the strictest sense, where the king's will is law, yet there is always one law above him. If his actions generally tend to destruction, instead of government, the people, who have no judge to appeal to, may lawfully do themselves right. *Salus populi est suprema lex.*

d) *Conjectural History in relation to Criminal Law*

From: *Historical Law-Tracts*, 4th ed. (1792), Tract I, 'Criminal Law', pp. 20-26

Having discoursed in general of the nature of punishment, and of some irregular notions that have been entertained about it, I am now ready to attend its progress through the different stages of the social life. Society, originally, did not make a strict union among individuals. Mutual defence against a more powerful neighbour, being in early times the chief or sole motive for joining in society, individuals never thought of surrendering to the public, any of their natural rights that could be retained consistently with mutual defence. In particular, the privileges of maintaining their own property, and of avenging their own wrongs, were reserved to individuals full and entire. In the dawn of society accordingly, we find no traces of a judge, properly so called, who had power to interpose in differences, and to force persons at variance to submit to his opinion. If a dispute about property, or about any civil right, could not be adjusted by the parties themselves, there was no other method, but to take the opinion of some indifferent person. This method of determining civil differences was imperfect; for what if the parties did not agree upon an arbiter? Or what if one of them proved refractory, after the chosen arbiter had given his opinion? To remedy these inconveniences, it was found expedient to establish judges, who at first differed in one circumstance only from arbiters, that they could not be declined. They had no magisterial authority, not even that of compelling parties to appear before them. This is evident from the Roman law, which subsisted many centuries before the notion obtained of a power in a judge to force a party into court. To bring a disputable matter to an issue, no other means occurred, but the making it lawful for the complainer to drag his party before the judge. [...] But jurisdiction, at first merely voluntary, came gradually to be improved to its present state of being compulsory, involving so much of the magisterial authority as is necessary for explicating jurisdiction, viz. power of calling a party into court, and power of making a sentence effectual. And in this manner, civil jurisdiction, in progress of time, was brought to perfection.

Criminal jurisdiction is in all countries of a much later date. Revenge, the darling privilege of undisciplined nature,[17] is never tamely given up; for the reason chiefly, that it is not gratified unless the punishment be inflicted by the person injured. The privilege of resenting injuries, was

---

17   [It is noteworthy that the first and second editions read 'the darling privilege of human nature'.]

therefore that private right which was the latest of being surrendered, or rather wrested from individuals in society. This revolution was of great importance with respect to government, which can never fully attain its end, where punishment in any measure is trusted in private hands. A revolution so contradictory to the strongest propensity of human nature, could not by any power, nor by any artifice, be instantaneous. It must have been gradual, and, in fact, the progressive steps tending to its completion, were slow, and, taken singly, almost imperceptible; as will appear from the following history. And to be convinced of the difficulty of wresting this privilege from individuals, we need but reflect upon the practice of duelling, so customary in times past; and which the strictest attention in the magistrate, joined with the severest punishment, have not altogether been able to repress.

No production of art or nature is more imperfect than is government in its infancy, comprehending no sort of jurisdiction, civil or criminal. What can more tend to break the peace of society, and to promote universal discord, than that every man should be the judge in his own cause, and inflict punishment according to his own judgment? But instead of wondering at the original weakness of government, our wonder would be better directed upon its present state of perfection, and upon the means by which it had arrived to that state, in opposition to the strongest and most active principles of human nature. This subject makes a great figure in the history of man; and that it partly comes under the present undertaking, I esteem a lucky circumstance.

A partiality rooted in the nature of man, makes private revenge a most dangerous privilege. The man who is injured, having a strong sense of the wrong done him, never dreams of putting bounds to his resentment. The offender, on the other hand, underrating the injury, judges a slight atonement sufficient. Further, the man who suffers is apt to judge rashly, and to blame persons without cause. To restrain the unjust effects of natural partiality, was not an easy task; and probably was not soon attempted. But early measures were taken to prevent the bad effects of rash judgment, by which the innocent were often oppressed. [...]

The necessity of applying to a judge, where any doubt arose about the author of the crime, was probably, in all countries, the first instance of the legislature's interposing in punishment. It was a novelty; but it was such as could not readily alarm individuals, being calculated not to restrain the privilege of revenge, but only to direct revenge to its proper object.

e) *Conjectural History in relation to Contractual Obligations*

From: *Historical Law-Tracts*, 4th ed. (1792), Tract II, 'Promises and Covenants', pp. 66–68

Moral principles, faint among savages, acquire strength by refinement of manners in polished societies. Promises and covenants, in particular, have full authority among nations disciplined in a long course of regular government: but among barbarians it is rare to find a promise or covenant of such authority as to counterbalance, in any considerable degree, the weight of appetite or passion. This circumstance, joined with the imperfection of a language in its infancy, are the causes why engagements are little regarded in original laws.

It is lucky, that among a rude people in the first stages of government, the necessity of engagements is not greater than their authority. Originally, every family subsisted by hunting, and by the natural fruits of the earth. The taming wild animals, and rendering them domestic, multiplied greatly the means of subsistence. The invention of agriculture produced to the industrious a superfluity, with which foreign necessaries were purchased. Commerce originally was carried on by barter or permutation,[18] to which a previous covenant is not necessary. And after money was introduced into commerce, we have reason to believe, that buying and selling also was at first carried on by exchanging goods for money, without any previous covenant. But in the progress of the social life, the wants and appetites of men multiply faster than to be readily supplied by commerce so narrow

---

[18] [*Permutatio* is the Roman law term for barter.]

and confined. There came to be a demand for interposed persons, who take care to be informed of what is redundant in one corner, and of what is wanted in another. This occupation was improved into that of a merchant, who provides himself from a distance with what is demanded at home. Then it was, and no sooner, that the use of a covenant comes to be recognised; for the business of a merchant cannot be carried on to any extent, or with any success, without previous agreements.

So far back as we can trace the Roman law, we find its authority interposed in behalf of sale, location,[19] and other contracts deemed essential to commerce. And that commerce was advanced in Rome before action was sustained upon such contracts, is evident from the contract of society or partnership[20] put in that class. Other covenants were not regarded, but left upon the obligation of the natural law.[21]

f) *Conjectural History in relation to Property*

i) From: *Historical Law-Tracts*, 4th ed. (1792), Tract III, 'Property', pp. 90–113

Hunting and fishing were originally the occupations of men, upon which chiefly they depended for food. A beast caught in a gin, or a fish with a hook, being the purchase of art and industry, were from the beginning, considered by all as belonging to the occupant: The appetite that man has for appropriation, vouches this to be true. But the extent of the relation thus created betwixt the hunter his prey, and the power acquired by the former over the latter in common estimation, are questions of more intricacy. That this relation implies a power to use for sustenance the creature thus taken, and to defend the possession against every invader, is clear. But supposing the creature to have been lost, and

---

[19] [This refers to the Roman law contract categories of *emptio venditio* (sale) and *locatio conductio* (hire, lease).]
[20] [The Roman law *societas* (partnership).]
[21] [This is a reference to the (late classical) Roman law (and the European *ius commune*) *obligatio naturalis*, an obligation which can be discharged through payment (so there is no unjustified enrichment), but cannot be enforced through court action.]

without violence to have come into the hands of another, I do not clearly see, that the original occupant would have any claim, or that restitution would be reckoned the duty of the possessor. This may be thought sceptical; for to one who has imbibed the refined principles of law, the conception is familiar of a relation betwixt a man and a subject, so intimate as not to be dissolvable without his consent: But, in the investigation of original laws, nothing is more apt to lead into error, than prepossession derived from modern improvements. It appears to me highly probable, that among savages, involved in objects of sense, and strangers to abstract speculation, property, and the rights or moral powers arising from it, never are with accuracy distinguished from the natural powers that must be exerted upon the subject to make it profitable to the possessor. The man who kills and eats, who sows and reaps, at his own pleasure, independent of another's will, is naturally deemed proprietor. The grossest savages understand power without right, of which they are made sensible by daily acts of violence: But property without possession is a conception too abstract for a savage, or for any person who has not studied the principles of law.[22] To this day the vulgar can form no distinct conception of property, otherwise than by figuring the man in possession, and using the subject without control. If such at present be the vulgar way of thinking, we may reasonably suspect a still greater obscurity in the conceptions of a savage.

Thus originally property was a very precarious right; and would have been of little value, had not nature provided means for recovering it when possession was lost. Where a man is deprived of his goods by theft or other criminal act,

---

[22] [The text of the first and second editions has an important variant of this passage: 'but it requires a habit of abstraction, to conceive right or moral power independent of natural power; because in this condition, right, being attended with no visible effect, is a mental conception merely. That a man may be deprived of a subject, and yet retain the property, is a lesson too intricate for a savage. For how can this be, it will be observed, when he has not the use of the subject, and has no power over it?' —See the definition of 'conception' in the *Appendix* of the *Elements of Criticism*, extract in chapter 1.]

the wrongdoer is in conscience bound to restore. He has indeed acquired the property with the possession; but he is bound to repair the injuries done to the former possessor; and the proper reparation is, to restore the subject to him. [...]

Man, by the frame of his body, is unqualified to be an animal of prey. His stomach requires more regular supplies of food, than can be obtained in a state where food is so precarious.[23] His necessities taught him the art of taming such of the wild creatures as are peaceable and docile. Large herds were propagated of horned cattle, sheep, and goats; which afforded plenty of food ready at hand for daily use. By this invention, the conveniences of living were greatly promoted: and in this state, which makes the second stage of the social life, the relation of property, though not entirely disjoined from possession, was considerably enlivened. The care and attention bestowed upon a domestic animal from the time of its birth, form in the mind of every one a strong connection betwixt the man and his beast, which, upon any casual interruption of possession, does not so readily vanish, as in the case of a wild beast seized by a hunter.

Thus, by a natural principle, the relation of property was in some measure fortified, and was considered as forming a stricter connection betwixt man and other animals than it did originally. In this condition, a political principle contributed to make the relation appear still more intimate. Experience demonstrated, that it is impracticable to repress theft and robbery, if purchasers be secure upon the pretext of *bona fides*.[24] For every purchase must be presumed honest, till the contrary be proved; and nothing is more easy than to contrive a dishonest purchase that shall be secure from detection. To remedy an evil which gave so great scope to

---

[23] [Footnote by Kames] When men were hunters, and lived like carnivorous animals upon prey, there could be no regular supplies of food; and after they became shepherds, the former habit of abstinence made their meals probably less frequent than at present, though food was at hand. In old times, there was but one meal a day; which continued to be the fashion, even after great luxury was indulged in other respects. [...]

[24] [Good faith.]

stealth and violence, the regulation above mentioned was introduced, prohibiting all buying and selling except in open market. After this regulation, a private purchase afforded no security, nor was the property transferred. The *nexus*, or lien, of property, was greatly strengthened, when it was now to become law, that no man could be deprived of his property without his own consent; except singly in the case of a purchase *bona fide* in open market. I add upon this head, that the notion of right, independent of natural power, once unfolded, acquired the greatest firmness and stability, by the regular establishment of courts of justice, the great purpose of which is, to afford natural power whenever it is of use to make right or moral power effectual. [...]

Property, it is certain, is a great favourite of human nature, and is frequently the object of a very strong affection. In the fluctuating state of human affairs, before regular governments were formed, property was seldom so permanent as to afford great scope for this affection. But in peaceable times, under a steady administration of law, the affection for property becomes exceeding warm, which fortifies greatly the relation of property. Thus there is discovered a natural resemblance between government and property: from the weak and infantine state in which both are found originally, they have equally arrived at that stability and perfection which they enjoy at present.

Having advanced so far in the history of moveable property, it is time to turn our view to the property of land. In the two first stages of the social life, while men were hunters or shepherds, there scarce could be any notion of land-property. Strangers to agriculture, and to the art of building, if it was not of huts which could be raised or demolished in a moment, men had no fixed habitation, but wandered about in hoards to find pasture for their cattle. In this vagrant life, men had scarce any connection with land more than with air or water. A field of grass might be considered as belonging to a hoard or clan, while they were in possession; and so might the air which they breathed, and the water of which they drank: but the moment they removed to another quarter, there no longer subsisted any connection betwixt them and the field that was deserted. It lay open to newcomers, who had the same right as if it had not been formerly occupied. Hence I conclude, that while men were shepherds, there was no relation formed betwixt them and land, in any manner so distinct as to obtain the name of property.

Agriculture, which makes the third stage of the social life, produced the relation of land-property. A man who has bestowed labour in preparing a field for the plough, and who has improved that field by artful culture, forms in his mind a very intimate connection with it. He contracts by degrees a singular affection for a spot, which in a manner is the workmanship of his own hands. He is fond to live there, and there to deposit his bones. It is an object that fills his mind, and is never out of thought at home or abroad. After a summer's expedition, or perhaps years of a foreign war, he returns with avidity to his own house, and to his own field, there to pass his time in ease and plenty. By such trials the relation of property is disjoined from possession; and to this disjunction, the lively perception of property with respect to an object so considerable, mainly contributes. If a proprietor happens to be dispossessed in his absence, the injustice is perceived and acknowledged. In the common sense of mankind, he continues proprietor, and a *rei vindicatio*[25] will be sustained to him against the possessor, to whom the property cannot be transferred by an immoral act. But what if the subject,[26] after a long interval, be purchased *bona fide*, and peaceable possession attained? [...] In ancient times, such a purchase transferred property, and extinguished the right of the former proprietor. Such undoubtedly was once the condition of moveable property, gradually altered, as observed above, by successive regulations. Land-property continued a much shorter time in this unstable condition. Of all subjects of property, land is that which engages our affection the most; by which means the relation of land-

---

[25] [In Roman law-based legal systems, the *rei vindicatio* or action for delivery is the exercise of the right of the owner against the possessor to claim the property object; it is the most fundamental right ownership confers.]

[26] [Here: object of property.]

property grew up much sooner to its present firmness and stability, than the relation of moveable property. [...]

It is highly probable, that the strong *nexus* of land-property, which cannot be loosened otherwise than by consent, had an influence upon moveable property, to make it equally stable. But if land-property led the way in this particular, moveable property undoubtedly led the way in what we are now to enter upon, viz. the power of aliening.[27] The connection of persons with moveables is more immediate than with land. A moveable may be locked up in a repository: Cattle are killed every day for the sustenance of the proprietor and his family. From this power, the transition is easy to that of alienation; for what doubt can there be of my power to alien what I can destroy? The right or power of alienation must therefore have been early recognised as a quality of moveable property. The power of disposing moveables by will, to take effect after death, is a greater stretch; and we shall have occasion to see, that this power was not early acknowledged as one of the qualities even of moveable property. We have reason beforehand to conjecture, that a power of aliening land, whether to take effect instantly or after death, was not early introduced; because land admits not, like moveables, a ready delivery from hand to hand. [...] Land, at the same time, is a desirable object; and a power to alien, after it came to be established in moveable property, could not long be separated from the property of land. [...]

Property, which originally bestowed no power of alienation, carries the mind naturally to the children of the possessor, who continue the possession after his death, and who must succeed if he cannot alien. Their right, being independent of his will, was conceived a sort of property. They make part of the family, live upon the land; and, in common with their parents, enjoy its product. When the father dies, they continue in possession without any alteration, but that the family is less by one than formerly. Such a right in children, which commenced at their birth, and which

---

[27] [Aliening, alienation is here it be understood in the technical sense of property transfer.]

was perfected by the father's death, was not readily to be distinguished from property. [...]

It is remarked above, that the enlarged notion of property, by annexing to it a power of alienation, obtained first in moveables: And indeed society could scarce subsist without such a power; at least so far as is necessary for exchanging commodities, and carrying on commerce. But the same power was not early annexed to the property of land, unless perhaps to support the alienation of some small part for value. This we know, that a proprietor of land that had descended to him from his ancestors, could not dispose upon it totally, even for a valuable consideration, unless he was reduced to want of bread; and even in that case, he was obliged to make the first offer to his heir. [...] The power of aliening for a valuable consideration, is now universally held to be inherent in the property of land as well as of moveables.

ii) From: *Essays upon Several Subjects concerning British Antiquities*, 2nd ed. (1749): Essay IV, 'Upon Succession or Descent', Part I, pp. 127–129

After Property was introduced, and had gained a firm establishment, the matter of succession could not be long neglected. The death of the very first man who acquired property, must have given occasion to the question, who was to succeed him? If his will was declared upon the point, no doubt could be that it was the rule.[28] If the estate was left *in*

---

[28] [Footnote by Kames] The author is aware, that while property was in its infancy, it was doubted whether a man's will, in whatever manner declared, could have the effect to regulate his succession. But when the thing is attended to, it will be found to resolve into a dispute about the nature of property. Occupation is allowed to have been the first foundation of property in land. When a piece of ground was taken out of the common, and cultivated by the occupier for the use of himself and family, it soon came to be settled, that this person was to have the undisturbed possession for his life; otherwise farewell to labour and industry. But as his interest in the subject behoved to die with himself, it was not readily conceived how his power over the subject should continue after his interest was at an end, or at any rate subsist after he was dead and gone. But this difficulty was plainly owing to the limited notion of property,

medio,[29] without a will to direct the succession, his children for whom he was bound to provide, would naturally be suggested to the mind. This pointed out the primary rule of succession, that children succeed *ab intestato*.[30] But what if there are no children? This is but following out the same rule, to pitch upon the nearest relation. For after a man's death, his children or other relations, will be considered as having a closer connection with his effects than strangers; and, by a natural transition of ideas, the property, that was in the deceased, will be readily transferred to his kindred.

2. Origin of Men and Human Races

From: *Sketches of the History of Man*, 3rd ed. (1788), book 1, 'Preliminary Discourse', pp. 3–77

Whether there are different races of men, or whether all men are of one race without any difference but what proceeds from climate or other external cause, is a question which philosophers differ widely about. As the question is of moment in tracing the history of man, I purpose to contribute my mite. And, in order to admit all the light possible, a

---

> which was entertained after its first introduction. In early times property was not much distinguished from what is now called *usufruct* [a proprietary right to use and enjoy the property of another]. No more was conceived in property, but the unlimited use of the subject. But experience pointed out a more extensive idea of property. Mankind are fond of power, especially over what is their own; and it came to be considered as an unreasonable hardship, after industry bestowed in acquiring and improving a field, that the occupier should not have it in his power to dispose of it at his pleasure. The power of disposal was relished, and became law, because it was every one's interest that it should be law. And when once this power was understood, it came by degrees to be extended the utmost length it was capable of [Kames quotes from Hugo Grotius here]. [...] Therefore, when we read of ancient laws among particular nations, introducing the power of making a testament, we must not consider these laws as bestowing peculiar privileges, but only as authorising a practice which was the consequence of an enlarged idea of property.

[29] [The estate or property left in the hands of the holder of the estate.]
[30] [Without a will or testament.]

view of brute animals as divided into different races or kinds, will make a proper introduction.

As many animals contribute to our well-being, and as many are noxious, man would be a being not a little imperfect, were he provided with no means but experience for distinguishing the one sort from the other. Did every animal make a species by itself (indulging the expression) differing from all others, a man would finish his course without acquiring as much knowledge of animals as is necessary even for self-preservation: he would be absolutely at a loss with respect to unknown individuals. The Deity has left none of his works imperfect. Animals are formed of different kinds; resemblance prevailing among animals of the same kind, dissimilitude among animals of different kinds. And, to prevent confusion, kinds are distinguished externally by figure, air, manner, so clearly as not to escape even a child. Nor does divine wisdom stop here: to complete the system, we are endued with an innate conviction, that each kind has properties peculiar to itself; and that these properties belong to every individual of the kind. Our road to the knowledge of animals is thus wonderfully shortened: the experience we have of the disposition and properties of any animal, is applied without hesitation to every one of the kind. By that conviction, a child, familiar with one dog, is fond of others that resemble it: A European, upon the first sight of a cow in Africa, strokes it as gentle and innocent: and an African avoids a tiger in Hindustan as at home.

If the foregoing theory be well founded, neither experience nor argument is required to prove, that a horse is not an ass, or that a monkey is not a man. In some individuals indeed, there is such a mixture of resemblance and dissimilitude, as to render it uncertain to what species they belong. But such instances are rare, and impinge not on the general law. Such questions may be curious, but they are of little use.

Whether man be provided by nature with a faculty to distinguish innocent animals from what are noxious, seems not a clear point: such a faculty may be thought unnecessary to man, being supplied by reason and experience. But as reason and experience have little influence on brute animals, they undoubtedly possess that faculty. A beast of prey would be ill-fitted for its station, if nature did not teach it what creatures to attack, what to avoid. A rabbit is the prey of the ferret. Present a rabbit, even dead, to a young ferret that never had seen a rabbit: it throws itself upon the body, and bites it with fury. A hound has the same faculty with respect to a hare; and most dogs have it. Unless directed by nature, innocent animals would not know their enemy till they were in its clutches. A hare flies with precipitation from the first dog it ever saw; and a chicken, upon the sight of a kite, cowers under its dam. Social animals, without scruple, connect with their own kind, and as readily avoid others. Birds are not afraid of quadrupeds; not even of a cat, till they are taught by experience that a cat is their enemy. They appear to be as little afraid of a man naturally; and upon that account are far from being shy when left unmolested. [...]

The division of animals into different kinds, serves another purpose, no less important than those mentioned; which is, to fit them for different climates. We learn from experience, that no animal nor vegetable is equally fitted for every climate; and from experience we also learn, that there is no animal nor vegetable but what is fitted for some climate, where it grows to perfection. Even in the torrid zone, plants of a cold climate are found upon mountains where plants of a hot climate will not grow; and the height of a mountain may be determined with tolerable precision from the plants it produces. Wheat is not an indigenous plant in Britain: no farmer is ignorant that foreign seed is requisite to preserve the plant in vigour. To prevent flax from degenerating in Scotland and Ireland, great quantities of foreign seed are annually imported. A camel is peculiarly fitted for the burning sands of Arabia; and Lapland would be uninhabitable but for reindeer, an animal so entirely fitted for piercing cold, that it cannot subsist even in a temperate climate. Arabian and Barbary horses degenerate in Britain; and, to preserve the breed in some degree of perfection, frequent supplies from their original climate are requisite. Spanish horses degenerate in Mexico; but improve in Chile, having more vigour and swiftness there, than even the Andalusian race, whose off-spring they are. [...]

To preserve the different kinds or species of animals entire, as far as necessary, providence is careful to prevent a mixed breed. Few animals of different species copulate together. Some may be brought to copulate, but without effect; and some produce a mongrel, a mule for example, which seldom procreates, if at all. In some few instances, where a mixture of species is harmless, procreation goes on without limitation. All the different species of the dog-kind copulate together; and the mongrels produced generate others without end.

M. Buffon,[31] in his natural history, borrows from Ray[32] a very artificial rule for ascertaining the different species of animals: 'Any two animals that can procreate together, and whose issue can also procreate, are of the same species'. A horse and an ass can procreate together; but they are not, says he, of the same species, because their issue, a mule, cannot procreate. He applies that rule to man; holding all men to be of the same species, because a man and a woman, however different in size, in shape, in complexion, can procreate together without end. And by the same rule he holds all dogs to be of the same species. With respect to other animals, the author should peaceably be indulged in his fancy; but as it comprehends also man, I cannot pass it without examination. Providence, to prevent confusion, has in many instances withheld from animals of different species a power of procreating together: but as our author has not attempted to prove that such restraint is universal without a single exception, his rule is evidently a *petitio principii*.[33] Why may not two animals different in species produce a mixed breed? M. Buffon must say, that it is contrary to a law of nature. But has he given any evidence of this supposed law of nature? On the contrary, he proves it by various instances not to be a law of nature. He admits the sheep and the goat to be of different species; and yet we have his authority for affirming, that a he-goat and a ewe produce a mixed breed which generate for ever. The camel and the dromedary, though nearly related, are however no less distinct than the

---

[31] [George Louis Leclerc Buffon (1707–88), author of the *Histoire naturelle*.]
[32] [Footnote by Kames] Wisdom of God in the works of creation.
[33] [A circular argument, circular reasoning in which the conclusion has been assumed in the premises.]

horse and the ass. The dromedary is less than the camel, more slender, and remarkably more swift of foot: it has but one bunch on its back, the camel has two: the race is more numerous than that of the camel, and more widely spread. One would not desire distinguishing marks more satisfying; and yet these two species propagate together, no less freely than the different races of men and of dogs. [...] At that rate, a horse and an ass are of the same species. Did it never once enter into the mind of this author, that the human race would be strangely imperfect, if they were unable to distinguish a man from a monkey, or a hare from a hedgehog, till it were known whether they can procreate together? [...]

What means are employed by providence to qualify different races of men for different climates, is a subject to which little attention has been given. It lies too far out of sight to expect a complete discovery; but facts carefully collected might afford some glimmering of light. In that view, I mention the following fact. The inhabitants of the kingdom of Senaar in Africa are true negroes, a jet black complexion, thick lips, flat nose, curled woolly hair. The country itself is the hottest in the world. From the report of a late traveller, they are admirably protected by nature against the violence of the heat. Their skin is to the touch remarkably cooler than that of a European; and is so in reality, no less than two degrees on Fahrenheit's thermometer. The young women there are highly prized by the Turks for that quality.

Thus it appears, that there are different races of men fitted by nature for different climates. Upon examination, another fact will perhaps also appear, that the natural productions of each climate make the most wholesome food for the people who are fitted to live in it. Between the tropics, the natives live chiefly on fruits, seeds, and roots; and it is the opinion of the most knowing naturalists, that such food is of all the most wholesome for the torrid zone; comprehending the hot plants, which grow there to perfection, and tend greatly to fortify the stomach. In a temperate climate, a mixture of animal and vegetable food is held to be the most wholesome; and there both animals and vegetables abound. In a cold climate, animals are in plenty, but few vegetables that can serve for food to man. What physicians pronounce upon that head, I know not; but, if we dare venture a conjecture from analogy, animal food will be found the most wholesome for such as are fitted by nature to live in a cold climate.

M. Buffon, from the rule, that animals which can procreate together, and whose progeny can also procreate, are of one species, concludes, that all men are of one race or species; and endeavours to support that favourite opinion, by ascribing to the climate, to food, or to other accidental causes, all the varieties that are found among men. But is he seriously of the opinion, that any operation of climate, or of other accidental cause, can account for the copper colour and smooth chin universal among the Americans, the prominence of the *pudenda* universal among Hottentot women, or the black nipple no less universal among female Samoides? The thick fogs of the island St. Thomas may relax the fibres of the natives, but cannot make them more rigid than they are naturally. Whence, then, the difference with respect to rigidity of fibres between them and Europeans, but from original nature? Can one hope for belief in ascribing to climate the low stature of the Esquimaux, the smallness of their feet, or the overgrown size of their head; or in ascribing to climate the low stature of the Laplanders, and their ugly visage. Lapland is indeed piercingly cold; but so is Finland, and the northern parts of Norway, the inhabitants of which are tall, comely, and well proportioned. The black colour of negroes, thick lips, flat nose, crisped woolly hair, and rank smell, distinguish them from every other race of men. The Abyssinians, on the contrary, are tall and well made, their complexion a brown olive, features well proportioned, eyes large, and of a sparkling black, lips thin, a nose rather high than flat. There is no such difference of climate between Abyssinia and Negroland as to produce these striking differences. At any rate, there must be a considerable mixture both of soil and climate in these extensive regions; and yet not the least mixture is perceived in the people. [...]

The kindness of some tribes to strangers deserves more attention, being not a little singular. Gonneville, commander of a French ship in a voyage to the East Indies in the year 1503, was driven by a tempest into an unknown country, and continued there six months, while his vessel was refitting.

The manners he describes were in all appearance original. The natives had not made a greater progress in the arts of life, than the savage Canadians have done; ill clothed; and worse lodged, having no light in their cabins but what came in through a hole in the roof. They were divided into small tribes, governed each by a king; who, though neither better clothed nor lodged than others, had power of life and death over his subjects. They were a simple and peaceable people, and in a manner worshipped the French, providing them with necessaries, and in return thankfully receiving knives, hatchets, small looking-glasses, and other such baubles. In a part of California the men go naked, and are fond of feathers and shells. They are governed by a king with great mildness; and of all savages are the most humane, even to strangers. An island discovered in the South Sea by Tasman, 21st degree of southern latitude, and 177th of longitude west from London, was called by him *Amsterdam*. The natives, who had no arms offensive or defensive, treated the Dutch with great civility, except in being given to pilfering. At no great distance, another island was discovered, named *Annamocha* by the natives, and *Rotterdam* by Tasman; possessed by a people resembling those last mentioned, particularly in having no arms. The Dutch, sailing round the island, saw abundance of cocoa-trees planted in rows, with many other fruit-bearing trees, kept in excellent order. Commodore Roggewein, commander of a Dutch fleet, discovered, anno 1721, a new island in the South Sea; inhabited by a people lively, active, and swift of foot; of a sweet and modest deportment: but timorous and faint-hearted; for having on their knees presented some refreshments to the Dutch, they retired with precipitation. Numbers of idols cut in stone were placed along the coast, in the figure of men with large ears, and the head covered with a crown; the whole nicely proportioned and highly finished. They fled for refuge to these idols: and they could do no better; for they had no weapons either offensive or defensive. Neither was there any appearance of government or subordination; for they all spoke and acted with equal freedom. This island, situated 28 degrees 30 minutes southern latitude, and about 115 degrees of longitude west from London, is by the Dutch called *Easter* or *Pasch Island*. [...]

To find the inhabitants of these remote islands differing so widely from the rest of the world, as to have no aversion to strangers, but on the contrary showing great kindness to the first they probably ever saw, is a singular phenomenon. It is vain here to talk of climate; because in all climates we find an aversion to strangers. From the instances given above, let us select two islands, or two clusters of islands, suppose for example Bowman's islands inhabited by whites, and those adjacent to New Guinea inhabited by blacks. Kindness to strangers is the national character of the former, and hatred to strangers is the national character of the latter. Virtues and vices of individuals depend on causes so various, and so variable, as to give an impression of chance more than of design. We are not always certain of uniformity in the conduct even of the same person; far less of different persons, however intimately related: how small is the chance, that sons will inherit their father's virtues or vices? In most countries, a savage who has no aversion to strangers, nor to neighbouring clans, would be noted as singular: to find the same quality in every one of his children, would be surprising: and would be still more so, were it diffused widely through a multitude of his descendants. Yet a family is as nothing compared with a whole nation; and when we find kindness to strangers a national character in certain tribes, we reject with disdain the notion of chance, and perceive intuitively that effects so regular and permanent must be owing to a constant and invariable cause. Such effects cannot be accidental, more than the uniformity of male and female births in all countries and at all times. They cannot be accounted for from education nor from example; which indeed may contribute to spread a certain fashion or certain manners, but cannot be their fundamental cause. Where the greater part of a nation is of one character, education and example may extend it over the whole; but the character of that greater part can have no foundation but nature. What resource then have we for explaining the opposite manners of the islanders above mentioned, but that they are of different races? [...]

A noted author[34] holds all savages to be bold, impetuous, and proud; assigning for a cause, their equality and independence. As in that observation he seems to lay no weight on climate, and as little on original disposition, it is with regret that my subject leads me in this public manner to differ from him with respect to the latter. The character he gives in general to all savages, is indeed applicable to many savage tribes, our European forefathers in particular; but not to all. It but faintly suits even the North-American savages, whom our author seems to have had in his eye; for in war they carefully avoid open force, relying chiefly on stratagem and surprise. They value themselves, it is said, upon saving men; but as that motive was no less weighty in Europe, and indeed every where, the proneness of our forefathers to open violence, demonstrates their superiority in active courage. [...]

But if the Americans abound not with active courage, their passive courage is beyond conception. Every writer expatiates on the torments they endure, not only patiently, but with singular fortitude; deriding their tormentors, and braving their utmost cruelty. North-American savages differ indeed so widely from those formerly in Europe, as to render it highly improbable that they are of the same race. Passive courage they have even to a wonder; but abound not in active courage: our European forefathers, on the contrary, were much more remarkable for the latter than for the former. [...]

In concluding from the foregoing facts that there are different races of men, I reckon upon strenuous opposition; not only from men biased against what is new or uncommon, but from numberless sedate writers, who hold every distinguishing mark, internal as well as external, to be the effect of soil and climate. Against the former, patience is my only shield; but I cannot hope for any converts to a new opinion, without removing the arguments urged by the latter. [...]

---

[34] [Footnote by Kames] Mr. Ferguson. [Most likely a loose reference to Adam Ferguson, *An Essay on the History of Civil Society* (1767), Part 1, Sections 1 and 2, and Part 2.]

The most formidable antagonist remains still on hand, the celebrated Montesquieu, who is a great champion for the climate; observing, that in hot climates people are timid like old men, and in cold climates bold like young men. This in effect is to maintain, that the torrid zone is an unfit habitation for men; that they degenerate in it, lose their natural vigour, and even in youth become like old men. That author certainly intended not any imputation on providence; and yet, does it not look like an imputation, to maintain, that so large a portion of the globe is fit for beasts only, not for men? Some men are naturally fitted for a temperate or for a cold climate: he ought to have explained, why other men may not be fitted for a hot climate. There does not appear any opposition between heat and courage, more than between cold and courage: on the contrary, courage seems more connected with the former than with the latter. [...] The Samoides and Laplanders are living instances of uncommon pusillanimity in the inhabitants of a cold climate; and instances, not few in number, have been mentioned of warlike people in a hot climate. To these I add the Hindus, whom our author will not admit to have any degree of courage; though he acknowledges, that, prompted by religion, the men voluntarily submit to dreadful tortures, and that even women are ambitious to burn themselves alive with their deceased husbands. [...]

It is my firm opinion, that neither temper nor talents have much dependence on climate. I cannot discover any probable exception, if it be not a taste for the fine arts. Where the influence of the sun is great, people are enervated with heat: where little, they are benumbed with cold. A clear sky, with moderate heat, exhibit a very different scene: the cheerfulness they produce disposes men to enjoyment of every kind. Greece, Italy, and the Lesser Asia, are delicious countries, affording variety of natural beauties to feast every sense: and men accustomed to enjoyment, search for it in art as well as in nature; the passage from the one to the other being easy and inviting. Hence the origin and progress of statuary and of painting, in the countries mentioned. It has not escaped observation, that the rude manners of savages are partly owing to the roughness and barrenness of uncultivated land. England has few natural beauties to boast of: even high mountains, deep valleys, impetuous torrents, and such other wild and awful beauties, are rare. But of late years, that country has received manifold embellishments from its industrious inhabitants; and in many of its scenes may now compare with countries that are more favoured by the sun or by nature. Its soil has become fertile, its verdure enlivening, and its gardens the finest in the world. The consequence is what might have been foreseen: the fine arts are gaining ground daily. May it not be expected, that the genius and sensibility of the inhabitants, will in time produce other works of art, to rival their gardens? How delightful to a true-hearted Briton is the prospect, that London, instead of Rome, may become the centre of the fine arts! [...]

The colour of the negroes [...] affords a strong presumption of their being a different species from the whites; and I once thought, that the presumption was supported by inferiority of understanding in the former. But it appears to me doubtful, upon second thoughts, whether that inferiority may not be occasioned by their condition. A man never ripens in judgment nor in prudence but by exercising these powers. At home, the negroes have little occasion to exercise either: they live upon fruits and roots, which grow without culture: they need little clothing: and they erect houses without trouble or art. Abroad, they are miserable slaves, having no encouragement either to think or to act. Who can say how far they might improve in a state of freedom, were they obliged, like Europeans, to procure bread with the sweat of their brows? Some nations in Negroland, particularly that of Whidah,[35] have made great improvements in government, in police, and in manners. [...]

Thus, upon an extensive survey of the inhabited parts of our globe, many nations are found differing so widely from each other, not only in complexion, features, shape, and other external circumstances, but in temper and disposition, particularly in two capital articles, courage, and behaviour to strangers, that even the certainty of different races could not make one expect more striking varieties. [...]

---

[35] [Formerly Kingdom of Whydah, 'Slave Coast', today in the state of Benin.]

It is thus ascertained beyond any rational doubt, that there are different races or kinds of men, and that these races or kinds are naturally fitted for different climates: whence we have reason to conclude, that originally each kind was placed in its proper climate, whatever change may have happened in later times by war or commerce.

There is a remarkable fact that confirms the foregoing conjectures. As far back as history goes, or tradition kept alive by history, the earth was inhabited by savages divided into many small tribes, each tribe having a language peculiar to itself. Is it not natural to suppose, that these original tribes were different races of men, placed in proper climates, and left to form their own language?

Upon summing up the whole particulars mentioned above, would one hesitate a moment to adopt the following opinion, were there no counterbalancing evidence, namely, 'That God created many pairs of the human race, differing from each other both externally and internally; that he fitted these pairs for different climates, and placed each pair in its proper climate; that the peculiarities of the original pairs were preserved entire in their descendants; who, having no assistance but their natural talents, were left to gather knowledge from experience, and in particular were left (each tribe) to form a language for itself; that signs were sufficient for the original pairs, without any language but what nature suggests; and that a language was formed gradually, as a tribe increased in numbers and in different occupations, to make speech necessary'? But this opinion, however plausible, we are not permitted to adopt; being taught a different lesson by revelation, namely, that God created but a single pair of the human species. Though we cannot doubt of the authority of Moses, yet his account of the creation of man is not a little puzzling, as it seems to contradict every one of the facts mentioned above. According to that account, different races of men were not created, nor were men framed originally for different climates. All men must have spoken the same language, that of our first parents. And what of all seems the most contradictory to that account, is the savage state: Adam, as Moses informs us, was endued by his maker with an eminent degree of knowledge; and he certainly must

3. Development of Reasoning

From: *Sketches of the History of Man*, 3rd ed. (1788), book 3, sketch 1, 'Progress of Reason', pp. 221–298

A progress from infancy to maturity in the mind of man, similar to that in his body, has been often mentioned. The external senses, being early necessary for self-preservation, arrive quickly at maturity. The internal senses are of a slower growth, as well as every other mental power: their maturity would be of little or no use while the body is weak, and unfit for action. Reasoning [...] requires two mental powers, the power of invention, and that of perceiving relations. By the former are discovered intermediate propositions, having the same relation to the fundamental proposition and to the conclusion; and that relation is verified by the latter. Both powers are necessary to the person who frames an argument, or a chain of reasoning: the latter only, to the person who judges of it. Savages are miserably deficient in both. With respect to the former, a savage may have from his nature a talent for invention; but it will stand him in little stead without a stock of ideas enabling him to select what may answer his purpose; and a savage has no opportunity to acquire such a stock. With respect to the latter, he knows little of relations. And how should he know, when both study and practice are necessary for distinguishing between relations? The understanding, at the same time, is among the illiterate obsequious to passion and prepossession; and among them the imagination acts without control, forming conclusions often no better than mere dreams. In short, considering the many causes that mislead from just reasoning, in days especially of ignorance, the erroneous and absurd opinions that have prevailed in the world, and that continue in some measure to prevail, are far from being surprising. Were reason our only guide in the conduct of life, we should have cause to complain; but our maker has provided us with the moral sense, a guide little subject to error in matters of importance. In the sciences, reason is essential; but in the conduct of life, which is our chief concern, reason may be a useful assistant; but to be our director is not its province.

The national progress of reason has been slower in Europe, than that of any other art: statuary, painting, architecture, and other fine arts, approach nearer perfection, as well as morality and natural history. Manners and every art that appears externally, may in part be acquired by imitation and example: in reasoning there is nothing external to be laid hold of. But there is beside a particular cause that regards Europe, which is the blind deference that for many ages was paid to Aristotle; who has kept the reasoning faculty in chains more than two thousand years. In his logic, the plain and simple mode of reasoning is rejected, that which nature dictates; and in its stead is introduced an artificial mode, showy but unsubstantial, of no use for discovering truth; but contrived with great art for wrangling and disputation. Considering that reason for so many ages has been immured in the enchanted castle of syllogism, where phantoms pass for realities; the slow progress of reason toward maturity is far from being surprising. The taking of Constantinople by the Turks in 1453, unfolded a new scene, which in time relieved the world from the usurpation of Aristotle, and restored reason to her privileges. All the knowledge of Europe was centred in Constantinople; and the learned men of that city, abhorring the Turks and their government, took refuge in Italy. The Greek language was introduced among the western nations of Europe; and the study of Greek and Roman classics became fashionable. Men, having acquired new ideas, began to think for themselves: they exerted their native faculty of reason: the futility of Aristotle's logic became apparent to the penetrating; and is now apparent to all. [...]

To exemplify erroneous and absurd reasonings of every sort, would be endless. The reader, I presume, will be satisfied with a few instances; and I shall endeavour to select what are amusing. For the sake of order, I divide them into three heads. First, instances showing the imbecility of human reason during its nonage. Second, erroneous reasoning occasioned by natural biases. Third, erroneous reasoning occasioned by acquired biases. With respect to the first, instances are endless of reasonings founded on erroneous premises. It was an Epicurean doctrine, that the gods have all of them a human figure; moved by the following argument, that no being of any other figure has the use of reason. Plato, taking for granted the following erroneous proposition, that every being which moves itself must have a soul, concludes that the world must have a soul, because it moves itself.[36] Aristotle taking it for granted, without the least evidence and contrary to truth, that all heavy bodies tend to the centre of the universe, proves the earth to be the centre of the universe by the following argument. 'Heavy bodies naturally tend to the centre of the universe: we know by experience that heavy bodies tend to the centre of the earth: therefore the centre of the earth is the centre of the universe.'[37] Appion ridicules the Jews for adhering literally to the precept of resting on their Sabbath, so as to suffer Jerusalem to be taken that day by Ptolemy, son of Lagos. Mark the answer of Josephus: 'Whoever passes a sober judgement on this matter, will find our practice agreeable to honour and virtue; for what can be more honourable and virtuous, than to postpone our country, and even life itself, to the service of God, and of his holy religion?' A strange idea of religion, to put it in direct opposition to every moral principle! A superstitious and absurd doctrine, that God will interpose by a miracle to declare what is right in every controversy, has occasioned much erroneous reasoning and absurd practice. The practice of determining controversies by single combat, commenced about the seventh century, when religion had degenerated into superstition, and courage was esteemed the only moral virtue. The parliament of Paris, in the reign of Charles VI appointed a single combat between two gentlemen, in order to have the judgement of God whether the one had committed a rape on the other's wife. In 1454, John Picard being accused by his son-in-law for too great familiarity with

---

[36] [Footnote by Kames] Cicero, *De natura Deorum*, lib. 2 § 12. [Cicero, *On the Nature of the Gods*, Book 2, section 12. Here Kames oversimplifies Plato's argument in *Timaeus* as related by Cicero.]

[37] [In this passage Kames refers to Aristotle's *De caelo* (*On the Heavens*) Book 2, Chapters 3, 13, and 14 [293b, 296b, 297a–b] (from which Kames's paraphrasing citation of Aristotle derives), and *Meteorologica* I, 2 [339a].]

his wife, a duel between them was appointed by the same parliament. Voltaire justly observes, that the parliament decreed a parricide to be committed, in order to try an accusation of incest, which possibly was not committed. The trials by water and by fire, rest on the same erroneous foundation. In the former, if the person accused sunk to the bottom, it was a judgement pronounced by God, that he was innocent: if he kept above, it was a judgement that he was guilty. Fleury[38] remarks, that if ever the person accused was found guilty, it was his own fault. In Sicily, a woman accused of adultery, was compelled to swear to her innocence: the oath, taken down in writing, was laid on water; and if it did not sink, the woman was innocent. We find the same practice in Japan, and in Malabar. One of the articles insisted on by the reformers in Scotland, was, that public prayers be made and the sacraments administered in the vulgar tongue. The answer of a provincial council was in the following words: 'That to conceive public prayers or administer the sacraments in any language but Latin, is contrary to the traditions and practice of the Catholic church for many ages past; and that the demand cannot be granted, without impiety to God and disobedience to the church.' Here it is taken for granted, that the practice of the church is always right; which is building an argument on a very rotten foundation. [...]

Next of reasonings where the conclusion follows not from the premises, or fundamental proposition. Plato endeavours to prove, that the world is endowed with wisdom, by the following argument. 'The world is greater than any of its parts: therefore it is endowed with wisdom; for otherwise a man who is endowed with wisdom would be greater than the world.'[39] The conclusion here does not follow; for though man is endowed with wisdom, it follows not, that he is greater than the world in point of size. Zeno endeavours to prove, that the world has the use of reason, by an argument

---

[38] [Footnote by Kames] *Histoire ecclésiastique* [Claude Fleury, French church historian (1640–1723)].

[39] [Footnote by Kames] Cicero, *De natura Deorum*, lib. 2 § 12. [Kames omits here Cicero's report of Plato's argument that there is world-heat as the source of all motion, so that heat is soul and thus the world is an animate being and possesses intelligence.]

of the same kind. To convince the world of the truth of the four gospels, Irenaeus[40] urges the following arguments, which he calls demonstration. 'There are four quarters of the world and four cardinal winds, consequently there are four gospels in the church, as there are four pillars that support it, and four breaths of life that render it immortal.' Again, 'The four animals in Ezekiel's vision[41] mark the four states of the Son of God. The lion is his royal dignity: the calf, his priesthood: the beast with the face of man, his human nature: the eagle, his spirit which descends on the church. To these four animals correspond the four gospels, on which our Lord is seated. John, who teaches his celestial origin, is the lion, his gospel being full of confidence: Luke, who begins with the priesthood of Zachariah, is the calf: Matthew, who describes the genealogy of Christ according to the flesh, is the animal resembling a man: Mark, who begins with the prophetic spirit coming from above, is the eagle.[42] This gospel is the shortest of all, because brevity is the character of prophecy.' Take a third demonstration of the truth of the four gospels. 'There have been four covenants; the first under Adam, the second under Noah, the third under Moses, the fourth under Jesus Christ.' Whence Irenaeus concludes, that they are vain, rash, and ignorant, who admit more or less than four gospels. St. Cyprian in his exhortation to martyrdom, after having applied the mysterious number seven, to the seven days of the creation, to the seven thousand years of the world's duration, to the seven spirits that stand before God, to the seven lamps of the tabernacle, to the seven candlesticks of the Apocalypse, to the seven pillars of wisdom, to the seven children of the barren woman, to the seven women who took one man for their husband, to the seven brothers of the Maccabees; observes, that St. Paul mentions that number as a privileged number; which, says he, is the reason why he did not write but to seven churches. Pope Gregory, writing

---

[40] [Footnote by Kames] Lib. 3, cap 2 [St Irenaeus († 202 CE), bishop of Lugdunum in the Roman Empire (Lyon), early Church Father].
[41] [Ezekiel 1, 6–28.]
[42] [Whether or not this is Kames's error, but actually Mark is symbolized with the lion and John with the eagle.]

in favour of the four councils, viz. Nice, Constantinople, Ephesus, and Chalcedon, reasons thus: 'That as there are four evangelists, there ought also to be four councils.' What would he have said, if he had lived 100 years later, when there were many more than four? In administering the sacrament of the Lord's supper, it was ordered, that the host should be covered with a clean linen cloth; because, says the Canon law, the body of our Lord Jesus Christ was buried in a clean linen cloth. Josephus, in his answer to Appion, urges the following argument for the temple of Jerusalem: 'As there is but one God, and one world, it holds in analogy, that there should be but one temple.' At that rate, there should be but one worshipper. And why should that one temple be at Jerusalem rather than at Rome, or at Pekin? [...]

Many reasonings have passed current in the world as good coin, where the premises are not true; nor, supposing them true, would they infer the conclusion. Plato in his Phaedo relies on the following argument for the immortality of the soul. 'Is not death the opposite of life? Certainly. And do they not give birth to each other? Certainly. What then is produced from life? Death. And what from death? Life. It is then from the dead that all things living proceed; and consequently souls exist after death.' God, says Plato, made but five worlds, because according to his definition there are but five regular bodies in geometry. Is that a reason for confining the Almighty to five worlds, not one less or more. Aristotle, who wrote a book upon mechanics, was much puzzled about the equilibrium of a balance, when unequal weights are hung upon it at different distances from the centre. Having observed, that the arms of the balance describe portions of a circle, he accounted for the equilibrium by a notable argument: 'All the properties of the circle are wonderful: the equilibrium of the two weights that describe portions of a circle is wonderful. *Ergo*, the equilibrium must be one of the properties of the circle.' What are we to think of Aristotle's Logic, when we find him capable of such childish reasoning? And yet that work has been the admiration of all the world for centuries upon centuries. Nay, that foolish argument has been espoused and commented upon by his disciples, for the same length of time. To proceed to another instance: Marriage within the fourth degree of consanguinity, as well as of affinity, is prohibited by the Lateran council, and the reason given is, that the body being made up of the four elements, has four different humours in it. The Roman Catholics began with beheading heretics, hanging them, or stoning them to death. But such punishments were discovered to be too slight, in matters of faith. It was demonstrated, that heretics ought to be burnt in a slow fire: it being taken for granted, that God punishes them in the other world with a slow fire; it was inferred, 'That as every prince and every magistrate is the image of God in this world, they ought to follow his example.' Here is a double error in reasoning: first, the taking for granted the fundamental proposition, which is surely not self-evident; and next, the drawing a conclusion from it without any connection. [...]

During the nonage of reason, men are satisfied with words merely, instead of an argument. A sea-prospect is charming; but we soon tire of an unbounded prospect. It would not give satisfaction to say, that it is too extensive; for why should not a prospect be relished, however extensive? But employ a foreign term and say, that it is *trop vaste*, we enquire no farther: a term that is not familiar, makes an impression, and captivates weak reason. This observation accounts for a mode of writing formerly in common use, that of stuffing our language with Latin words and phrases. These are now laid aside as useless; because a proper emphasis in reading, makes an impression deeper than any foreign term can do. [...]

Reason, with respect to its progress, is singular. Morals, manners, and every thing that appears externally, may in part be acquired by imitation and example; which have not the slightest influence upon the reasoning faculty. The only means for advancing that faculty to maturity, are indefatigable study and practice; and even these will not carry a man one step beyond the subjects he is conversant about: examples are not rare of men extremely expert in one science, and grossly deficient in others. Many able mathematicians are novices in politics, and even in the common arts of life: study and practice have ripened them in every relation of equality, while they remain ignorant, like the vulgar, about other relations. A man, in like manner, who has bestowed much time and thought in political matters, may be a child as to other branches of knowledge. [...]

I proceed to the second article, containing erroneous reasoning occasioned by natural biases. The first bias I shall mention has an extensive influence. What is seen, makes a deeper impression than what is reported, or discovered by reflection. Hence it is, that in judging of right and wrong, the ignorant and illiterate are struck with the external act only, without penetrating into will or intention which lie out of sight. Thus with respect to covenants, laws, vows, and other acts that are completed by words, the whole weight in days of ignorance is laid upon the external expression, with no regard to the meaning of the speaker or writer. [...]

Reason is easily warped by habit. In the disputes among the Athenians about adjusting the form of their government, those who lived in the high country were for democracy; the inhabitants of the plains were for oligarchy; and the seamen for monarchy. Shepherds are all equal: in a corn country, there are a few masters and many servants: on shipboard, there is one commander, and all the rest subjects. Habit was their adviser: none of them thought of consulting reason, in order to judge what was the best form upon the whole. Habit of a different kind has an influence no less powerful. Persons who are in the habit of reasoning, require demonstration for every thing: even a self-evident proposition is not suffered to escape. Such demonstrations occur more than once in the *Elements* of Euclid, nor has Aristotle, with all his skill in logic, entirely avoided them. Can any thing be more self-evident, than the difference between pleasure and motion? Yet Aristotle attempts to demonstrate, that they are different. 'No motion,' says he, 'except circular motion, is perfect in any one point of time; there is always something wanting during its course, and it is not perfected till it arrive at its end. But pleasure is perfect in every point of time; being the same from the beginning to the end.'[43] The difference is clear from perception: but instead of being clear from this demonstration, it should rather follow from it, that pleasure is the

---

[43] [Reference to Aristotle, *De caelo* (*On the Heavens*), Book 1 [268b–269b].]

same with motion in a circle. Plato also attempts to demonstrate a self-evident proposition, that a quality is not a body. 'Every body,' says he, 'is a subject: quality is not a subject, but an accident;[44] *ergo*, quality is not a body. Again, a body cannot be in a subject: every quality is in a subject; *ergo*, quality is not a body.'[45] But Descartes affords the most illustrious instance of the kind. He was the greatest geometer of the age he lived in, and one of the greatest of any age; which insensibly led him to overlook intuitive knowledge, and to admit no proposition but what is demonstrated or proved in the regular form of syllogism. He took a fancy to doubt even of his own existence, till he was convinced of it by the following argument. *Cogito, ergo sum*: I think, therefore I exist.[46] And what sort of a demonstration is this after all? In the very fundamental proposition he acknowledges his existence by the term *I*; and how absurd is it, to imagine a proof necessary of what is admitted in the fundamental proposition? In the next place, how does our author know that he thinks? If nothing is to be taken for granted, an argument is no less necessary to prove that he thinks, than to prove that he exists. It is true, that he has intuitive knowledge of his thinking; but has he not the same of his existing? [...]

In every subject of reasoning, to define terms is necessary in order to avoid mistakes: and the only possible way of defining a term, is to express its meaning in more simple terms. Terms expressing ideas that are simple without parts, admit not of being defined, because there are no terms more simple to express their meaning. To say that every term is capable of a definition, is in effect to say, that terms resemble matter; that as the latter is divisible without end, so the former is reducible into simpler terms without end. The habit however of defining is so inveterate in some men, that they will attempt to define words signifying simple ideas.

---

[44] [Read: 'attribute' (thus also in the original quote).]

[45] [It appears that this particular quote comes from the *Handbook of Platonism* (chapter 11) by Alcinous, the Middle Platonist philosopher from the 2nd cent. AD.]

[46] [Reference to Descartes, *Discours de la méthode* (*Discourse on the Method*), part 4, sections 1 and 3 (in the original: 'je pense, donc je suis'), also in *Principa Philosophiae* (*Principles of Philosophy*).]

4. Progress of Religion and Worshipping

From: *Sketches of the History of Man*, 3rd ed. (1788), book 3, sketch 3, 'Principles and Progress of Theology', pp. 192–241

That there exist beings, one or many, powerful above the human race, is a proposition universally admitted as true, in all ages, and among all nations. I boldly call it universal, notwithstanding what is reported of some gross savages; for reports that contradict what is acknowledged to be general among men, require more able vouchers than a few illiterate voyagers. Among many savage tribes, there are no words but for objects of external sense: is it surprising, that such people are incapable to express their religious perceptions, or any perception of internal sense? and from their silence can it be fairly presumed, that they have no such perception? The conviction that men have of superior powers in every country where there are words to express it, is so well vouched, that in fair reasoning it ought to be taken for granted among the few tribes where language is deficient. Even the grossest idolatry affords evidence of that conviction. No nation can be so brutish as to worship a stock or a stone, merely as such: the visible object is always imagined to be connected with some invisible power; and the worship paid to the former, is as representing the latter, or as in some manner connected with it. [...] The ancient Egyptians were not idiots, to pay divine honours to a bull or a cat, as such: the divine honours were paid to a deity, as residing in these animals. The sun is to man a familiar object; being frequently obscured by clouds, and totally eclipsed during night, a savage naturally conceives it to be a great fire, sometimes flaming bright, sometimes obscured, and sometimes extinguished. Whence then sun-worship, once universal among savages? Plainly from the same cause: it is not properly the sun that is worshipped, but a deity who is supposed to dwell in that luminary.

Taking it then for granted, that our conviction of superior powers has been long universal, the important question is, from what cause it proceeds. A conviction so universal and so permanent, cannot proceed from chance; but must have a cause operating constantly and invariably upon all men in all ages. Philosophers, who believe the world to be eternal and self-existent, and imagine it to be the only deity though without intelligence, endeavour to account for our conviction of superior powers, from the terror that thunder and other elementary convulsions raise in savages; and thence conclude that such belief is no evidence of a deity.[47] [...]

It will readily be yielded to these gentlemen, that savages, grossly ignorant of causes and effects, are apt to take fright at every unusual appearance, and to think that some malignant being is the cause. And if they mean only, that the first perception of deity among savages is occasioned by fear, I heartily subscribe to their opinion. But if they mean, that such perceptions proceed from fear solely, without having any other cause, I wish to be informed from what source is derived the belief we have of benevolent deities. Fear cannot be the source: [...] though malevolent deities were first recognised among savages, yet that in the progress of society, the existence of benevolent deities was universally believed. The fact is certain; and therefore fear is not the sole cause of our believing the existence of superior beings.

It is beside to me evident, that the belief even of malevolent deities, once universal among all the tribes of men, cannot be accounted for from fear solely. I observe, first, that there are many men, to whom an eclipse, an earthquake, and even thunder, are unknown: Egypt, in particular, though the country of superstition, is little or not at all acquainted with the two latter; and in Peru, though its government was a theocracy, thunder is not known. Nor do such appearances strike terror into every one who is acquainted with them. The universality of the belief, must then have some cause more universal than fear. [...]

If fear be a cause altogether insufficient for our conviction of a Deity, universal among all tribes; and if reasoning from effects to their causes can have no influence upon ignorant savages; what other cause is there to be laid hold of? One still remains, and imagination cannot figure another: to make this conviction universal, the image of the Deity must be stamped upon the mind of every human being, the ignorant equally

---

[47] [Kames quotes here Lucretius and Petronius Arbiter for providing evidence.]

with the knowing: nothing less is sufficient. And the original perception we have of Deity, must proceed from an internal sense, which may be termed the *sense of Deity*.

Included in the sense of Deity, is the duty we are under to worship him. And to enforce that duty, the principle of devotion is made a part of our nature. All men accordingly agree in worshipping superior beings, however they may differ in the mode of worship. And the universality of such worship, proves devotion to be an innate principle. [...]

Thus our maker has revealed himself to us, in a way perfectly analogous to our nature: in the mind of every human creature, he has lighted up a lamp, which renders him visible even to the weakest sight. Nor ought it to escape observation, that here, as in every other case, the conduct of providence to man, is uniform. It leaves him to be directed by reason, where liberty of choice is permitted; but in matters of duty, he is provided with guides less fallible than reason: in performing his duty to man, he is guided by the moral sense; in performing his duty to God, he is guided by the sense of Deity. In these mirrors, he perceives his duty intuitively.

It is no slight support to this doctrine, that if there really be a Deity, it is highly presumable, that he will reveal himself to man, fitted by nature to adore and worship him. To other animals, the knowledge of a Deity is of no importance: to man, it is of high importance. Were we totally ignorant of a Deity, this world would appear to us a mere chaos: under the government of a wise and benevolent Deity, chance is excluded; and every event appears to be the result of established laws: good men submit to whatever happens, without repining; knowing that every event is ordered by divine providence: they submit with entire resignation; and such resignation is a sovereign balsam for every misfortune. [...]

The sense of Deity, like the moral sense, makes no capital figure among savages; the perceptions of both senses being in them faint and obscure. But in the progress of nations to maturity, these senses become more and more vigorous, so as among enlightened nations to acquire a commanding influence; leaving no doubt about right and wrong, and as little about the existence of a Deity. [...]

The sense of Deity, like many other delicate senses, is in savages so faint and obscure as easily to be biased from truth. Among them, the belief of many superior beings, is universal. And two causes join to produce that belief. The first is, that being accustomed to a plurality of visible objects, men, mountains, trees, cattle, and such like, they are naturally led to imagine a like plurality in things not visible; and from that slight bias, slight indeed but natural, is partly derived the system of polytheism, universal among savages. The other is, that savages know little of the connection between causes and effects, and still less of the order and government of the world: every event that is not familiar, appears to them singular and extraordinary; and if such event exceed human power, it is without hesitation ascribed to a superior being. But as it occurs not to a savage, nor to any person who is not a philosopher, that the many various events exceeding human power and seemingly unconnected, may all proceed from the same cause; they are readily ascribed to different beings. [...]

This stage is distinguishable from others, by a belief that all superior beings are malevolent. Man, by nature weak and helpless, is prone to fear, dreading every new object and every unusual event. Savages, having no protection against storms, tempests, nor other external accidents, and having no pleasures but in gratifying hunger, thirst, and animal love; have much to fear, and little to hope. In that disconsolate condition, they attribute the bulk of their distresses to invisible beings, who in their opinion must be malevolent. [...]

Conviction of superior beings, who, like men, are of a mixed nature, sometimes doing good, sometimes mischief, constitutes the second stage. This came to be the system of theology in Greece. The introduction of writing among the Greeks while they were little better than savages, produced a compound of character and manners, that has not a parallel in any other nation. They were acute in science, skilful in fine arts, extremely deficient in morals, gross beyond conception in theology, and superstitious to a degree of folly; a strange jumble of exquisite sense and absurd nonsense. They held their gods to resemble men in their external figure, and to be corporeal. [...]

Two: Philosophical History 115

It appears from Cicero,[48] that when Greek philosophers began to reason about the deity, their notions were wonderfully crude. One of the hardest morsels to digest in Plato's philosophy, was a doctrine, that God is incorporeal; which by many was thought absurd, for that, without a body, he could not have senses, nor prudence, nor pleasure. The religious creed of the Romans seems to have been little less impure than that of the Greeks. It was a ceremony of theirs, in besieging a town, to evocate the tutelary deity, and to tempt him by a reward to betray his friends and votaries. In that ceremony, the name of the tutelary deity was thought of importance; and for that reason, the tutelary deity of Rome was a profound secret. [...]

A division of invisible beings into benevolent and malevolent, without any mixture of these qualities, makes the third stage. The talents and feelings of men, refine gradually under good government: social amusements begin to make a figure: benevolence is highly regarded; and some men are found without gall. Having thus acquired a notion of pure benevolence, and finding it exemplified in some eminent persons, it was an easy step in the progress of theological opinions, to bestow the same character upon some superior beings. This led men to distinguish their gods into two kinds, essentially different, one entirely benevolent, another entirely malevolent; and the difference between good and ill, which are diametrically opposite, favoured that distinction. Fortunate events out of the common course of nature, were accordingly ascribed to benevolent deities; and unfortunate events of that kind to malevolent. In the time of Pliny the elder, malevolent deities were worshipped at Rome. He mentions a temple dedicated to *Bad Fortune*, another to the disease termed a *Fever*. The Lacedemonians[49] worshipped *Death* and *Fear*; and the people of Cadiz *Poverty* and *Old Age*; in order to deprecate their wrath. Such gods were by the Romans termed *Averrunci*, as putting away evil.

---

[48] [Footnote by Kames] Lib. 1 *De natura Deorum* [Kames had probably in mind Book 1, from section 8 onwards].

[49] [Inhabitants of Sparta.]

Conviction of one supreme benevolent Deity, and of inferior deities, some benevolent, some malevolent, is the fourth stage. Such conviction, which gains ground in proportion as morality ripens, arises from a remarkable difference between gratitude and fear. Willing to show my gratitude for some kindness proceeding from an unknown hand, several persons occur to my conjectures; but I always fix at last upon one person as the most likely. Fear is of an opposite nature: it expands itself upon every suspicious person, and blackens them all. Thus, upon providential good fortune above the power of man, we naturally rest upon one benevolent Deity as the cause; and to him we confine our gratitude and veneration. When, on the other hand, we are struck with an uncommon calamity, every thing that possibly may be the cause raises terror. Hence the propensity in savages to multiply objects of fear; but to confine their gratitude and veneration to a single object. Gratitude and veneration, at the same time, are of such a nature, as to raise a high opinion of the person who is their object; and when a single invisible being is understood to pour out blessings with a liberal hand, good men, inflamed with gratitude, put no bounds to the power and benevolence of that being. And thus one supreme benevolent Deity comes to be recognised among the more enlightened savages. With respect to malevolent deities, as they are supposed to be numerous, and as there is no natural impulse for elevating one above another; they are all of them held to be of an inferior rank, subordinate to the supreme Deity.

Unity in the supreme being has, among philosophers, a more solid foundation, namely, unity of design and of order in the creation and government of this world.[50] At the same time, the passion of gratitude, which leads even savages to the attribute of unity in the supreme being, prepares the

---

[50] [Footnote by Kames] All things in the universe are evidently of a piece. Every thing is adjusted to every thing; one design prevails through the whole: and this uniformity leads the mind to acknowledge one author; because the conception of different authors without distinction of attributes or operations, serves only to perplex the imagination, without bestowing any satisfaction on the understanding. *Natural History of Religion, by David Hume, Esquire.*

mind for relishing the proof of that unity, founded on the unity of his works. [...]

As unity in the Deity was not an established doctrine in the countries where the Christian religion was first promulgated, Christianity could not fail to prevail over Paganism; for improvements in the mental faculties lead by sure steps, though slow, to one God.

The fifth stage is, the belief of one supreme benevolent Deity, as in that immediately foregoing, with many inferior benevolent deities, and one only who is malevolent. As men improve in natural knowledge and become skilful in tracing causes from effects, they find much less malice and ill-design than was imagined: humanity at last prevails, which with improved knowledge banish the suspicion of ill-design, in every case where an event can be explained without it. In a word, a settled opinion of good prevailing in the world, produced conviction among some nations, less ignorant than their neighbours and less brutal, that there is but one malevolent subordinate deity, and good subordinate deities without number. The ancient Persians acknowledged two principles; one all good and all powerful, named *Hormuz*, and by the Greeks corruptly *Oromazes*; the other evil, named *Ahariman*, and by the Greeks *Arimanes*. [...] Plutarch acquaints us, that Hormuz and Ahariman, ever at variance, formed each of them creatures of their own stamp; that the former created good genii, such as goodness, truth, wisdom, justice; and that the latter created evil genii, such as infidelity, falsehood, oppression, theft. This system of theology, commonly termed the *Manichean system*,[51] is said to be also the religious creed of Pegu,[52] with the following addition, that the evil principle only is to be worshipped; which is abundantly probable, as fear is a predominant passion in barbarians. [...]

Having traced the sense of deity, from its dawn in the grossest savages to its approaching maturity among enlightened nations, we proceed to the last stage of the

---

[51] [Kames equates here the old Persian cult of Mazdaism with the Manichaean system, which is an inaccurate oversimplification.]

[52] Today Bago, Myanmar (Burma).]

progress, which makes the true system of theology; and that is, conviction of a supreme being, boundless in every perfection, without subordinate deities, benevolent or malevolent. Savages learn early to trace the chain of causes and effects, with respect to ordinary events: they know that fasting produces hunger, that labour occasions weariness, that fire burns, that the sun and rain contribute to vegetation. But when they go beyond such familiar events, they lose sight of cause and effect: the changes of weather, of winds, of heat and cold, impress them with a notion of chance: earthquakes, hurricanes, storms of thunder and lightning, which fill them with terror, are ascribed to malignant beings of greater power than man. In the progress of knowledge light begins to break in upon them: they discover, that such phenomena, however tremendous, come under the general law of cause and effect; and that there is no ground for ascribing them to malignant spirits. At the same time, our more refined senses ripen by degrees: social affections come to prevail, and morality makes a deep impression. In maturity of sense and understanding, benevolence appears more and more; and beautiful final causes are discovered in many of nature's productions, that formerly were thought useless, or perhaps hurtful: and the time may come, we have solid ground to hope that it will come, when doubts and difficulties about the government of providence, will all of them be cleared up; and every event be found conducive to the general good. Such views of providence banish malevolent deities; and we settle at last in a most comfortable opinion; either that there are no such beings; or that, if they exist and are permitted to perpetrate any mischief, it is in order to produce greater good. Thus, through a long maze of errors, man arrives at true religion, acknowledging but one Being, supreme in power, intelligence, and benevolence, who created all other beings, to whom all other beings are subjected, and who directs every event to answer the best purposes. This system is true theology.

Three

Moral Philosophy and Legal Philosophy

1. Reasoning: Principles

From: *Sketches of the History of Man*, 3rd ed. (1788), book 3, sketch 1, 'Principles of Reason', pp. 190–221

Affirmation is that sort of expression which the speaker uses, when he desires to be believed. What he affirms is termed a *proposition*.

Truth and error are qualities of propositions. A proposition that says a thing is what it is in reality, is termed a *true proposition*. A proposition that says a thing is what it is not in reality, is termed an *erroneous proposition*.

Truth is so essential in conducting affairs, that man would be a disjointed being were it not agreeable to him. Truth accordingly is agreeable to every human being, and falsehood or error disagreeable. The pursuit of truth is no less pleasant than the pursuit of any other good.[1]

Our knowledge of what is agreeable and disagreeable in objects is derived from the sense of beauty, handled in Elements of Criticism.[2] Our knowledge of right and wrong in actions, is derived from the moral sense[3] [...]. Our knowledge of truth and error is derived from various sources.

---

[1] [Footnote by Kames] It has been wisely observed, that truth is the same to the understanding that music is to the ear, or beauty to the eye.

[2] [See relevant extracts in chapter 1.]

[3] [See in this chapter, below under 2.]

Our external senses are one source of knowledge: they lay open to us external subjects, their qualities, their actions, with events produced by these actions. The internal senses are another source of knowledge: they lay open to us things passing in the mind; thinking, for example, deliberating, inclining, resolving, willing, consenting, and other acts; and they also lay open to us our emotions and passions. There is a sense by which we perceive the truth of many propositions; such as, that every thing which begins to exist must have a cause;[4] that every effect adapted to some end or purpose, proceeds from a designing cause; and, that every effect adapted to a good end or purpose, proceeds from a designing and benevolent cause. A multitude of axioms in every science, particularly in mathematics, are equally perceived to be true. By a peculiar sense [...] we know that there is a Deity.[5] There is a sense by which we know, that the external signs of passion are the same in all men; that animals of the same external appearance, are of the same species, and that animals of the same species, have the same properties. There is a sense that dives into futurity: we know that the sun will rise tomorrow; that the earth will perform its wonted course round the sun; that winter and summer will follow each other in succession; that a stone dropped from the hand will fall to the ground; and a thousand other such propositions.

There are many propositions, the truth of which is not so apparent: a process of reasoning is necessary, of which afterward.

Human testimony is another source of knowledge. So framed we are by nature, as to rely on human testimony; by which we are informed of beings, attributes, and events, that never came under any of our senses.

The knowledge that is derived from the sources mentioned, is of different kinds. In some cases, our knowledge includes absolute certainty, and produces the highest degree of conviction: in other cases, probability comes in place of certainty, and the conviction is inferior in degree. Knowledge

---

[4] [See in this chapter, below under 4.]
[5] [See relevant extracts in chapter 2.]

of the latter kind is distinguished into belief, which concerns facts; and opinion, which concerns relations, and other things that fall not under the denomination of facts. In contradistinction to opinion and belief, that sort of knowledge which includes absolute certainty, and produces the highest degree of conviction, retains its proper name. To explain what is here said, I enter into particulars.

The sense of seeing, with very few exceptions, affords knowledge properly so termed: it is not in our power to doubt of the existence of a person we see, touch, and converse with. When such is our constitution, it is a vain attempt to call in question the authority of our sense of seeing, as some writers pretend to do. No one ever called in question the existence of internal actions and passions, laid open to us by internal sense; and there is as little ground for doubting of what we see. The sense of seeing, it is true, is not always correct: through different mediums the same object is seen differently: to a jaundiced eye every thing appears yellow; and to one intoxicated with liquor, two candles sometimes appear four. But we are never left without a remedy in such a case: it is the province of the reasoning faculty to correct every error of that kind.

An object of sight recalled to mind by the power of memory, is termed an *idea* or secondary perception. An original perception, as said above, affords knowledge in its proper sense; but a secondary perception affords belief only. And nature in this, as in all other instances, is faithful to truth; for it is evident, that we cannot be so certain of the existence of an object in its absence, as when present.

With respect to many abstract propositions, of which instances are above given, we have an absolute certainty and conviction of their truth, derived to us from various senses. We can, for example, entertain as little doubt that every thing which begins to exist must have a cause, as that the sun is in the firmament; and as little doubt that he will rise tomorrow, as that he is now set. There are many other propositions, the truth of which is probable only, not absolutely certain; as, for example, that winter will be cold and summer warm. That natural operations are performed in the simplest manner, is an axiom of natural philosophy: it may be probable, but is far from being certain.[6]

In every one of the instances given, conviction arises from a single act of perception: for which reason, knowledge acquired by means of that perception, not only knowledge in its proper sense but also opinion and belief, are termed *intuitive knowledge*.[7] But there are many things, the knowledge of which is not obtained with so much facility. Propositions for the most part require a process or operation in the mind, termed *reasoning*; leading, by certain intermediate steps, to the proposition that is to be demonstrated or made evident; which, in opposition to intuitive knowledge, is termed *discursive knowledge*. This process or operation must be explained, in order to understand the nature of reasoning. And as reasoning is mostly employed in discovering relations, I shall draw my examples from them. Every proposition concerning relations, is an affirmation of a certain relation between two subjects. If the relation affirmed appear not intuitively, we must search for a third subject, intuitively connected with each of the others by the relation affirmed: and if such a subject be found, the proposition is demonstrated; for it is intuitively certain, that two subjects connected with a third by any particular relation, must be connected together by the same relation. The longest chain of reasoning may be linked together in this manner. Running over such a chain, every one of the subjects must appear intuitively to be connected with that immediately preceding, and with that immediately subsequent, by the relation

---

[6] [Footnote by Kames] I have given this proposition a place, because it is assumed as an axiom by all writers on natural philosophy. And yet there appears some room for doubting, whether our conviction of it do not proceed from a bias in our nature, rather than from an original sense. Our taste for simplicity, which undoubtedly is natural, renders simple operations more agreeable than what are complex, and consequently makes them appear more natural. It deserves a most serious discussion, whether the operations of nature be always carried on with the greatest simplicity, or whether we be not misled by our taste for simplicity to be of that opinion.

[7] [This whole section is obviously strongly influenced by John Locke's *An Essay Concerning Human Understanding* (1690), especially book 4, chapter 2, and following chapters.]

affirmed in the proposition; and from the whole united, the proposition, as above mentioned, must appear intuitively certain. The last step of the process is termed a *conclusion*, being the last or concluding perception.

No other reasoning affords so clear a notion of the foregoing process, as that which is mathematical. Equality is the only mathematical relation; and comparison therefore is the only means by which mathematical propositions are ascertained. To that science belong a number of intuitive propositions, termed *axioms*, which are all founded on equality. For example: Divide two equal lines, each of them, into a thousand equal parts, a single part of the one line must be equal to a single part of the other. Second: Take ten of these parts from the one line, and as many from the other, and the remaining parts must be equal; which is more shortly expressed thus: From two equal lines take equal parts, and the remainders will be equal; or add equal parts, and the sums will be equal. Third: If two things be, in the same respect, equal to a third, the one is equal to the other in the same respect. I proceed to show the use of these axioms. Two things may be equal without being intuitively so; which is the case of the equality between the three angles of a triangle and two right angles. To demonstrate that truth, it is necessary to search for some other angles that intuitively are equal to both. If this property cannot be discovered in any one set of angles, we must go more leisurely to work, and try to find angles that are equal to the three angles of a triangle. These being discovered, we next try to find other angles equal to the angles now discovered; and so on in the comparison, till at last we discover a set of angles, equal not only to those thus introduced, but also to two right angles. We thus connect the two parts of the original proposition, by a number of intermediate equalities; and by that means perceive, that these two parts are equal among themselves; it being an intuitive proposition, as mentioned above, that two things are equal, each of which, in the same respect, is equal to a third.

I proceed to a different example, which concerns the relation between cause and effect. The proposition to be demonstrated is, 'That there exists a good and intelligent Being, who is the cause of all the wise and benevolent effects that are produced in the government of this world.' That there are such effects, is in the present example the fundamental proposition; which is taken for granted, because it is verified by experience. In order to discover the cause of these effects, I begin with an intuitive proposition mentioned above, 'That every effect adapted to a good end or purpose, proceeds from a designing and benevolent cause.' The next step is, to examine whether man can be the cause: he is provided indeed with some share of wisdom and benevolence; but the effects mentioned are far above his power, and no less above his wisdom. Neither can this earth be the cause, nor the sun, the moon, the stars; for, far from being wise and benevolent, they are not even sensible. If these be excluded, we are unavoidably led to an invisible being, endowed with boundless power, goodness, and intelligence; and that invisible being is termed *God*.

Reasoning requires two mental powers, namely, the power of invention, and the power of perceiving relations. By the former are discovered intermediate propositions, equally related to the fundamental proposition and to the conclusion: by the latter we perceive, that the different links which compose the chain of reasoning, are all connected together by the same relation.

We can reason about matters of opinion and belief, as well as about matters of knowledge properly so termed. Hence reasoning is distinguished into two kinds; demonstrative, and probable. Demonstrative reasoning is also of two kinds: in the first, the conclusion is drawn from the nature and inherent properties of the subject: in the other, the conclusion is drawn from some principle, of which we are certain by intuition. With respect to the first, we have no such knowledge of the nature or inherent properties of any being, material or immaterial, as to draw conclusions from it with certainty. I except not even figure considered as a quality of matter, though it is the object of mathematical reasoning. As we have no standard for determining with precision the figure of any portion of matter, we cannot with precision reason upon it: what appears to us a straight line may be a curve, and what appears a rectilinear angle may be curvilinear. How then comes mathematical reasoning to be demonstrative? This question may appear at first sight puzzling; and I know not that it has anywhere been distinctly explained. Perhaps what follows may be satisfactory.

The subjects of arithmetical reasoning are numbers. The subjects of mathematical reasoning are figures. But what figures? Not such as I see; but such as I form an idea of, abstracting from every imperfection. I explain myself. There is a power in man to form images of things that never existed; a golden mountain, for example, or a river running upward. This power operates upon figures: there is perhaps no figure existing the sides of which are straight lines; but it is easy to form an idea of a line that has no waving or crookedness, and it is easy to form an idea of a figure bounded by such lines. Such ideal figures are the subjects of mathematical reasoning; and these being perfectly clear and distinct, are proper subjects for demonstrative reasoning of the first kind. Mathematical reasoning however is not merely a mental entertainment: it is of real use in life, by directing us to operate upon matter. There possibly may not be found any where a perfect globe, to answer the idea we form of that figure: but a globe may be made so near perfection, as to have nearly the properties of a perfect globe. In a word, though ideas are, properly speaking, the subject of mathematical evidence; yet the end and purpose of that evidence is, to direct us with respect to figures as they really exist; and the nearer any real figure approaches to its ideal perfection, with the greater accuracy will the mathematical truth be applicable. [...]

Numbers considered by themselves, abstractedly from things, make the subject of arithmetic. And with respect both to mathematical and arithmetical reasonings, which frequently consist of many steps, the process is shortened by the invention of signs, which, by a single dash of the pen, express clearly what would require many words. By that means, a very long chain of reasoning is expressed by a few symbols; a method that contributes greatly to readiness of comprehension. [...]

Arithmetical reasoning, like mathematical, depends entirely upon the relation of equality, which can be ascertained with the greatest certainty among many ideas. [...]

As to the other kind of demonstrative reasoning, founded on propositions of which we are intuitively certain; I justly call it *demonstrative*, because it affords the same conviction that arises from mathematical reasoning. In both, the means of conviction are the same, viz. a clear perception of the relation between two ideas: and there are many relations of which we have ideas no less clear than of equality; witness substance and quality, the whole and its parts, cause and effect, and many others. From the intuitive proposition, for example, that nothing which begins to exist can exist without a cause, I can conclude, that some one being must have existed from all eternity, with no less certainty, than that the three angles of a triangle are equal to two right angles.

What falls next in order, is that inferior sort of knowledge which is termed *opinion*; and which, like knowledge properly so termed, is founded in some instances upon intuition, and in some upon reasoning. But it differs from knowledge properly so termed in the following particular, that it produces different degrees of conviction, sometimes approaching to certainty, sometimes sinking toward the verge of improbability. The constancy and uniformity of natural operations, is a fit subject for illustrating that difference. The future successive changes of day and night, of winter and summer, and of other successions which have hitherto been constant and uniform, fall under intuitive knowledge, because of these we have the highest conviction. As the conviction is inferior of successions that hitherto have varied in any degree, these fall under intuitive opinion. We expect summer after winter with the utmost confidence; but we have not the same confidence in expecting a hot summer or a cold winter. And yet the probability approaches much nearer to certainty, than the intuitive opinion we have, that the operations of nature are extremely simple, a proposition that is little relied on.

As to opinion founded on reasoning, it is obvious, that the conviction produced by reasoning, can never rise above what is produced by the intuitive proposition upon which the reasoning is founded. And that it may be weaker, will appear from considering, that even where the fundamental proposition is certain, it may lead to the conclusive opinion by intermediate propositions, that are probable only, not certain. In a word, it holds in general with respect to every sort of reasoning, that the conclusive proposition can never rise higher in point of conviction, than the very lowest of the intuitive propositions employed as steps in the reasoning.

The perception we have of the contingency of future events, opens a wide field to our reasoning about probabilities. That perception involves more or less doubt according to its subject. In some instances, the event is perceived to be extremely doubtful; in others, it is perceived to be less doubtful. It appears altogether doubtful, in throwing a die, which of the six sides will turn up; and for that reason, we cannot justly conclude for one rather than for another. If one only of the six sides be marked with a figure, we conclude, that a blank will turn up; and five to one is an equal wager that such will be the effect. In judging of the future behaviour of a man who has hitherto been governed by interest, we may conclude with a probability approaching to certainty, that interest will continue to prevail.

Belief comes last in order, which, as defined above, is knowledge of the truth of facts that falls below certainty, and involves in its nature some degree of doubt. It is also of two kinds; one founded upon intuition, and one upon reasoning. Thus, knowledge, opinion, belief, are all of them equally distinguishable into intuitive and discursive. Of intuitive belief, I discover three different sources or causes. First, a present object. Second, an object formerly present. Third, the testimony of others.

To have a clear conception of the first cause, it must be observed, that among the simple perceptions that compose the complex perception of a present object, a perception of real and present existence is one. This perception rises commonly to certainty; in which case it is a branch of knowledge properly so termed; and is handled as such above. But this perception falls below certainty in some instances; as where an object, seen at a great distance or in a fog, is perceived to be a horse, but so indistinctly as to make it a probability only. The perception in such a case is termed *belief*. Both perceptions are fundamentally of the same nature; being simple perceptions of real existence. They differ only in point of distinctness: the perception of reality that makes a branch of knowledge, is so clear and distinct as to exclude all doubt or hesitation: the perception of reality that occasions belief, being less clear and distinct, makes not the existence of the object certain to us, but only probable.

With respect to the second cause; the existence of an absent object, formerly seen, amounts not to a certainty; and therefore is the subject of belief only, not of knowledge. Things are in a continual flux from production to dissolution; and our senses are accommodated to that variable scene: a present object admits no doubt of its existence; but after it is removed, its existence becomes less certain, and in time sinks down to a slight degree of probability.

Human testimony, the third cause, produces belief, more or less strong, according to circumstances. In general, nature leads us to rely upon the veracity of each other; and commonly the degree of reliance is proportioned to the degree of veracity. Sometimes belief approaches to certainty, as when it is founded on the evidence of persons above exception as to veracity. Sometimes it sinks to the lowest degree of probability, as when a fact is told by one who has no great reputation for truth. The nature of the fact, common or uncommon, has likewise an influence: an ordinary incident gains credit upon very slight evidence; but it requires the strongest evidence to overcome the improbability of an event that deviates from the ordinary course of nature. At the same time, it must be observed, that belief is not always founded upon rational principles. [...]

We proceed to the other kind of belief, that which is founded on reasoning; to which, when intuition fails us, we must have recourse for ascertaining certain facts. Thus, from known effects, we infer the existence of unknown causes. That an effect must have a cause, is an intuitive proposition; but to ascertain what particular thing is the cause, requires commonly a process of reasoning. This is one of the means by which the Deity, the primary cause, is made known to us, as mentioned above. Reason, in tracing causes from known effects, produces different degrees of conviction. It sometimes produces certainty, as in proving the existence of the Deity; which on that account is handled above, under the head of knowledge. For the most part it produces belief only, which, according to the strength of the reasoning, sometimes approaches to certainty, sometimes is so weak as barely to turn the scale on the side of probability. [...]

When we investigate the causes of certain effects, the reasoning is often founded upon the known nature of man. In the high country, for example, between Edinburgh and Glasgow, the people lay their coals at the end of their houses, without any fence to secure them from theft: whence it is rationally inferred, that coals are there in plenty. In the west of Scotland, the corn-stacks are covered with great care and nicety: whence it is inferred, that the climate is rainy. [...]

Analogical reasoning, founded upon the uniformity of nature, is frequently employed in the investigation of facts; and we infer, that facts of which we are uncertain, must resemble those of the same kind that are known. The reasonings in natural philosophy are mostly of that kind. Take the following examples. We learn from experience, that proceeding from the humblest vegetable to man, there are numberless classes of beings rising one above another by differences scarce perceptible, and leaving nowhere a single gap or interval: and from conviction of the uniformity of nature we infer, that the line is not broken off here, but is carried on in other worlds, till it end in the Deity. I proceed to another example. Every man is conscious of a self-motive power in himself; and from the uniformity of nature, we infer the same power in every one of our own species. The argument here from analogy carries great weight, because we entertain no doubt of the uniformity of nature with respect to beings of our own kind. We apply the same argument to other animals; though their resemblance to man appears not so certain, as that of one man to another. But why not also apply the same argument to infer a self-motive power in matter? When we see matter in motion without an external mover, we naturally infer, that, like us, it moves itself. [...]

After a fatiguing investigation of numberless particulars which divide and scatter the thought, it may not be unpleasant to bring all under one view by a succinct recapitulation.

We have two means for discovering truth and acquiring knowledge, viz. intuition and reasoning. By intuition we discover subjects and their attributes, passions, internal action, and in short every thing that is matter of fact. By intuition we also discover several relations. There are some facts and many relations, that cannot be discovered by a single act of intuition, but require several such acts linked together in a chain of reasoning.

Knowledge acquired by intuition, includes for the most part certainty: in some instances it includes probability only. Knowledge acquired by reasoning, frequently includes certainty; but more frequently includes probability only.

Probable knowledge, whether founded on intuition or on reasoning, is termed *opinion* when it concerns relations; and is termed *belief* when it concerns facts. Where knowledge includes certainty, it retains its proper name.

Reasoning that produces certainty, is termed *demonstrative*; and is termed *probable*, when it only produces probability.

Demonstrative reasoning is of two kinds. The first is, where the conclusion is derived from the nature and inherent properties of the subject: mathematical reasoning is of that kind; and perhaps the only instance. The second is, where the conclusion is derived from some proposition, of which we are certain by intuition.

Probable reasoning is endless in its varieties; and affords different degrees of conviction, depending on the nature of the subject upon which it is employed.

2. Moral Sense, Duty and Justice

From: *Essays on the Principles of Morality and Natural Religion*, 3rd ed. (1779), part 1, essay 2, chapters 2 and 3, pp. 29–47

As we are placed in a great world, surrounded with beings and things, some beneficial, some hurtful; we are so constituted, that scarce any object is indifferent to us: it either gives pleasure or pain; witness sounds, tastes, and smells. This is the most remarkable in objects of sight, which affect us in a more lively manner than objects of any other external sense. Thus, a spreading oak, a verdant plain, a large river, are objects that afford delight. A rotten carcase, a distorted figure, create aversion; which, in some instances, goes the length of horror.

With regard to objects of sight, whatever gives pleasure is said to be *beautiful*: whatever gives pain, is said to be *ugly*. The terms *beauty* and *ugliness*, in their proper signification, are confined to objects of sight. And indeed such objects, being more highly agreeable or disagreeable than others, deserve well to be distinguished by a proper name. But, as it happens with words that convey a more lively idea than ordinary, the terms are applied in a figurative sense to almost everything that gives a high relish or disgust. Thus, we talk of a beautiful theorem, a beautiful thought, and a beautiful passage in music. And this way of speaking has become so familiar, that it is scarce reckoned a figurative expression.

Objects considered simply as existing, without relation to any end or any designing agent, are in the lowest rank or order with respect to beauty and ugliness; a smooth globe for example, or a vivid colour. But when external objects, such as works of art, are considered with relation to some end, we feel a higher degree of pleasure or pain. Thus, a building regular in all its parts, pleases the eye upon the very first view: but considered as a house for dwelling in, which is the end purposed, it pleases still more, supposing it to be well fitted to its end. A similar sensation arises in observing the operations of a well-ordered state, where the parts are nicely adjusted to the ends of security and happiness.

This perception of beauty in works of art or design, which is produced not barely by a sight of the object, but by viewing the object as fitted to some use, and as related to some end, includes in it what is termed *approbation*: for approbation, when applied to works of art, means our being pleased with them or conceiving them beautiful, in the view of being fitted to their end. *Approbation* and *disapprobation* are not applicable to the lowest class of beautiful and ugly objects. To say, that we approve a sweet taste, or a flowing river, is really saying no more but that we are pleased with such objects. But the term is justly applied to works of art, because it means more than being pleased with such an object merely as existing. It imports a peculiar beauty, which is perceived, upon considering the object as fitted to the use intended.

It must be further observed to avoid obscurity, that the beauty which arises from the relation of an object to its end, is independent of the end itself, whether good or bad, whether beneficial or hurtful: it arises from considering its fitness to the end purposed, whatever that end be.

When we take the end itself under consideration, there is discovered a beauty or ugliness of a higher kind than the two former. A beneficial end strikes us with a peculiar pleasure; and approbation belongs also to this feeling. Thus, the mechanism of a ship is beautiful, in the view of means well fitted to an end. But the end itself, of carrying on commerce and procuring so many conveniences to mankind, exalts the object, and heightens our approbation and pleasure. By an end, I mean what it serves to procure and bring about, whether it be an ultimate end, or subordinate to something farther. Considered with respect to its end, the degree of its beauty depends on the degree of its usefulness. Let it be only kept in view, that as the end or use of a thing is an object of greater dignity and importance than the means, the approbation bestowed on the former rises higher than that bestowed on the latter.

These three orders of beauty may be blended together in many different ways, to have very different effects. If an object in itself beautiful be ill-fitted to its end, it will, upon the whole, be disagreeable. This may be exemplified in a house regular in its architecture and beautiful to the eye, but incommodious for dwelling. If there be in an object an aptitude to a bad end, it will, upon the whole, be disagreeable, though it have the second modification of beauty in perfection. A constitution of government formed with the most perfect art for enslaving the people, may be an instance of this. If the end be good but the object not well fitted to the end, it will be beautiful, or ugly, as the goodness of the end, or unfitness of the means, is prevalent. Of this instances will occur at first view, without being suggested.

The foregoing modifications of beauty and deformity, apply to all objects, animate and inanimate. A voluntary agent produces a peculiar species of beauty and deformity, which may be distinguished from all others. The actions of living creatures are more interesting than the actions of matter. The instincts and principles of action of the former, give us more delight than the blind powers of the latter; or, in other words, are more beautiful. No one can doubt of this fact, who is in any degree conversant with the poets. In Homer every thing lives: even darts and arrows are endued with voluntary motion. And we are sensible, that nothing animates a poem more than the frequent use of this figure.

Hence a new circumstance in the beauty and deformity of actions, considered as proceeding from intention, deliberation, and choice. This circumstance, which is of the utmost importance in the science of morals, concerns chiefly human actions: for we discover little of intention, deliberation, and choice, in the actions of inferior creatures. Human actions are not only agreeable or disagreeable, beautiful or deformed, in the different views above mentioned, but are further distinguished in our perception of them, as *fit* and *meet* to be done, or as *unfit* and *unmeet*. These are simple perceptions, capable of no definition. But let any man attentively examine what passes in his mind, when the object of his thought is an action proceeding from deliberate intention, and he will soon discover the meaning of these words, and the perceptions which they denote. Let him reflect upon a signal act of generosity to a person of merit, relieving him from want or from a cruel enemy: let him reflect on a man of exemplary patriotism bearing patiently rank oppression, rather than break the peace of society. Such conduct will not only be agreeable to him, and appear beautiful, but will be agreeable and beautiful, as *fit* and *meet* to be done. He will approve the action in that quality, and he will approve the actor for his humanity and disinterestedness. This distinguishing circumstance entitles the beauty and deformity of human actions to peculiar names: they are termed *moral beauty* and *moral deformity*. Hence the *morality* and *immorality* of human actions; founded on a faculty termed the *moral sense*.

It gives no clear notion of morality, to rest it upon simple approbation, as some writers do. I approve a well-constructed plough or waggon for its usefulness. I approve a fine picture or statue for the justness of its representation; and I approve the maker for his skill. I approve an elegant dress on a fine woman; and I approve her taste. But such approbation is far from being the same with that which is occasioned by human actions deliberately done in order to some end. If the end be beneficial, the action is approved as right and fit to have been done: if hurtful, it is disapproved as wrong and unfit to have been done. None of these qualities are applicable to the instances first given.

Of all objects whatever, human actions are the most highly delightful or disgustful, and possess the highest degree of beauty or deformity. In these every circumstance concurs: the fitness or unfitness of the means, the goodness or badness of the end, the intention of the actor; which give them the peculiar character of *fit* and *meet*, or *unfit* and *unmeet*.

Thus we find the nature of man so constituted, as to approve certain actions, and to disapprove others; to consider some actions as *fit* and *meet* to be done, and others as *unfit* and *unmeet*. What distinguishes actions to make them objects of the one or the other perception, will be explained in the following chapter. And with regard to some of our actions, another circumstance will be discovered, different from what have been mentioned, sounding the well known terms of *duty* and *obligation*, directing our conduct, and constituting what in the strictest sense may be termed a law. With regard to other beings, we have no *data* to discover the laws of their nature, other than their frame and constitution. We have the same *data* to discover the laws of our own nature; and over and above, a peculiar sense of approbation or disapprobation, termed the moral sense. And one thing extremely remarkable will be explained afterwards, that the laws which are fitted to the nature of man and to his external circumstances, are the same that we approve by the moral sense.

Though these terms are of the utmost importance in morals, I know not that any author has attempted to explain them, by pointing out those principles or perceptions which they express. This defect I shall endeavour to supply, by tracing these terms to their proper source, without which the system of morals cannot be complete; because these terms point out to us the most precise and essential branch of morality.

Lord Shaftesbury, to whom the world is greatly indebted for his inestimable writings, has clearly and convincingly made out, 'that virtue is the good, and vice the ill of every one'.[8] But he has not proved virtue to be our duty, other ways than by showing it to be our interest; which comes not up to the idea of duty. For this term plainly implies somewhat indispensable in our conduct; what we ought to do, what we ought to submit to. Now, a man may be considered as foolish for acting against his interest; but he cannot be considered as wicked or vicious. His Lordship indeed, in his essay upon virtue, approaches to an explanation of duty and obligation, by asserting the subordinacy of the self-affections to the social. But though he states this as a proposition to be made out, he drops it in the subsequent part of his work, and never again brings it into view.

Hutcheson, in his essay upon beauty and virtue, founds the morality of actions on a certain quality of actions, that procures approbation and love to the agent. But this account of morality is also imperfect, as it makes no distinction between duty and simple benevolence. It is scarce applicable to justice; for the man who, confining himself strictly to it, is true to his word and avoids harming others, is a just and moral man, is entitled to some share of esteem; but will never be the object of love or friendship. He must show a disposition to the good of mankind, of his friends at least and neighbours, he must exert acts of humanity and benevolence; before he can hope to procure the affection of others.

But it is chiefly to be observed, that in this account of morality, the terms *obligation*, *duty*, *ought* and *should*, have no distinct meaning; which shows, that the entire foundation of morality is not taken in by this author. It is true, that toward the close of his work, he attempts to explain the meaning of the term *obligation*; but without success. He explains it to be, either, 'a motive from self-interest, sufficient to determine those who duly consider it to a certain course of action'; which surely is not moral obligation; or 'a determination, without regard to our own interest, to approve actions, and to perform them; which determination shall also make us displeased with ourselves, and uneasy upon having acted

---

[8] [Anthony Ashley Cooper, Third Earl of Shaftesbury (1671–1713). The quoted passage comes from *Inquiry Concerning Virtue or Merit*, in: *Characteristics of Men, Manners, Opinions, Times* (1711).]

contrary to it';[9] in which sense, he says, there is naturally an obligation upon all men to benevolence. But this account falls short of the true idea of obligation; because it makes no distinction betwixt it and that simple approbation of the moral sense which can be applied to heroism, magnanimity, generosity, and other exalted virtues, as well as to justice. Duty however belongs to the latter only; and no man reckons himself under an obligation to perform any action that belongs to the former.

Neither is the author of the treatise upon human nature more successful, when he endeavours to resolve the moral sense into pure sympathy.[10] According to that author, there is no more in morality, but approving or disapproving an action, after we discover by reflection that it tends to the good or hurt of society. This would be too faint a principle to control our irregular appetites and passions. It would scarce be sufficient to restrain us from encroaching upon our friends and neighbours; and, with regard to strangers, would be the weakest of all restraints. We shall by and by show, that morality has a more solid foundation. In the meantime, it is of importance to observe, that, upon this author's system,[11] as well as Hutcheson's, the noted terms of *duty*, *obligation*, *ought* and *should*, etc. have no meaning.

We shall now proceed to explain these terms, by pointing out the perceptions which they express. And, in performing this task, there will be discovered a wonderful and beautiful contrivance of the author of our nature, to give authority to morality, by putting the self-affections in a due subordination to the social. The moral sense has in part been explained above; that by it we perceive some actions to be *fit* and *meet* to be *done*; and others to be *unfit* and *unmeet*. When this

---

[9] [Francis Hutcheson (1694–1746), Professor of Moral Philosophy at the University of Glasgow from 1730 and one of the founding figures of the Scottish Enlightenment. The text Kames quotes is from *An Inquiry into the Original of Our Ideas of Beauty and Virtue* (1725), second essay ('An Inquiry concerning the Original of our Ideas of Virtue or Moral Good').]

[10] [The reference here is to David Hume's *A Treatise of Human Nature* (1739–40), book 3, part 3, section 1.]

[11] [That is: David Hume.]

observation is applied to particulars, it is an evident fact, that we have a sense of *fitness* in kindly and beneficent actions: we approve ourselves and others for performing actions of this kind: as, on the other hand, we disapprove the unsociable, peevish, and hard-hearted. But in one class of actions, an additional circumstance is regarded by the moral sense. Submission to parents, gratitude to benefactors, and the acting justly to all, are perceived not only as fit and meet, but as our indispensable duty. On the other hand, the injuring others in their persons, in their fame, or in their goods are perceived not only as *unfit* to be done, but as absolutely *wrong* to be done, and what, upon no account, we *ought* to do. What is here asserted, is a matter of fact, which can admit of no other proof than an appeal to every man's own perceptions. [...]

It is proper here to be remarked, that benevolent and generous actions are not objects of this peculiar sense. Hence, such actions, though considered as *fit* and *right* to be done, are not however considered to be our *duty*, but as virtuous actions beyond what is strictly our duty. Benevolence and generosity are more beautiful, and more attractive of love and esteem, than justice. Yet, not being so necessary to the support of society, they are left upon the general footing of approbatory pleasure; while justice, faith, truth, without which society cannot subsist, are objects of the foregoing peculiar sense, to take away all shadow of liberty, and to put us under a necessity of performance. The virtues that are exacted from us as duties, may be termed *primary*: the other which are not exacted as duties, may be termed *secondary*. [...]

We may observe, in the next place [...] that conscience, or the moral sense, is none of our principles of action, but their guide and director. It is still of greater importance to observe, that the authority of conscience does not consist merely in an act of reflection. It arises from a direct perception, which we have upon presenting the object, without the intervention of any sort of reflection. And the authority lies in this circumstance, that we perceive the action to be our duty, and what we are indispensably bound to perform. It is in this manner that the moral sense, with regard to some actions, plainly bears upon it the marks of authority over all our appetites and passions. It is the voice of God within us, which commands our strictest obedience, just as much as when his will is declared by express revelation.

What is here stated will I hope clearly distinguish duty or moral obligation from benevolence: I know of no words in our language to make the distinction more clear. The overlooking this distinction is a capital defect in the writers who acknowledge morality to be founded on an innate sense: it has led them to reduce the whole of virtue to benevolence; and consequently, to hold mankind as bound to perform the highest acts of benevolence, because such acts produce the highest approbation. This doctrine cannot be altogether harmless, because it converts benevolence into indispensable duty, contrary to the system of nature. [...]

A very important branch of the moral sense remains still to be unfolded. In the matters above mentioned, performing of promises, gratitude, and abstaining from harming others, we have the peculiar sense of duty and obligation: but in transgressing these duties, we have not only the sense of vice and wickedness, but we have further the sense of merited punishment, and dread of its being inflicted upon us. This dread may be but slight in the more venial transgressions. But, in crimes of a deep dye, it rises to a degree of anguish and despair. Hence remorse of conscience, which, upon the commission of certain crimes, is a dreadful torture. This dread of merited punishment operates for the most part so strongly upon the imagination, that every unusual accident, every extraordinary misfortune, is by the criminal judged to be a punishment purposely inflicted upon him. During prosperity, he makes a shift to blunt the stings of his conscience. But no sooner does he fall into distress or into any depression of mind, than his conscience lays fast hold of him: his crime stares him in the face; and every accidental misfortune is converted into a real punishment. [...]

One material circumstance is here to be remarked, which widens the difference still more betwixt the primary and secondary virtues. As justice, and the other primary virtues, are more essential to society, than generosity, benevolence, or any other secondary virtue, they are more indispensable. Friendship, generosity, softness of manners, form peculiar characters, and serve to distinguish one person from another.

But the sense of justice and of the other primary virtues, belongs to man as such. Though it exists in very different degrees of strength, there perhaps never was a human creature altogether void of it. And it makes a delightful appearance in the human constitution, that even where this sense is weak, as it is in some individuals, it notwithstanding retains its authority as the director of their conduct. If there be a sense of justice, it must distinguish right from wrong, what we *ought* to do from what we *ought not* to do; and, by that very distinguishing faculty, justly claims to be our guide and governor. This consideration may serve to justify human laws, which make no distinction among men, as endued with a stronger or weaker sense of justice.

And here we must pause a moment, to indulge some degree of admiration upon this part of the human system. Man is evidently intended to live in society; and because there can be no society among creatures who prey upon one another, it was necessary, in the first place, to provide against mutual injuries. Further, man is the weakest of all creatures separately, and the very strongest in society; therefore mutual assistance is the chief end of society; and to this end it was necessary, that there should be mutual trust and reliance upon engagements, and that favours received should be thankfully repaid. Now, nothing can be more finely adjusted than the human heart, to answer these purposes. It is not sufficient that we approve every action that is essential to the preservation of society: it is not sufficient, that we disapprove every action that tends to its dissolution. Approbation or disapprobation merely, is not sufficient to subject our conduct to the authority of a law. These sentiments have in this case the peculiar modification of duty, that such actions are what we ought to perform, and what we are indispensably bound to perform. This circumstance converts into a law, what without it can only be considered as a rational measure, and a prudential rule of conduct. Nor is any thing omitted to give it the most complete character of a law. The transgression is attended with apprehension of punishment, nay with actual punishment; as every misfortune which befalls the transgressor is considered by him as a punishment. Nor is this the whole of the matter. Sympathy is a principle implanted in the breast of every man; we cannot hurt another without suffering for it, which is an additional punishment. And we are still further punished for our injustice or ingratitude, by incurring the aversion and hatred of all men.

3. Liberty and Necessity

i) From: *Essays on the Principles of Morality and Natural Religion*, 3rd ed. (1779), part 1, essay 3, pp. 151–169

When we apply our thoughts to final causes, no subject more readily presents itself than the material world, which is stamped with the brightest characters of wisdom and goodness. The moral world, being less in view, has been generally overlooked, though it yields not to the other in rich materials. Man's inward system will be found no less admirable, than the external system of which he makes a part. The subject is the more curious, that the traces of wisdom and design discernible in our internal frame, lie more out of common sight. They are touches, as it were, of a finer pencil and of a nicer hand, than are discovered in the material world. Thought is more subtle than motion; and more of exquisite art is displayed in the laws of voluntary action, than in the laws of mere matter.

That nothing can happen without a cause, is a principle embraced by all men, the illiterate and ignorant as well as the learned. Nothing that happens is conceived as happening of itself, but as an *effect* produced by some other thing. However ignorant of the cause, we notwithstanding conclude, that every thing which happens must have a cause. We should perhaps be at a loss to deduce this proposition from any premises, by a chain of reasoning. But perception affords conviction, where reason leaves us in the dark. We perceive the proposition to be true. [...] Events thus viewed in a chain of causes and effects, should naturally be considered, one would think, as necessary and fixed: for the relation betwixt a cause and its effect implies somewhat precise and determinate, and leads our thoughts to what must be, and cannot be other ways than it is.

That we have such a sense as is above described, cannot be controverted; and yet, when we search farther into human nature, a sense of chance or contingency in events seems to be no less deeply rooted in our nature than the former. This sense of chance or contingency is most conspicuous when we look forward to future events. Some things we indeed always consider as certain or necessary; such as, the revolution of seasons, and the rising and setting of the sun. These as experience teaches, are regulated by fixed laws. But many things appear to us loose, fortuitous, uncertain; uncertain not only with respect to us on account of our ignorance of the cause, but uncertain in themselves, or not tied down and predetermined to fall out by any invariable law. We naturally make a distinction betwixt things that *must be*, and things that *may be*, or *may not be*. Thus, with respect to future events, we have a sense of chance, or of contingency, which seems to banish the other sense of the dependency of events upon precise and determinate causes.

When we consider in what view our own actions are perceived by the mind, there is somewhat equally strange and mysterious. It is admitted by all men, that we act from motives. The plain man, as well as the philosopher, perceives the connection betwixt an action and its motive to be so strong, that from this perception both of them reason with full confidence about the future actions of others. That an avaricious man will take every fair opportunity of acquiring riches, is as little doubted, as that rain and sunshine will make plants grow. The motive of gain is judged to operate as certainly and infallibly upon his temper, as heat and moisture upon the soil, each to produce its proper effect. If we be uncertain what part any particular man will act, the uncertainty arises not from our doubting whether he will act from a motive, for this is never called in question: it arises from our not being able to judge, what motive will prevail. If so, it should seem, that all the train of human actions would occur to the mind as necessary and fixed. Yet human actions do not always appear to us in that light. Previous to any particular action, we indeed always judge, that it will be the necessary result of some motive. But in a retrospect the judgment seems to vary. Has a man done what is wrong and shameful? We accuse, and we condemn him for acting the wrong and shameful part. We conceive that he had power to act otherwise, and *ought* to have acted otherwise. Nay he himself gives the same impartial judgment of his conduct.

The whole train of our perceptions, in a moment, accommodate themselves to the supposition of his being a free agent. [...]

Taking a view of the material world, we find all things there proceeding in a fixed and settled train of causes and effects. It is a point indisputable, that all the changes produced in matter and all the different modifications it assumes, are the result of fixed laws. Every effect is so precisely determined, that no other effect could, in such circumstances, have resulted from the operation of the cause: which holds even in the minutest changes of the different elements, as all philosophers admit. Casual and fluctuating as these seem, even their slightest variations are the result of pre-established laws. There is a chain of causes and effects which hang one upon another, running through this whole system; and not the smallest link of the chain can be broken, without altering the whole constitution of things, or suspending the regular operation of the laws of nature. Here then, in the material world, there is nothing that can be called *contingent*; nothing that is left loose; but every thing must be precisely what it is, and be found in that state in which we find it.

In the moral world, this necessary chain of causes and effects appears not so clearly. 'Man is the actor here. He is endued with will, and he acts from choice. He has a power of beginning motion, which is subject to no mechanical laws; and therefore he is not under what is called physical necessity. He has appetites and passions which prompt him to gratify them: but he is under no necessity of blindly submitting to their impulse. For reason has a power of restraint. It suggests motives from the cool views of good and evil. He deliberates upon these. In consequence of his deliberation he chooses: and here lies our liberty.'[12] Let us examine to what this liberty amounts. That motives have some influence in determining the mind, is certain; and that they have this influence in different degrees, is equally certain. The sense of honour and gratitude for example, are powerful motives with a man to serve a friend. Let the man's private interest

---

[12] [Kames quotes himself here, from the first edition of the *Essays*, essay 3 (1751).]

concur; and the motives become more powerful. Add the certain prospect of poverty, shame, or bodily suffering, if he shall act a different part; and you leave him no choice; the motives to action become irresistible. Motives being once allowed to have a determining influence in any degree, it is easy to suppose the influence so augmented, whether of the same or of accumulated motives, as to leave little freedom to the mind, or rather none at all. In such a case, there is no denying that we are under a necessity to act. And though this arises from the constitution of the mind, not from external compulsion; yet in this case the consequence is no less certain, fixed, and unavoidable, than in that of external compulsion. So evident this is, that, in some instances, moral and physical necessity seem to coincide, or scarcely to be distinguished. A criminal walks to the scaffold in the midst of his guards. No man will deny that he is under an absolute necessity in this case. Why? because he knows, that if he refuse to go, they will drag him. I ask, is this a physical or a moral necessity? The answer at first view is not obvious. And yet, strictly speaking, the necessity is only moral: for it is the force of a motive that determines the criminal to walk to the scaffold; to wit, that resistance is vain. The idea of necessity however in the mind of the spectators, when they view the criminal in this situation, is no less strong, than if they saw him bound and carried on a sledge. Nothing is more common, than to talk of an action which one must do, and cannot avoid. He was compelled to it, we say, and it was impossible he could act otherwise; when all the compulsion we mean, is only the application of some very strong motive to the mind. This shows, that, in the judgment of all men, a motive may, in certain circumstances, carry in it the power of rendering an action necessary. In other words, we expect such an action in consequence of such a motive, with equal confidence, as when we expect to see a stone fall to the ground when dropped from the hand.

'This', it will be said, 'may hold in some instances, but not in all. For, in the greater part of human actions, there is really a sense of liberty. When the mind hesitates betwixt two things, examines and compares, and at last resolves, is there any compulsion or necessity here?'[13] No compulsion, it is granted; but as to necessity, let us pause, and examine more accurately. The resolution being taken, the choice being made, upon what is it founded? Certainly upon some reason or motive, however silent or weak. No man in his senses ever made choice of one thing before another, without being able to assign a reason, weak or strong, for the preference. It would be a pregnant mark of idiocy, to say that one has come to are solution and cannot say why. If this be an undoubted fact, it follows that the determination must result from that motive which has the greatest influence for the time; or from what appears the best and most eligible upon the whole. If motives be different with regard to strength and influence, which is plainly the case; it is involved in the very idea of the strongest motive, that it must have the strongest effect in determining the mind. This can no more be doubted, than that in a balance the greater weight must turn the scale. [...]

It is true, that, in debating upon human liberty, a man may attempt to show that motives have no necessary influence, by eating perhaps the worst apple that is before him, or, in some such trifling matter, preferring an obviously less good to a greater. But is it not plain, that the humour of showing that he can act against motives, is the very motive of the whimsical preference?

Comparing the laws that govern human actions with those that govern the actions of matter, they will be found equally operative, and their effects equally necessary. Where the motives to any action are perfectly full, cogent, and clear, the sense of liberty, as we showed before, entirely vanishes. In other cases, where the field of choice is wider, and where opposite motives counter balance and work against each other, the mind fluctuates for a while, and feels itself more loose: but at last, must as necessarily be determined to the side of the most powerful motive, as the balance, after several vibrations, to the side of the preponderating weight. The laws of mind, and the laws of matter, are in this respect

---

[13] [Again, Kames quotes himself here, from the first edition of the *Essays*, essay 3 (1751).]

perfectly similar; though, in making the comparison, we are apt to deceive ourselves. In forming a notion of physical necessity, we seldom think of any force, but what has visibly a full effect. A man in prison, or tied to a post, must remain there: if dragged along, he cannot resist. Whereas motives, which are very different, do not always produce sensible effects. Yet, when the comparison is accurately instituted, the very same thing holds in the actions of matter. A weak motive makes some impression: but, in opposition to one more powerful, it has no effect to determine the mind. In the precise same manner, a small force will not overcome a great resistance; nor an ounce in one scale, counter balance a pound in the other. Comparing together the actions of mind and of matter, similar causes will in both equally produce similar effects.

But admitting all that has been contended for, of the necessary influence of motives to bring on the choice or last judgment of the understanding, it is urged by Dr Clarke, that man is still a free agent, because he has a power of acting or beginning motion according to his will.[14] In this he places human liberty, that motives are not physical efficient causes of motion. Man is a free agent undoubtedly, because he acts as he wills; but he is equally a necessary agent, as being necessarily influenced by motives to act. The motive, according to his own concession, necessarily determines the will; and the will necessarily produces the action, unless it be obstructed by some foreign force. 'But,' says he, 'it is only a moral necessity which is produced by motives; and a moral necessity is no necessity at all, being consistent with the highest liberty.' The Doctor's error lies in opposing moral necessity to liberty. Man is a free agent, because he acts according to his own will. He is at the same time a necessary agent, because his will is necessarily influenced by motives. These are perfectly consistent. The laws of action which respect the human mind, are as fixed as those which respect

---

[14] [Samuel Clarke (1675–1729), English rationalist philosopher and clergyman. Kames quotes from *A Demonstration of the Being and Attributes of God*, Proposition 10, in: *A Discourse concerning the Being and Attributes of God* (1705).]

matter. The idea of *necessary, certain, unavoidable*, equally agrees to both.

One great source of confusion, in reflecting upon this subject, seems to be, our not distinguishing betwixt *necessity* and *constraint*. In common language, these are used as equivalent terms; but they ought to be distinguished when we treat of this subject. A person having a strong desire to escape, remains in prison because the doors are guarded. Finding his keepers gone, he makes his escape. His escape now is as necessary, i.e. as certain and infallible a consequence of the circumstances he finds himself in, as his confinement was before; though in the one case there is constraint, in the other none. When, being under no constraint, we act according to our inclination and choice, our actions are justly reckoned free. At the same time they are strictly necessary; because every inclination and choice is unavoidably caused or occasioned by the prevailing motive.

The preceding reasonings may perhaps make a stronger impression upon being reduced into a short argument, after the following manner. When a being acts merely by instinct and without any view to consequences, every one must see that it acts necessarily. Though not so obvious, the case comes to the same where an action is exerted in order to bring about some end or event. This end or event must be the object of desire; for no man in his senses who uses means in order to a certain end, but must desire the means to be effectual: if we do not desire to accomplish an event, we cannot possibly act in order to bring it about. Desire and action are then intimately connected; so intimately, that no action can be exerted where there is no antecedent desire: the event is first the object of desire, and then we act in order to bring it about. This being so, it follows clearly, that our actions cannot be free in any sense opposed to their being morally necessary. Our desires obviously are not under our own power, but are raised by means that depend not upon us. And if our desires are not under our power, neither can our actions be under our power. Liberty, as opposed to moral necessity, if it have any meaning, must signify a power to act in contradiction to desire; or, in other words, a power to act in contradiction to any view, purpose, or design, we can have in acting; which power, beside that no man was ever conscious of it, seems to be an absurdity altogether inconsistent with a rational being. [...]

As there is scarce room for overdoing in explaining the doctrine of moral necessity, which in some particulars goes cross to vulgar notions, I shall endeavour to set it in a clear light, by opposing it to physical necessity. In the first place, a man under the influence of a physical cause is passive: he is acted upon, and does not act. Under the influence of a moral cause, he himself acts; and the moral cause operates by influencing and determining him to act. Secondly, a physical cause is generally exerted against a man's inclination and will. If the force applied overcome his resistance, he must submit; and in this case, the necessity is involuntary: it is constraint or coaction.[15] On the other hand, moral necessity is always *voluntary*. A moral cause operates not by force or coaction, but by solicitation and persuasion. It applies to the judgment, and generally affords conviction. But whether or not, it never fails to succeed with the sensitive part of our nature, by raising desire; and when a man is under no restraint, he naturally and necessarily proceeds to action, in order to accomplish his desire. The action is performed as a means to an end. It is directed by will, and is in the strictest sense voluntary. It is at the same time necessary: for such is the nature of man, that desire always determines the will. The necessity here is of the same kind with that of being pleased with a beautiful object, or of being displeased with one that is ugly. But as this necessity is altogether voluntary, it is directly opposite to what arises from external force. Thirdly, physical necessity, except when voluntary which rarely happens, is extremely disagreeable. But moral necessity, which is always voluntary, is for that reason always agreeable. To nothing is human nature more averse

---

[15] [Footnote by Kames] Physical necessity, however, is not always involuntary. Force may be applied to bring about an agreeable event. In this case the necessity is *voluntary*. A ship having in a storm lost its masts and rigging, is driven towards the port by a violent wind: the seamen being under the power of physical necessity, are entirely passive; but their desire is to be on shore. The necessity they are under, corresponds with their desire, and is thereby *voluntary*. [...]

than to constraint: on the other hand, our condition is always agreeable when we enjoy the freedom of our own will. Fourthly, a man impelled by a physical cause and acted upon involuntarily, must be sensible of the force and coaction, and consequently of the necessity he is under. A moral cause is in a very different condition. As it influences by persuasion, and not force, it may well be supposed to operate without discovering itself to be a necessary cause. And in fact that it so operates, is evident from constant experience. And hence the ignorance, almost universal, of our being necessary agents.

And this luckily suggests a comparison between moral necessity, and a power to act against motives, termed commonly *liberty of indifference*. [...] Moral necessity [...] is always agreeable. An action, provided it be voluntary, is not the less agreeable by being necessary: so far from it, that the necessity and agreeableness are inseparable, as proceeding from the same cause. An action is necessary, because it is directed by desire: it is at the same time agreeable, because it tends to the accomplishment of desire. And from this it clearly follows, that the greater the necessity is, the greater must also be the pleasure. And now to the other member of the comparison. It is difficult to form a conception of a power to act, without motives or any thing to influence the mind. But supposing such a power, it must be devoid of all pleasure or satisfaction, even when exercised without crossing any appetite or passion. It is still more difficult to form a conception of a power to act in contradiction to motives, or in other words in contradiction to desire. But such power, if it can exist, must be extremely disagreeable: for here a man acting in contradiction to his desires, must of course render himself miserable. In this particular, liberty of indifference resembles perfectly physical necessity: for when a man lies open to have his most rational and best-concerted schemes disappointed, it comes to the same in point of distress, whether the disappointment be occasioned by an internal or an external cause. [...]

ii) From: *Essays on the Principles of Morality and Natural Religion*, 1st ed. (1751), part 1, essay 3, pp. 192–216

The extent of human liberty is above ascertained. It consists in spontaneity, or acting according to our inclination and choice. It may be therefore distinguished from *constraint*, but must not be opposed to necessity. For, as has been fully shown, the mind, in the most calm choice, the most deliberate action, is necessarily, i.e. unavoidably and certainly, determined by the prepollent motive. When we examine accurately, how far our feelings correspond to this system; we find, as was hinted before, first, that, antecedent to any particular action, we generally think and reason upon the scheme of necessity. In considering or guessing at future events, we always conclude, that a man will act consistently with his character; we infer what his actions will be, from the knowledge we have of his temper, and the motives that are fitted to influence it; and never dream of any man's having a power of acting against motives. [...] Our actions are not considered as proceeding in a necessary unavoidable train: but we accuse and blame others, for not having acted the part they *might* and *ought* to have acted, and condemn ourselves, and feel remorse, for having been guilty of a wrong we *might have* refrained from. The operations of moral conscience plainly proceed upon this supposition, that there is such a power in man of directing his actions, as rendered it possible for the person accused, to have acted a better part. This affords an argument, which the advocates for liberty have urged in its full force, against the doctrine of necessity. They reason thus: if actions be necessary, and not in our own power, and if we know it to be so, what ground can there be for reprehension and blame, for self-condemnation and remorse? If a clock had understanding to be sensible of its own motions, knowing, at the same time, that they proceed according to necessary laws, could it find fault with itself for striking wrong? Would it not blame the artist, who had ill adjusted the wheels on which its movements depended? So that, upon this scheme, say they, all the moral constitution of our nature is overturned. There is an end to all the operations of conscience about right and wrong. Man is no longer a moral agent, nor the subject of praise or blame for what he does.

This difficulty is great, and never has been surmounted by the advocates for necessity. They endeavour to surmount it, by reconciling feeling to philosophic truth, in the following manner. We are so constituted, they say, that certain affections, and the actions which proceed from them, appear odious and base; and others agreeable and lovely; that, wherever they are beheld, either in ourselves or others, the moral sense necessarily approves of the one, and condemns the other; that this approbation is immediate and instinctive, without any reflection on the liberty or necessity of actions; that, on the contrary, the more any person is under the power of his affections and passions, and, by consequence, the greater necessity he is under, the more virtuous or vicious he is esteemed.

But this account of the matter is not satisfactory. All that is here said, is in the main true, but is not the whole truth. I appeal to any man who has been guilty of a bad action, which gives him uneasiness, whether there is not somewhat more in the inward feeling, than merely a dislike or disapprobation of the affection, from which his action proceeded? [...] The sting is indeed much sharper, and for very wise reasons, when a man has trespassed against the rules of strict morality. But, in both cases, the uneasiness proceeds upon the supposition, that he was free, and had it in his power to have acted a better part. [...] The person, thus under the dominion of bad passions, is accused, is condemned, singly upon this ground, that it was *through his own fault* he became so subject to them; in other words, that it was in his power, to have kept his mind free from the enslaving influence of corrupt affections. Were not this the case, brute animals might be the objects of moral blame, as well as man. Some beasts are reckoned savage and cruel, others treacherous and false: we dislike, we hate creatures so ill constituted: but we do not blame nor condemn them, as we do rational agents; because they are not supposed to have a sense of right and wrong, nor freedom and power of directing their actions according to that inward rule. We must therefore admit, that the idea of freedom, of a power of regulating our will and actions according to certain rules, is essential to the moral feeling. On the system of universal necessity, abstracted from this feeling, though certain affections and actions might excite our approbation, and others our dislike, there could be no place for blame or remorse. All the ideas would entirely vanish, which at present are suggested by the words *ought* and *should*, when applied to moral conduct. [...]

After having ascertained the foundation, upon which the doctrine of necessity is built, and which seems incapable of being shaken, let us fairly and candidly take our nature as we find it, which will lead us to this conclusion, that though man, in truth, is a necessary agent, having all his actions determined by fixed and immutable laws; yet that, this being concealed from him, he acts with the conviction of being a free agent. It is concealed from him, I say, as to the purposes of action: for whatever discoveries he makes as a philosopher, these affect not his conduct as a man. In principle and speculation, let him be a most rigid fatalist; he has nevertheless all the feelings which would arise from power over his own actions. He is angry at himself when he has done wrong. He praises and blames just like other men: nor can all his principles set him above the reach of self-condemnation and remorse, when conscience at any time smites him. It is true, that a man of this belief, when he is seeking to make his mind easy, after some bad action, may reason upon the principles of necessity, that, according to the constitution of his nature, it was impossible for him to have acted any other part. But this will give him little relief. In spite of all reasonings, his remorse will subsist. Nature never intended us to act upon this plan; and our natural principles are too deeply rooted, to give way to philosophy. This case is precisely similar to that of contingency. A feeling of liberty, which I now scruple not to call deceitful, is so interwoven with our nature, that it has an equal effect in action, as if we were really endued with such a power.

Having explained [...] this remarkable feeling of liberty, and examined, as we went along, some arguments against necessity that are founded upon it; we now proceed to handle this feeling, as we have done that of contingency, with regard to its final cause. And in this branch of our nature are displayed the greatest wisdom, and the greatest goodness. Man must be so constituted, in order to attain the proper improvement of his nature, in virtue and happiness. Put the case, he were entirely divested of his present ideas of liberty: suppose him to see and conceive his own nature, and the constitution of things, in the light of strict philosophic truth; in the same light they are beheld by the deity: to conceive himself, and all his actions, necessarily linked into the great chain of causes and effects, which renders the whole order both of the natural and moral world unalterably determined in every article: suppose, I say, our natural feelings, our practical ideas to suit and tally with this, which is the real plan; and what would follow? Why, an entire derangement of our present system of action, especially with regard to the motives which now lead us to virtue. There would still indeed be ground for the love of virtue, as the best constitution of nature, and the only sure foundation of happiness; and, in this view, we might be grieved when we found ourselves deficient in good principles. But this would be all. We could feel no inward self-approbation on doing well, no remorse on doing ill; because both the good and the ill were necessary and unavoidable. There would be no more place for applause or blame among mankind: none of that generous indignation we now feel at the bad, as persons who have abused and perverted their rational powers: no more notion of accountableness for the use of those powers: no sense of ill desert, or just punishment annexed to crimes as their due; nor of any reward merited by worthy and generous actions. All these ideas, and feelings, so useful to men in their moral conduct, vanish at once with the feeling of liberty. There would be field for no other passions but love and hatred, sorrow and pity: and the sense of *duty*, of being obliged to certain things which we *ought* to perform, must be quite extinguished; for we can have no conception of moral *obligation*, without supposing a power in the agent over his own actions.

It appears then most fit and wise, that we should be endued with a sense of liberty; without which, man must have been ill qualified for acting his present part. That artificial light, in which the feeling of liberty presents the moral world to our view, answers all the good purposes of making the actions of man entirely dependent upon himself.

His happiness and misery appear to be in his own power. He appears praiseworthy or culpable, according as he improves or neglects his rational faculties. The idea of his being an accountable creature arises. Reward seems due to merit; punishment to crimes. He feels the force of moral obligation. In short, new passions arise, and a variety of new springs are set in motion, to make way for new exertions of reason and activity. In all which, though man is really actuated by laws of necessary influence, yet he seems to move himself: and whilst the universal system is gradually carried on to perfection by the first mover, that powerful hand, which winds up and directs the great machine, is never brought into sight.

It will now be proper to answer some objections, which may be urged against the doctrine we have advanced. One, which at first, may seem of considerable weight, is, that we found virtue altogether upon a deceitful feeling of liberty, which, it may be alleged, is neither a secure nor an honourable foundation. But, in the first place, I deny that we have founded it altogether upon a deceitful feeling. For, independent of the deceitful feeling of liberty, there is in the nature of man a firm foundation for virtue. He must be sensible that virtue is essentially preferable to vice; that it is the just order, the perfection and happiness of his nature. For, supposing him only endued with the principle of self-love; this principle will lead him to distinguish moral good from evil, so far as to give ground for loving the one, and hating the other: as he must needs see that benevolence, justice, temperance, and the other virtues, are the necessary means of his happiness, and that all vice and wickedness introduce disorder and misery. But man is endued with a social as well as a selfish principle, and has an immediate satisfaction and pleasure in the happiness of others, which is a further ground for distinguishing and loving virtue. All this, I say, takes place, laying aside the deceitful feeling of liberty, and supposing all our notions to be adjusted to the system of necessity. I add, that there is nothing in the above doctrine, to exclude the perception, of a certain beauty and excellency in virtue, according to Lord *Shaftesbury* and the ancient philosophers; which may, for ought we know, render it lovely and admirable to all rational beings. It appears to us, unquestionably, under the form of intrinsic excellency, even when we think not of its tendency to our happiness. Ideas of moral obligation, of remorse, of merit, and all that is connected with this way of thinking, arise from, what may be called, a wise delusion in our nature concerning liberty: but, as this affects only a certain modification of our ideas of virtue and vice, there is nothing in it, to render the foundation of virtue, either unsecure or dishonourable. Unsecure it does not render it, because, as now observed, virtue partly stands firm upon a separate foundation, independent of these feelings; and even where built upon these feelings, it is still built upon human nature. For though these feelings of liberty vary from the truth of things, they are, nevertheless, essential to the nature of man. We act upon them, and cannot act otherwise. And therefore, though the distinction betwixt virtue and vice, had no other foundation but these feelings (which is not the case), it would still have an immoveable and secure foundation in human nature. As for the supposed dishonour done to virtue, by resting its authority, in any degree, on a deceitful feeling, there is so little ground for this part of the objection, that, on the contrary, our doctrine most highly exalts virtue. For the above described artificial sense of liberty, is wholly contrived to support virtue, and to give its dictates the force of a law. Hereby it is discovered to be, in a singular manner, the care of the Deity; and a peculiar sort of glory is thrown around it. The author of nature, has not rested it, upon the ordinary feelings and principles of human nature, as he has rested our other affections and appetites, even those which are most necessary to our existence. But a sort of extraordinary machinery is introduced for its sake. Human nature is forced, as it were, out of its course, and made to receive a nice and artificial set of feelings; merely that conscience may have a commanding power, and virtue be set as on a throne. This could not otherwise be brought about, but by means of the deceitful feeling of liberty, which therefore is a greater honour to virtue, a higher recommendation of it, than if our conceptions were, in every particular, correspondent to the truth of things.

A second objection which may be urged against our system, is, that it seems to represent the Deity, as acting deceitfully by his creatures. He has given them certain ideas of contingency in events, and of liberty in their own actions, by which he has, in a manner, forced them to act upon a false hypothesis; as if he were unable, to carry on the government of this world, did his creatures conceive things, according to the real truth. This objection is, in a great measure, obviated, by what we observed in the introduction to this essay, concerning our sensible ideas. It is universally allowed by modern philosophers, that the perceptions of our external senses, are not always agreeable to strict truth, but so contrived, as rather to answer the purposes of use. Now, if it be called a deceit in our senses, not to give us just representations of the material world, the Deity must be the author of this deceit, as much as he is, of that which prevails in our moral ideas. But no just objection can lie against the conduct of the Deity, in either case. Our senses, both internal and external, are given us for different ends and purposes; some to discover truth, others to make us happy and virtuous. The senses which are appropriated to the discovery of truth, unerringly answer their end. So do the senses, which are appropriated to virtue and happiness. And, in this view, it is no material objection, that the same sense does not answer both ends. As to the other part of the objection, that it must imply imperfection in the Deity, if he cannot establish virtue but upon a delusive foundation; we may be satisfied how fallacious this reasoning is, by reflecting upon the numberless appearances, of moral evil and disorder in this world. From these appearances, much more strongly, were there any force in this reasoning, might we infer imperfection in the Deity; seeing the state of this world, in many particulars, does not answer the notions we are apt to form, of supreme power conducted by perfect wisdom and goodness. But, in truth, there is nothing in our doctrine, which can justly argue imperfection in the Deity. For it is abundantly plain, first, that it is a more perfect state of things, and more worthy of the Deity, to have all events going on with unbroken order, in a fixed train of causes and effects; than to have every thing desultory and contingent. And, if such a being as man, was to be placed in this world, to act his present part; it was necessary, that he should have a notion of contingency in events, and of liberty in his own actions. The objection therefore, on the whole, amounts to no more, than that the Deity cannot work contradictions. For, if it was fit and wise, that man should think and act, as a free agent, it was impossible this could be otherwise accomplished, than by endowing him with a sense of liberty: and if it was also fit and wise, that universal necessity should be the real plan of the universe, this sense of liberty could be no other than a deceitful one.

Another objection may perhaps be raised against us in this form. If it was necessary for man to be constituted, with such an artificial feeling, why was he endowed with so much knowledge, as to unravel the mystery? What purpose does it serve, to let in just so much light, as to discover the disguised appearance of the moral world, when it was intended, that his conduct should be adjusted to this disguised appearance? To this, I answer, first, that the discovery, when made, cannot possibly be of any bad consequence; and next, that a good consequence, of very great importance, results from it. No bad consequence, I say, ensues from the discovery, that liberty and contingency are deceitful feelings; for the case is confessedly parallel in the natural world, where no harm has ensued. After we have discovered, by philosophy, that several of the appearances of nature, are only useful illusions, that secondary qualities exist not in matter, and that our sensible ideas, in various instances, do not correspond to philosophic truth; after these discoveries are made, do they, in the least, affect even the philosopher himself in ordinary action? Does not he, in common with the rest of mankind, proceed, as it is fit he should, upon the common system of appearances and natural feelings? As little, in the present case, do our speculations about liberty and necessity, counteract the plan of nature. Upon the system of liberty we do, and must act: and no discoveries, made concerning the illusive nature of that feeling, are capable of disappointing, in any degree, the intention of the Deity. [...]

iii) From: *Essays on the Principles of Morality and Natural Religion*, 3rd ed. (1779), part 1, essay 3, pp. 110–111

The sum of what is discovered concerning the impressions we have of contingency in events, and liberty in actions, is this. Comparing together the moral and the material world, every thing is as much the result of established laws in the one as in the other. There is nothing in the whole universe that can properly be called contingent, that may be, or may not be; nothing loose and fluctuating in any part of nature: but every motion in the material, and every action in the moral world, are directed by immutable laws; so that, whilst these laws remain in force, not the smallest link of the universal chain of causes and effects can be broken, nor any one thing be otherwise than it is.[16]

4. Causation

From: *Essays on the Principles of Morality and Natural Religion*, 3rd ed. (1779), part 2, essay 5, pp. 296–304

The author of the treatise of human nature[17] has employed a world of reasoning, in searching for the foundation of our idea of power, and of necessary connection. And, after all his anxious researches, he can make no more of it, but, 'That the idea of necessary connection, *alias power* or *energy*, arises from a number of instances, of one thing always following another, which connects them in the imagination; whereby we can readily foretell the existence of the one from the appearance of the other.' And he pronounces, 'That this connection can never be suggested from any one of these

---

[16] [Footnote by Kames] As to an objection of making God the author of sin, which may seem to arise from our system, it is rather popular than philosophical. Sin, or moral turpitude, lies in the evil intention of him who commits it. It consists in some wrong or depraved affection supposed to be in the sinner. Now the intention of the Deity is unerringly good. The end purposed by him is order and general happiness; and there is the greatest reason to believe, that all events are so directed by him, as to work towards this end. In the present system of things, some moral disorders are indeed included. No doubt it is a considerable difficulty, how evil comes to be in the world, seeing God is perfectly good. But this difficulty is not peculiar to our doctrine; but recurs upon us at last with equal force, whatever hypothesis we embrace. For moral evil cannot exist, without being, at least, permitted by the Deity. And with regard to a first cause, *permitting* is the same thing with *causing*; since against his will nothing can possibly happen. All the schemes that have been contrived for answering this objection, are but the tortoise introduced to support the elephant. They put the difficulty a step further off, but never remove it.

[17] [David Hume. *The Treatise of Human Nature* appeared in 1739 and 1740.]

instances, surveyed in all possible lights and positions.'[18] Thus, he places the essence of power or necessary connection upon that propensity which custom produces to pass from an object to the idea of its usual attendant. And from these premises, he draws a conclusion of a very extraordinary nature, and which he himself acknowledges to be not a little paradoxical. His words are: 'Upon the whole, necessity is something that exists in the mind, not in objects; nor is it possible for us even to form the most distant idea of it, considered as a quality in bodies. The efficacy or energy in causes, is neither placed in the causes themselves, nor in the Deity, nor in the concurrence of these two principles; but belongs entirely to the soul, which considers the union of two or more objects in all past instances. It is here that the real power of causes is placed, along with their connection and necessity.'[19]

He may well admit this doctrine to be a violent paradox; because it wages war with the common sense of mankind. [...]

To what a cruel situation does a man reduce himself, when he is led unhappily to adopt a system inconsistent with common sense. Even his own conviction of a gross absurdity, is not sufficient to convert him. Upon such reasoners demonstration itself makes no impression; yet nothing is more clear, than that the very sight of a body in motion suggests to the mind the idea of power.

And to show, that our author's account of this matter comes far short of truth, it will be plain, from one or two instances, that though a constant connection of two objects, may by custom produce a similar connection in the imagination; yet that a constant connection, whether in the imagination or betwixt the objects themselves, does by no means come up to our idea of power. Far from it. In a garrison, the soldiers constantly turn out at a certain beat of the drum. The

---

[18] [Kames refers to David Hume, *An Enquiry concerning Human Understanding*, Section 7, part II, especially para. 59. Kames paraphrases here, it is not a direct quote.]

[19] [This is a direct quote from David Hume's *A Treatise of Human Nature*, book 1, part 3, section 14. Kames leaves out two sentences of the original between the first and the second sentence quoted.]

gates of the town are opened and shut regularly, as the clock points at a certain hour. These connected facts are observed by a child, are associated in his mind, and the association becomes habitual during a long life. The man however, if not a changeling,[20] never imagines the beat of the drum to be the cause of the motion of the soldiers; nor the pointing of the clock to a certain hour, to be the cause of the opening or shutting of the gates. He perceives the cause of these operations to be very different; and is not led into any mistake by the above-mentioned circumstances, however closely connected. Let us put another instance, still more apposite. Such is the human constitution, that we act necessarily upon motives. The prospect of victuals makes a hungry man accelerate his pace: respect to an ancient family moves him to take a wife: an object of distress prompts him to lay out his money, or venture his person. Yet no man dreams a motive to be the cause of action; though here is not only a constant, but a necessary connection.[21]

The reader will take notice, that this author founds the idea of power upon instances of one thing always following another, which connects them in the imagination. According to that account, our idea of power includes two objects, one going before, another following. But what is to be said with respect to a single object, as where we see a man walking? Here there is no connection of one thing following another. It ought therefore to be admitted, that the idea of power is independent of that connection; otherwise, when a man is seen walking, it must be maintained that we have no idea of his having a power to walk. We have a conviction of power from every action, even of the simplest kind. Every man is conscious of having himself a power to act; and he readily transfers the idea to other beings, animate and inanimate. [...]

---

[20] [Here: someone with an abnormality or mental defect. Kames stresses in this way his harsh criticism of Hume's supposedly 'absurd' concept of causation.]

[21] [Footnote by Kames] A thought or idea, it is obvious, cannot be the cause of action, cannot, of itself, produce motion. It is the mind itself that is the agent. Its power indeed is so regulated as that it cannot be exerted but by means of certain motives present to it.

We cannot discover power in any object, otherwise than by seeing it exert its power [...]. Therefore, we can never discover any object to be a cause, otherwise than from the effect produced. But with regard to things caused or produced, the case is different. For we know an object to be an effect, when the cause is not seen. No one is at a loss to say, that a table or a chair is an effect produced: a child will ask who made it? We know from the light of nature every event, every new object, to be an effect or production, and consequently to have a cause. Hence the maxim, 'That nothing can fall out, nothing begin to exist, without a cause'; in other words, 'That every thing which begins to exist, must have a cause.' This maxim cannot be the result of experience, for it is applied to unknown objects and singular events as readily as to the most familiar. [...]

Further, the sense of any object as an effect leads us to infer a cause proportioned to it. If the object be an effect properly adapted to some end, we infer an intelligent designing cause. If the effect be some good end brought about by proper means, we infer a designing and benevolent cause. Nor is it in our power, by any sort of constraint, to vary these inferences. It may be in our power to conceive, but it is not in our power to believe, that a fine painting, a pathetic poem, or a beautiful piece of architecture, can ever be the effect of chance, or of blind fatality. It may be possible, for ought we know to the contrary, that a blind and undesigning cause may be productive of excellent effects. But we have intuitive conviction, that every object which appears beautiful as adapted to an end or purpose, is the effect of a designing cause; and that every object which appears beautiful as fitted to a good end or purpose, is the effect of a designing and benevolent cause. We are so constituted, that we cannot entertain a doubt of this, if we would. And as far as we gather from experience, we are not deceived.

5. Application of Moral Philosophy in the Law: Contract, Tort and Crime

i) From: *Sketches of the History of Man*, 3rd ed. (1788), book 3, sketch 2, sections 2, 3, 5 and 6, 'Principles and Progress of Morality', pp. 11–72

The qualities of right and wrong in voluntary actions, are secondary, like beauty and ugliness and the other secondary qualities mentioned. Like them, they are objects of intuitive perception, and depend not in any degree on reason. No argument is requisite to prove, that to rescue an innocent babe from the jaws of a wolf, to feed the hungry, to clothe the naked, are right actions: they are perceived to be so intuitively. As little is an argument requisite to prove, that murder, deceit, perjury, are wrong actions: they are perceived to be so intuitively. The Deity has bestowed on man, different faculties for different purposes. Truth and falsehood are investigated by the reasoning faculty. Beauty and ugliness are objects of a sense, known by the name of *taste*. Right and wrong are objects of a sense termed the *moral sense* or *conscience*. And supposing these qualities to be hid from our perception, in vain would we try to discover them by any argument or process of reasoning: the attempt would be absurd; no less so than an attempt to discover by reasoning colour, or taste, or smell.

Right and wrong, as mentioned above, are qualities of voluntary actions, and of no other kind. An instinctive action may be agreeable, may be disagreeable; but it cannot properly be denominated either right or wrong. An involuntary act is hurtful to the agent, and disagreeable to the spectator; but it is neither right nor wrong. These qualities also depend in no degree on the event. Thus, if to save my friend from drowning I plunge into a river, the action is right, though I happen to come too late. And if I aim a stroke at a man behind his back, the action is wrong, though I happen not to touch him.

The qualities of right and of agreeable, are inseparable; and so are the qualities of wrong and of disagreeable. A right action is agreeable, not only in the direct perception, but equally so in every subsequent recollection. And in both circumstances equally, a wrong action is disagreeable.

Right actions are distinguished by the moral sense into two kinds, what *ought* to be done, and what *may* be done, or left undone. Wrong actions admit not that distinction: they are all prohibited to be done. To say that an action ought to be done, means that we are tied or obliged to perform; and to say that an action ought not to be done, means that we are restrained from doing it. Though the necessity implied in the being tied or obliged, is not physical, but only what is commonly termed *moral*; yet we conceive ourselves deprived of liberty or freedom, and necessarily bound to act or to forbear acting, in opposition to every other motive. The necessity here described is termed *duty*. The moral necessity we are under to forbear harming the innocent, is a proper example: the moral sense declares the restraint to be our duty, which no motive whatever will excuse us for transgressing.

The duty of performing or forbearing any action, implies a *right* in some person to exact performance of that duty; and accordingly, a duty or obligation necessarily infers a corresponding right. My promise to pay £100 to John, confers a right on him to demand performance. The man who commits an injury, violates the *right* of the person injured; which entitles that person to demand reparation of the wrong.

Duty is twofold; duty to others, and duty to ourselves. With respect to the former, the doing what we ought to do, is termed *just*: the doing what we ought not to do, and the omitting what we ought to do, are termed *unjust*. With respect to ourselves, the doing what we ought to do, is termed *proper*: the doing what we ought not to do, and the omitting what we ought to do, are termed *improper*. Thus, *right*, signifying a quality of certain actions, is a genus; of which *just* and *proper* are species: *wrong*, signifying a quality of other actions, is a genus; of which *unjust* and *improper* are species.

Right actions left to our free will, to be done or left undone, come next in order. They are, like the former, right when done; but they differ, in not being wrong when left undone. To remit a just debt for the sake of a growing family, to yield a subject in controversy rather than go to law with a neighbour, generously to return good for ill, are examples of this species. They are universally approved as right actions:

Three: Moral Philosophy and Legal Philosophy   163

but as no person has a right or title to oblige us to perform such actions, the leaving them undone is not a wrong: no person is injured by the forbearance. Actions that come under this class, shall be termed *arbitrary* or *discretionary*, for want of a more proper designation.

So much for right actions, and their divisions. Wrong actions are of two kinds, *criminal* and *culpable*. What are done intentionally to produce mischief, are *criminal*: rash or unguarded actions that produce mischief without intention, are *culpable*. The former are restrained by punishment, [...] the latter by reparation [...].

The divisions of voluntary actions are not yet exhausted. Some there are that, properly speaking, cannot be denominated either right or wrong. Actions done merely for amusement or pastime, without intention to produce good or ill, are of that kind; leaping, for example, running, jumping over a stick, throwing a stone to make circles in the water. Such actions are neither approved nor disapproved: they may be termed *indifferent*. [...]

That there is in mankind a uniformity of opinion with respect to right and wrong, is a matter of fact of which the only infallible evidence is observation and experience: and to that evidence I appeal; entering only a caveat, that, for the reason above given, the inquiry be confined to enlightened nations. In the meantime, I take liberty to suggest an argument from analogy, that if there be great uniformity among the different tribes of men in seeing and hearing, in pleasure and pain, in judging of truth and error, the same uniformity ought to be expected with respect to right and wrong. Whatever minute differences there may be to distinguish one person from another, yet in the general principles that constitute our nature, internal and external, there is wonderful uniformity.

This uniformity of sentiment, which may be termed *the common sense of mankind with respect to right and wrong*, is essential to social beings. Did the moral sentiments of men differ as much as their faces, they would be unfit for society:

discord and controversy would be endless, and *major vis*[22] would be the only rule of right and wrong.

But such uniformity of sentiment, though general, is not altogether universal: men there are, as above mentioned, who differ from the common sense of mankind with respect to various points of morality. What ought to be the conduct of such men? Ought they to regulate their conduct by that standard, or by their private conviction? There will be occasion afterward to observe, that we judge of others as we believe they judge of themselves; and that private conviction is the standard for rewards and punishments. But with respect to every controversy about property and pecuniary interest, and, in general, about every civil right and obligation, the common sense of mankind is to every individual the standard, and not private conviction or conscience; for proof of which take what follows.

We have an innate sense of a common nature, not only in our own species, but in every species of animals. And that our perception holds true in fact, is verified by experience; for there appears a remarkable uniformity in creatures of the same kind, and a deformity, no less remarkable, in creatures of different kinds. It is accordingly a subject of wonder, to find an individual deviating from the common nature of the species, whether in its internal or external structure: a child born with aversion to its mother's milk, is a wonder, no less than if born without a mouth, or with more than one.

Secondly, this sense dictates, that the common nature of man in particular, is invariable as well as universal; that it will be the same hereafter as it is at present, and as it was in time past; the same among all nations, and in all corners of the earth: nor are we deceived; because, allowing for slight differences occasioned by culture and other accidental circumstances, the fact corresponds to our perception.

Thirdly, we perceive that this common nature is *right* and *perfect*, and that it *ought* to be a model or standard for every

---

[22] [Irresistible violence or calamity; here probably understood in a wider sense than in law only where '*vis major*' denotes 'act of God', 'force majeure', that is, an unavoidable overpowering event (storm, natural disaster) which relieves from liability.]

human being. Any remarkable deviation from it in the structure of an individual, appears imperfect or irregular; and raises a painful emotion: a monstrous birth, exciting curiosity in a philosopher, fails not at the same time to excite aversion in every spectator.

This sense of perfection in the common nature of man, comprehends every branch of his nature, and particularly the common sense of right and wrong; which accordingly is perceived by all to be perfect, having authority over every individual as the ultimate and unerring standard of morals, even in contradiction to private conviction. Thus, a law in our nature binds us to regulate our conduct by that standard: and its authority is universally acknowledged; as nothing is more ordinary in every dispute about *meum* et *tuum*,[23] than an appeal to common sense as the ultimate and unerring standard.

At the same time, as that standard, through infirmity or prejudice, is not conspicuous to every individual; many are misled into erroneous opinions, by mistaking a false standard for that of nature. And hence a distinction between a right and a wrong sense in morals; a distinction which every one understands, but which, unless for the conviction of a moral standard, would have no meaning.

The final cause of this branch of our nature is conspicuous. Were there no standard of right and wrong for determining endless controversies about matters of interest, the strong would have recourse to force, the weak to cunning, and society would dissolve. Courts of law could afford no remedy; for without a standard of morals, their decisions would be arbitrary, and of no authority. Happy it is for men to be provided with such a standard: it is necessary in society that our actions be uniform with respect to right and wrong; and in order to uniformity of action, it is necessary that our perceptions of right and wrong be also uniform: to produce such uniformity, a standard of morals is indispensable. Nature has provided us with that standard, which is daily applied by courts of law with success.

---

[23] ['Mine and yours' — this alludes to property rights.]

In reviewing what is said, it must afford great satisfaction, to find morality established upon the solid foundations of intuitive perception; which is a single mental act complete in itself, having no dependence on any antecedent proposition. The most accurate reasoning affords not equal conviction; for every sort of reasoning [...] requires not only self-evident truths or axioms to found upon, but employs over and above various propositions to bring out its conclusions. By intuitive perception solely, without reasoning, we acquire knowledge of right and wrong; of what we may do, of what we ought to do, and of what we ought to abstain from: and considering that we have thus greater certainty of moral laws than of any proposition discoverable by reasoning, man may well be deemed a favourite of heaven, when he is so admirably qualified for doing his duty. The moral sense or conscience is the voice of God within us; constantly admonishing us of our duty, and requiring from us no exercise of our faculties but attention merely. [...]

It follows from the standard of right and wrong, that an action is right or wrong, independent of what the agent may think. Thus, when a man, excited by friendship or pity, rescues a heretic from the flames, the action is right, even though he think it wrong, from a conviction that heretics ought to be burnt. But we apply a different standard to the agent: a man is approved and held to be innocent in doing what he himself thinks right: he is disapproved and held to be guilty in doing what he himself thinks wrong. Thus, to assassinate an atheist for the sake of religion, is a wrong action; and yet the enthusiast who commits that wrong, may be innocent: and one is guilty, who against conscience eats meat in Lent, though the action is not wrong. In short, an action is perceived to be right or wrong, independent of the actor's own opinion: but he is approved or disapproved, held to be innocent or guilty, according to his own opinion. [...]

We are now prepared for investigating the laws that result from the foregoing principles. The several duties we owe to others shall be first discussed, taking them in order according to the extent of their influence. [...] Of our duties to others, one there is so extensive, as to have for its object all the innocent part of mankind. It is the duty that prohibits us to hurt others: than which no law is more clearly dictated by the moral sense; nor is the transgression of any other law more deeply stamped with the character of wrong. A man may be hurt externally in his goods, in his person, in his relations, and in his reputation. Hence the laws, do not steal; defraud not others; do not kill nor wound; be not guilty of defamation. A man may be hurt internally, by an action that occasions to him distress of mind, or by being impressed with false notions of men and things. Therefore conscience dictates, that we ought not to treat men disrespectfully; that we ought not causelessly to alienate their affections from others; and, in general, that we ought to forbear whatever may tend to break their peace of mind, or tend to unqualify them for being good men and good citizens.

The duties mentioned are duties of restraint. Our active duties regard particular persons; such as our relations, our friends, our benefactors, our masters, our servants. It is our duty to honour and obey our parents; and to establish our children in the world, with all advantages internal and external: we ought to be faithful to our friends, grateful to our benefactors, submissive to our masters, kind to our servants; and to aid and comfort every one of these persons when in distress. To be obliged to do good to others beyond these bounds, must depend on positive engagement; for [...] universal benevolence is not a duty. [...]

One great advantage of society, is the co-operation of many to accomplish some useful work, where a single hand would be insufficient. Arts, manufactures, and commerce, require many hands: but as hands cannot be secured without a previous engagement, the performance of promises and covenants is, upon that account, a capital duty in society. In their original occupations of hunting and fishing, men living scattered and dispersed, have seldom opportunity to aid and benefit each other; and in that situation, covenants, being of little use, are little regarded: but husbandry, requiring the co-operation of many hands, draws men together for mutual assistance; and then covenants make a figure: arts and commerce make them more and more necessary; and in a polished society great regard is paid to them.

But contracts and promises are not confined to commercial dealings: they serve also to make benevolence a duty; and are even extended to connect the living with the dead: a man would die with regret, if he thought his friends were not bound by their promises to fulfil his will after his death: and to quiet the minds of men with respect to futurity, the moral sense makes the performing such promises our duty. Thus, if I promise to my friend to erect a monument for him after his death, conscience binds me, even though no person alive be entitled to demand performance: every one perceives this to be my duty; and I must expect to suffer reproach and blame, if I neglect my engagement.

To fulfil a rational promise or covenant, deliberately made, is a duty no less inflexible than those duties are which arise independent of consent. But as man is fallible, often misled by ignorance, and liable to be deceived, his condition would be deplorable, did the moral sense compel him to fulfil every engagement, however imprudent or irrational. Here the moral sense gives way to human infirmity: it relieves from deceit, from imposition, from ignorance, from error; and binds a man by no engagement but what answers the end fairly intended. [...]

The other branch of duties, those we owe to ourselves, shall be discussed in a few words. *Propriety*, a branch of the moral sense, regulates our conduct with respect to ourselves; as *Justice*, another branch of the moral sense, regulates our conduct with respect to others. Propriety dictates, that we ought to act up to the dignity of our nature, and to the station allotted us by providence: it dictates in particular, that temperance, prudence, modesty, and uniformity of conduct, are self-duties. These duties contribute to private happiness, by preserving health, peace of mind, and self-esteem; which are inestimable blessings: they contribute no less to happiness in society, by gaining the love and esteem of others, and aid and support in time of need. [...]

A crime against any primary virtue is attended with severe and never-failing punishment, more efficacious than any that have been invented to enforce municipal laws: on the other hand, the preserving primary virtues inviolate, is attended with little merit. The secondary virtues are directly opposite: the neglecting them is not attended with any punishment; but the practice of them is attended with illustrious rewards. Offices of undeserved kindness, returns of good for ill, generous toils and sufferings for our friends or for our country, are attended with consciousness of self-merit, and with universal praise and admiration; the highest rewards a generous mind is susceptible of.

From what is said, the following observation will occur: The pain of transgressing justice, fidelity, or any duty, is much greater than the pleasure of performing; but the pain of neglecting a generous action, or any secondary virtue, is as nothing compared with the pleasure of performing. Among the vices opposite to the primary virtues, the most striking moral deformity is found; among the secondary virtues, the most striking moral beauty.

The principle of reparation is made a branch of the moral system for accomplishing two ends: which are, to repress wrongs that are not criminal, and to make up the loss sustained by wrongs of whatever kind. With respect to the former, reparation is a species of punishment: with respect to the latter, it is an act of justice. These ends will be better understood, after ascertaining the nature and foundation of reparation; to which the following division of actions is necessary. First, actions that we are bound to perform. Second, actions that we perform in prosecution of a right or privilege. Third, indifferent actions, described above. Actions of the first kind subject not a man to reparation, whatever damage ensues; because it is his duty to perform them, and it would be inconsistent with morality that a man should be subjected to reparation for doing his duty. The laws of reparation that concern actions of the second kind, are more complex. The social state, highly beneficial by affording opportunity for mutual good offices, is attended with some inconveniences; as where a person happens to be in a situation of necessarily harming others by exercising a right or privilege. If the foresight of harming another restrain me not from exercising my right, the interest of that other is made subservient to mine: on the other hand, if such foresight restrain me from exercising my right, my interest is made subservient to his. What does the moral sense provide in that case? To preserve as far as possible an equality among persons born free and by nature equal in rank, the moral sense dictates a rule, no less beautiful than salutary; which is, that the exercising a right will not justify me for doing direct mischief; but will justify me, though I foresee that mischief may possibly happen. The first branch of the rule resolves into a proposition established above, that no interest of mine, not even life itself, will authorize me to hurt an innocent person. The other branch is supported by expediency: for if the bare possibility of hurting others were sufficient to restrain a man from prosecuting his rights and privileges; men would be too much cramped in action, or rather would be reduced to a state of absolute inactivity. With respect to the first branch, I am criminal, and liable even to punishment: with respect to the other, I am not even culpable, nor bound to repair the mischief that happens to ensue. But this proposition admits a temperament, which is, that if any danger be foreseen, I am in some degree culpable, if I be not at due pains to prevent it. For example, where in pulling down an old house I happen to wound one passing accidentally, without calling aloud to beware.

With respect to indifferent actions, the moral sense dictates, that we ought carefully to avoid doing mischief, either direct or consequential. As we suffer no loss by forbearing actions that are done for pastime merely, such an action is *culpable* or *faulty*, if the consequent mischief was foreseen or might have been foreseen; and the actor of course is subjected to reparation. As this is a cardinal point in the doctrine of reparation, I shall endeavour to explain it more fully. Without intending any harm, a man may foresee, that what he is about to do will probably or possibly produce mischief; and sometimes mischief follows that was neither intended nor foreseen. The action in the former case is not criminal; because ill intention is essential to a crime: but it is culpable or faulty; and if mischief ensue, the actor blames himself, and is blamed by others, for having done what he ought not to have done. Thus, a man who throws a large stone among a crowd of people, is highly culpable; because he must foresee that mischief will probably ensue, though he has no intention to hurt any person. As to the latter case, though mischief was neither intended nor foreseen, yet if it might have been foreseen, the action is rash or incautious, and consequently culpable or faulty in some degree. Thus, if a man, shooting at a mark for recreation near a high road, happen to wound one passing accidentally, without calling aloud to keep out of the way, the action is in some degree culpable, because the mischief might have been foreseen. But though mischief ensue, an action is not culpable or faulty if all reasonable precaution have been adhibited: the moral sense declares the author to be innocent and blameless: the mischief is accidental; and the action may be termed *unlucky*, but comes not under the denomination of either right or wrong. In general, when we act merely for amusement, our nature makes us answerable for the harm that ensues, if it was either foreseen or might with due attention have been foreseen. But our rights and privileges would profit us little, if their exercise were put under the same restraint: it is more wisely ordered, that the probability of mischief, even foreseen, should not restrain a man from prosecuting his concerns, which may often be of consequence to him; provided that he act with due precaution. He proceeds accordingly with a safe conscience, and is not afraid of being blamed either by God or man.

With respect to rash or incautious actions, where the mischief might have been foreseen though not actually foreseen; it is not sufficient to escape blame, that a man, naturally rash or inattentive, acts according to his character: a degree of precaution is required, both by himself and by others, such as is natural to the generality of men: he perceives that he might and *ought* to have acted more cautiously; and his conscience reproaches him for his inattention, no less than if he were naturally more sedate and attentive. Thus the circumspection natural to mankind in general, is applied as a standard to every individual; and if a man fall short of that standard he is culpable and blameable, however unforeseen by him the mischief may have been.

What is said upon culpable actions, is equally applicable to culpable omissions; for by these also mischief may be occasioned, entitling the sufferer to reparation. If we forbear to do our duty with an intention to occasion mischief, the forbearance is criminal. The only question is, how far forbearance without such intention is culpable: supposing the probability of mischief to have been foreseen, though not intended, the omission is highly culpable; and though neither intended nor foreseen, yet the omission is culpable in a lower degree, if there have been less care and attention than are proper in performing the duty required. But supposing all due care, the omission of extreme care and diligence is not culpable.

ii) From: *Historical Law-Tracts*, 4th ed. (1792), Tract I, 'Criminal Law', pp. 1-2

Of the human system no part, external or internal, is more remarkable than a class of principles intended obviously to promote society, by restraining men from harming each other. These principles, as the source of the criminal law, must be attentively examined: and, to form a just notion of them, we need but reflect upon what we feel when we commit a crime, or witness it. Upon certain actions, hurtful to others, the stamp of *impropriety* and *wrong* is impressed in legible characters, visible to all, not excepting even the delinquent. Passing from the action to its author, we perceive that he is *guilty*; and we also perceive that he ought to be punished for his guilt. He himself, having the same perception, is filled with remorse; and, which is extremely remarkable, his remorse is accompanied with an anxious dread that the punishment will be inflicted, unless it be prevented by his making reparation or atonement. Thus in the breast of man a tribunal is erected for conscience: sentence passes against him for every delinquency; and he is delivered over to the hand of providence, to be punished in proportion to his guilt. The wisdom of this contrivance is conspicuous. A sense of wrong is of itself not sufficient to restrain the excesses of passion: but the dread of punishment, which is felt even where there is no visible hand to punish, is a natural restraint so efficacious, that none more perfect can be imagined. This dread, when the result of atrocious or unnatural crimes, is itself a tremendous punishment, far exceeding all that have been invented by men. Happy it is for society, that instances are rare of crimes so gross as to produce this natural dread in its higher degrees: it is, however, still more rare to find any person so singularly virtuous, as never to have been conscious of it in any degree.

6. Legal History and Legal Science

i) From: *Historical Law-Tracts*, 4th ed. (1792), Preface, pp. iii–xiv

The history of man is a delightful subject. A rational inquirer is no less entertained than instructed, in tracing the progress of manners, of laws, of arts, from their birth to their present maturity. Events and subordinate incidents are, in each of these, linked together, and connected in a regular chain of causes and effects. Law in particular becomes then only a rational study, when it is traced historically, from its first rudiments among savages, through successive changes, to its highest improvements in a civilized society. And yet the study is seldom conducted in this manner. Law, like geography, is taught as if it were a collection of facts merely: the memory is employed to the full, rarely the judgment. This method, were it not rendered familiar by custom, would appear strange and unaccountable. With respect to the political constitution of Britain, how imperfect must the knowledge be of that man who confines his reading to the present times? If he follow the same method in studying its laws, have we reason to hope that his knowledge of them will be more perfect?

Such neglect of the history of law is the more strange, that in place of a dry, intricate and crabbed science, law treated historically becomes an entertaining study; entertaining not only to those whose profession it is, but to every person who has any thirst for knowledge. With the generality of men, it is true, the history of law makes not so great a figure, as the history of wars and conquests. Singular events, which by the prevalence of chance or fortune excite wonder, are much relished by the vulgar. But readers of solid judgment find more entertainment, in studying the constitution of a state, its government, its laws, the manners of its people; where reason is exercised in discovering causes and tracing effects through a long train of dependencies.

The history of law, in common with other histories, enjoys the privilege of gratifying curiosity. [...] A statute, or any regulation, if we confine ourselves to the words, is seldom so perspicuous as to prevent errors, perhaps gross ones. In order to form a just notion about any statute, and to discover its spirit and intendment, we ought to be well informed how the law stood at the time, what defect was meant to be supplied, or what improvement made. These particulars require historical knowledge; and therefore, with respect to statute law at least, such knowledge appears indispensible.

In the foregoing respects I have often amused myself with a fanciful resemblance of law to the river Nile. When we enter upon the municipal law of any country in its present state, we resemble a traveller, who, crossing the Delta, loses his way among the numberless branches of the Egyptian river. But when we begin at the source and follow the current of law, it is in that course not less easy than agreeable; and all its relations and dependencies are traced with no greater difficulty, than are the many streams into which that magnificent river is divided before it is lost in the sea. [...]

I have often reflected upon it as an unhappy circumstance, that different parts of the same kingdom should be governed by different laws. This imperfection could not be remedied in the union betwixt England and Scotland; for what nation will tamely surrender its laws more than its liberties? But if the thing was unavoidable, its bad consequences were not altogether so. These might have been prevented, and may yet be prevented, by establishing public professors of both laws, and giving suitable encouragement for carrying on together the study of both. [...] I know none more rational, than a careful and judicious comparison of the laws of different countries. Materials for such comparison are richly furnished by the laws of England and of Scotland. They have such resemblance, as to bear a comparison almost in every branch; and they so far differ, as to illustrate each other by their opposition. Our law will admit of many improvements from that of England; and if the author be not in a mistake, through partiality to his native country, we are rich enough to repay with interest, all we have occasion to borrow. A regular institute of the common law of this island, deducing historically the changes which that law has undergone in the two nations, would be a valuable present to the public; because it would make the study of both laws a task easy and agreeable. Such institute, it is true, is an undertaking too great for any one hand. But if men of knowledge and genius would undertake particular branches, a general system might in time be completed from their works. [...] There are men of genius in this country, and good writers. Were our law treated as a rational science, it would find its way into England, and be studied there for curiosity as well as for profit.

ii) From: *Elucidations Respecting The Common and Statute Law of Scotland* (1777), Preface, pp. vii–xiii

No science affords more opportunity for exerting the reasoning faculty, than that of law; and yet, in no other science is authority so prevalent. What are our law-books but a mass of naked propositions, drawn chiefly from the decisions of our supreme courts, rarely connected either with premises or consequences? Our supreme civil court consists of many members: can uniformity be expected from a fluctuating body, as if all men were actuated with the same spirit? Yet in none of our law-books is there the slightest attempt to separate the chaff from the wheat. [...] Our law-students, trained to rely upon authority, seldom think of questioning what they read: they husband their reasoning faculty, as if it would rust by exercise.

Nor is the exercise of reasoning promoted in any degree by public professors. [...] They load the weak mind with a heap of uninteresting facts, without giving any exercise to the judgment. Is it surprising, that the Roman law, so taught, is held to be a dry and fatiguing study?[24] Is there no cause to fear, that many of our law-students, contracting an aversion to study in general, will sink into idleness, and prove no less useless to themselves than to their country? Are there no traces to be discovered of this malady? Many, many. [...]

In other sciences reason begins to make a figure: why should it be excluded from the science of law? The authority of men of eminence has deservedly great weight; for nature

---

[24] [Footnote by Kames] I should merit censure equal to what I do liberally bestow on others, did I not except Mr John Millar, Professor of Roman law in the college of Glasgow. [The jurist, philosopher and historian John Millar (1735–1801), Regius Professor of Civil Law at the University of Glasgow, was also one of Kames's protégés and for some time tutor of Kames's son.]

gives it weight. But authority ought to be subservient to reason; which the God of nature has bestowed on man, as his chief guide in thinking as well as in acting. The great Descartes commenced his philosophical inquiries with doubting of everything:[25] he endeavoured not to believe even his own existence, without an argument. This indeed was carrying scepticism to an extravagance: it was however erring on the safer side; for excess in scepticism is less unmanly, than excess in deference to authority: reason may profit by the former; it is stifled by the latter. [...]

Were law taught as a rational science, its principles unfolded, and its connection with manners and politics, it would prove an enticing study to every person who has an appetite for knowledge. We might hope to see our lawyers soaring above their predecessors; and giving splendour to their country, by purifying and improving its laws.

As my intention is only to give examples of reasoning, free from the shackles of authority, I pretend not to say what our law actually is, but what it ought to be.

---

[25] [Here Kames alludes especially to the First and the Second Meditation of the *Meditations of First Philosophy* (*Meditations de Prima Philosophia*) by René Descartes (1596–1650).]

Four

Property and Equity

1. Concept of Property

i) From: *Historical Law-Tracts*, 4th ed. (1792), Tract III, 'Property', pp. 88–90

That peculiar relation which connects a person with a subject, signified by the term *Property*, is one of the capital objects of law. The privileges founded on this relation, are at present extensive, but were not always so. Property originally bestowed no other privilege, but merely that of using or enjoying the subject. A privilege essential to commerce was afterwards introduced, *viz.* to alien for a valuable consideration: And at present the relation of property is so intimate, as to comprehend a power or privilege of making donations to take effect after death, as well as during life. Laws have been made, and decisions pronounced in every age, conformable to the different ideas that have been entertained of this relation. These laws and decisions are rendered obscure, and perhaps scarce intelligible, to those who are unacquainted with the history of property […].[1]

Man by his nature is fitted for society; and society is fitted for man by its manifold conveniences. The perfection of

---

[1] [Footnote by Kames] The term *property* has three different significations. It signifies properly, as above, a peculiar relation betwixt a person and certain subjects, as land, houses, moveables, etc.; sometimes it is made to signify the privileges a person has with relation to such a subject; and sometimes it signifies the subject itself, considered with relation to the person. I have not scrupled to use the term, in these different senses, as occasion offered.

human society consists in that just degree of union among individuals, which to each reserves freedom and independency, so far as is consistent with peace and good order. The bonds of society may be too lax; but they may also be overstretched. A society where every man should be bound to dedicate the whole of his industry to the common interest, would be unnatural and uncomfortable, because destructive of liberty and independence. The enjoyment of the goods of fortune in common, would be not less unnatural and uncomfortable: There subsists in man a remarkable propensity for appropriation; and a communion of goods is not necessary to society, though it may be indulged in some singular cases. And happy it is for man to be thus constituted. Industry, in a great measure, depends on property; and a much greater blessing depends on it, which is the gratification of the most dignified natural affections. What place would there be for generosity, benevolence, or charity, if the goods of fortune were common to all? These noble principles, being destitute of objects and exercise, would for ever lie dormant; and what would man be without them? — a very grovelling creature; distinguishable indeed from the brutes, but scarce elevated above them. Gratitude and compassion might have some slight exercise; but how much greater is the figure they make in a state of divided property? The springs and principles of man are adjusted with admirable wisdom to his external circumstances; and these in conjunction form one regular constitution, harmonious in all its parts.

ii) From: *Essays upon Several Subjects in Law* (1732), Essay 4: 'Observations upon Prescription', pp. 100–103

As man is not formed complete in himself, but an indigent being, standing in need of daily supplies from without; the Deity has bestowed the earth upon man, and men upon one another. Towards this end he has wisely implanted in our natures the remarkable affections to *property* and *society*. In this equally provident as in his other dispensations to mankind, not only to furnish us sufficient *means*, but, which is admirable, to compel us in the most agreeable manner to make choice of, and embrace these *means*. Possibly at first, when the world was thinly peopled, and great plenty of common necessaries of life, the affection for *property* was small, and the natural notions of *appropriation* little cultivated. But as mankind grew numerous, and the necessaries of life not so easily come at, labour and industry became of value, and *property* to be considered: for without property, labour and industry was in vain. The foundation of property *a posteriori* is apparent; that it is also founded *a priori* in the nature of man, and consequently in the original laws, is also certain. Evident from this, that nature, which makes nothing in vain, has provided every person with an *affection* to property, wherein is founded that connection betwixt men and things, which we call commonly by the name of property, and whereby nature prompts a man to be differently *affected* to one thing from another; and which affection leads us to bestow care in preserving, labour and industry in improving what we thus consider as our own; and frequently enhances the value of it in our imagination above reality, and above the value we attribute to any other thing that does not stand with us in that relation. This *affection* is as much founded in nature as that we bear to our children, or any affection whatever. And the design is admirable: for it is this affection that is the *primum mobile*[2] of all that industry and diligence men bestow upon their affairs. Providence foresaw appropriation necessary, and it fitted us with *affections* and *faculties* leading to that end. And thus *property* is founded *a priori* in the nature of man, or, which is the same, in the abstract Laws of Nature: the abstract laws, relating to whatever species of beings, being nothing else but the regulations their natures and constitution prompt and direct them to govern themselves by.

Property being thus founded in the Law of Nature, there are *means* of acquiring and losing it, founded also in the same law. *Occupation* is the primary *means* of acquiring property, and *dereliction* of losing it. When we relinquish our property by any express positive act of the will, nobody questions the effect. But it has not been so clearly understood, that the same effect may be wrought negatively by *neglect, desertion*

---

[2] ['First moved', a term from the Middle Ages and the Renaissance denoting the motion of the outermost sphere in the geocentric universe; here: the first mover, the first moving force.]

or *disuse*. Most writers agree that prescription is a creature only of positive statute, not at all founded in the Law of Nature; thus *Grotius, Jur. Bell. L. 2. C. 4.* Thus *Puffendorf, L. 4. C. 12.*[3] But let us examine human nature: let us see what it says as to this dispute; for to it must lie the ultimate appeal. Let us suppose, that by some accident one loses a jewel, he's concerned, and contrives all means for recovery. The affection of property exerts itself; and during that time the thing is as much his as ever. His attempts prove unsuccessful, hope loses ground, he despairs. By degrees his loss wears out of his mind. His affection cools, and at last vanishes. He loses entirely the consciousness of property. Thus the matter lies over for many years. My position is, that the connection betwixt the man and his jewel is by those means as thoroughly dissolved, as if he had relinquished it by the most positive act, or as if it had never been his. The affection and consciousness ceases, upon which his property is founded, and property ceases of consequence. It is upon this foundation that things lost by shipwreck, after such long time as the proprietor has given over all hope of recovery, go to the first finder [...]. It is upon the same, that a hunter, so soon as he gives over hope of his quarry, loses that title of prevention which he had by the pursuit; after which the law gives access to the next finder. If this hold with respect to the person himself who once had the affection of property, much more with respect to his heirs, who never were in possession, and possibly in time may have entirely lost the knowledge of their predecessors' right. Thus then dereliction may be distinguished into two kinds, positive, or active, and negative, or passive. The positive act is properly *abdication*; and hereafter, when we intend to express the negative, we shall indifferently use the terms of *dereliction* or *desertion*.

---

[3] [Kames refers here to the Natural Law jurists Hugo Grotius, *De jure belli ac pacis* (1625) and Samuel Pufendorf, *De jure naturae et gentium* (1672), who were widely influential on law and legal science especially in the seventeenth and eighteenth centuries.]

2. Abolition of Feudalism

i) From: *Historical Law-Tracts*, 4th ed. (1792), Tract III, 'Property', pp. 140-142

Entails[4] [imposed] limitations [...] upon heirs to prevent aliening or contracting debt. This followed from the very nature of the feudal system; for the vassal's right, being a liferent or usufruct only,[5] gave him no power of alienating the property which remained with the superior. It was only unlucky for entails, that during the vigour of the feudal law, constant wars and commotions, a perpetual hurry in attacking or defending, afforded very little time for indulging views of perpetuity. In times only of peace, security, and plenty, do men dream of distant futurity, and of perpetuating their estates in their families. The feudal law lost ground in times of peace. It was a violent and unnatural system, which could not be long supported in contradiction to love of independence and property, the most steady and industrious of all the human appetites. After a regular government was introduced in Britain, which favoured the arts of peace, all men conspired to overthrow the feudal system. The vassal was willing to purchase independence with his money; and the superior, who had no longer occasion for military tenants, disposed of his land to better advantage. In this manner, land, which is the chief object of avarice, came again to be the chief subject of commerce: And that this was early the case in Britain, we have undoubted evidence from the famous statute, *Quia emptores terrarum*[6]

---

[4] [An entail, in Scots law also 'tailzie' (pronounce: 'tailie'), is an estate held under a settlement which confined the inheritance to a special line of succession, for example the eldest son, so as to avoid the division of the family estate because it prevented the heirs from disposing of the family property.]

[5] [A liferent is the right to use and enjoy someone else's property and income from it during one's lifetime. *Usufruct* is the Roman law/ civilian term for the right to use and enjoy someone else's property (but not necessarily for life, although Scots law often uses this term synonymously with liferent).]

[6] [The statute *Quia Emptores (terrarum)* ('Forasmuch as purchasers of lands') was passed in England in 1290 under Edward I. The statute *Quia Emptoris* which is technically still the ultimate legal basis for

[...]. By this time the strict principles of the feudal law had vanished, and scarce any thing was left but the form only. Land, now restored to commerce, was mostly in the hands of purchasers who had paid a valuable consideration; and consequently, instead of being beneficiary as formerly, it had now become patrimonial.[7] The property being thus transferred from the superior to the vassal, the vassal's power of alienation was a necessary consequence.[8]

ii) From: *Historical Law-Tracts*, 4th ed. (1792), Tract IV, 'Securities upon Land for Payment of Debt', pp. 174–176

When land came universally to be patrimonial, and no longer beneficiary, the forms of feudal law indeed remained, but the substance wore out gradually. [...]

And when time discovered that the feudal forms could be squeezed and moulded into a new shape, so as to correspond in some measure with a patrimonial estate, it is not wonderful[9] that our forefathers acquiesced in the forms that were in use, improper as they were.

But it will be a harder task to justify our forefathers for deserting the established form of a rent-charge, substituting in its place and infeftment of annualrent,[10] than which

---

freehold transfers of land in England and Wales today introduced land transfer by way of substitution of vassals (the seller and old vassal is substituted by a new vassal, the buyer, while before this transfer was effected by subinfeudation, being the creation of a new feudal bond with a new vassal.]

[7] [That means, no longer land granted for use, but being in outright ownership.]
[8] [Kames's explanation is probably acceptable from a sociological and economical viewpoint, but does not correspond accurately to feudal property law.]
[9] [Here to be read as: 'it is no wonder'.]
[10] [Infeftment is technically the feudal entry of a vassal with his superior with a symbolic granting of possession. In an infeftment of an annualrent the creditor obtained feudally a real burden, a kind of restricted property right, similar to a servitude, which entitled the creditor to a certain sum of money from the land each year. This and other baroque forms of security rights in Scots law disappeared finally only in 1970 and were replaced by a modern version of a mortgage.]

nothing in my apprehension can be more absurd. For here a man, who has no other intention but to obtain a real security[11] for his money, is transformed, by a sort of hocus-pocus trick, into a servant or vassal, either of his debtor or of his debtor's superior. And to prevent a mistake, as if this were for the sake of form only, I must observe, that the creditor is even held to be a military vassal, bound to serve his superior in war; if the contrary be not specified in the bond.[12] [...] In a word, it is impossible to conceive any form less consistent with the nature and substance of the deed to which it relates, than an infeftment of annualrent is. The wonder is, how it ever came to be introduced in opposition to the more perfect form of a rent-charge. I can discover no other cause but one, which had an arbitrary sway in law as well as in more trivial matters, and that is the prevalence of fashion. We had long been accustomed to the feudal law, and to consider a feudal tenure as the only complete title to land: No man thought himself secure with a title of any other sort: Jurisdictions and offices must be brought under a feudal tenure; and even creditors, influenced by the authority of fashion, were not satisfied till they got their securities in the same form.

iii) From: *Elucidations Respecting The Common and Statute Law of Scotland* (1777), Article XI, 'Dominium directum et utile',[13] pp. 76–77

The superior's right to the land[14] is, in its nature, unlimited, extending over the whole. The vassal's right, on the contrary,

---

[11] [A restricted/subordinate proprietary security right over the property of another to secure a debt, for example, a pledge (moveable property) or, untechnically, a mortgage (land).]
[12] [Footnote by Kames] Stair, p. 268. [Kames refers here to the Institutional Writer of Scots law, Viscount of Stair (1619–1695), more precisely to his *Institutions of the Law of Scotland*, book II, 5, 4.]
[13] [*Dominium directum*: the superior's ownership right in the land; *dominium utile*: the vassal's ownership right in the land. Medieval jurists romanized the feudal system by devising this concept of divided ownership, but it is alien to classical Roman law where there could not be different qualities of ownership simultaneously.]
[14] [This is the *dominium directum*, being the superior's property right of ownership in the land.]

is in its nature limited, being in effect a burden on the superiority. Accordingly, when the vassal's right is by any means annihilated, the superior's property, like air formerly compressed, expands itself over the whole, and becomes unlimited, precisely as before the vassal's right existed. The vassal's right, on the contrary, being originally limited, would not turn more extensive by extinction of the superior's property, if such a thing could be.

From this definition, the following consequences are derived. First, a resignation *ad remanentiam*,[15] or even a simple renunciation, is sufficient to extinguish the vassal's right,[16] and to render the superiority unlimited as originally; because a simple renunciation is sufficient to extinguish a real burden,[17] though not to convey it. But a renunciation by the superior in favour of the vassal, avails nothing: because property cannot be extinguished like a real burden; nor can one divest himself of his property, otherwise than by conveying it to another.

Second, a discharge to the vassal of the future casualties of superiority,[18] though good against the granter, has no effect against the purchaser of the superiority. The reason is, that these casualties, being inherent in the superiority, cannot be separated from it. They are in reality so many effects of the original property reserved to the superior; feu-duties, for example, liferent-escheat, ward, nonentry.[19]

---

[15] [This is the formal and permanent returning of the feudally held land (fee) to the superior by the vassal.]

[16] [Kames follows here the French Renaissance jurist Jacques Cujas (Cujacius, 1522–1590) who said that the vassal really has a *usufruct* or proprietary right of use which is a burden on the superior's right. This view was not shared by the prevalent opinion of the lawyers of Kames's time. Kames's argumentation aims here at the weakening of the feudal system on a technical-legal ground: if the vassal can simply renounce the vassal's right, that also eliminates the vassal's social position as a vassal.]

[17] [A real burden in this context and in Kames's time was a proprietary security right over land.]

[18] [Casualties were proprietary rights the superior could exercise against the vassal under certain circumstances ('*casus*').]

[19] [These are examples of casualties: e.g. liferent-escheat was the forfeiture or confiscation of a vassal's estate in form of a liferent which

This affords a satisfactory reason, why casualties of superiority are not lost by negative prescription. Being inherent in the property, they must subsist with it. And as property is not lost by negative prescription, neither can these casualties be lost, except as to arrears.

iv) From: *Sketches of the History of Man*, 3rd ed. (1788), Appendix, sketch 1, 'Scotch Entails considered in Moral and Political Views', pp. 447–463

Man is by nature a hoarding animal; and to secure what is acquired by honest industry, the sense of property is made a branch of human nature. During the infancy of nations, when artificial wants are unknown, the hoarding appetite makes no figure. The use of money produced a great alteration in the human heart. Money having at command the goods of fortune, introduced inequality of rank, luxury, and artificial wants without end. No bounds are set to hoarding, where an appetite for artificial wants is indulged: love of money becomes the ruling passion: it is coveted by many, in order to be hoarded; and means are absurdly converted into an end.

The sense of property, weak among savages, ripens gradually till it arrives at maturity in polished nations. In every stage of the progress, some new power is added to property; and now, for centuries, men have enjoyed every power over their own goods, that a rational mind can desire: they have the free disposal during life, and even after death, by naming an heir. These powers are sufficient for accomplishing every rational purpose: they are sufficient for commerce, and they are sufficient for benevolence. But the artificial wants of men are boundless: not content with the full enjoyment of their property during life, nor with the prospect of its being enjoyed by a favourite heir, they are anxiously bent to preserve it to themselves for ever. A man who has amassed a great estate in land, is miserable at the prospect of being obliged to quit his hold: to soothe his

---

returns to his superior; ward was the superior's right to be the vassal's guardian if the vassal was a pupil or minor.]

diseased fancy, he makes a deed securing it for ever to certain heirs; who must without end bear his name, and preserve his estate entire. Death, it is true, must at last separate him from his idol: it is some consolation, however, that his will governs and gives law to every subsequent proprietor. How repugnant to the frail state of man are such swollen conceptions! Upon these, however, are founded entails, which have prevailed in many parts of the world, and unhappily at this day infest Scotland. Did entails produce no other mischief but the gratification of a distempered appetite, they might be endured, though far from deserving approbation: but, like other transgressions of nature and reason, they are productive of much mischief, not only to commerce, but to the very heirs for whose sake alone it is pretended that they are made.

Considering that the law of nature has bestowed on man every power of property that is necessary either for commerce or for benevolence, how blind was it in the English legislature to add a most irrational power, that of making an entail! But men will always be mending; and, when a lawgiver ventures to tamper with the laws of nature, he hazards much mischief. We have a pregnant instance above, of an attempt to mend the laws of God in many absurd regulations for the poor; and that the law authorizing entails is another instance of the same kind, will be evident from what follows.

The mischievous effects of English entails were soon discovered: they occasioned such injustice and oppression, that even the judges ventured to relieve the nation from them by an artificial form, termed *fine* and *recovery*. And yet, though no moderate man would desire more power over his estate than he has by common law, the legislature of Scotland enabled every land-proprietor to fetter his estate for ever; to tyrannize over his heirs; and to reduce their property to a shadow, by prohibiting them to alien, and by prohibiting them to contract debt, were it even to redeem them from death or slavery. Thus, many a man, fonder of his estate than of his wife and children, grudges the use of it to his natural heirs, reducing them to the state of mere liferenters.[20] Behold the consequences. A number of noblemen and gentlemen among us lie in wait for every parcel of land that comes to market. Intent upon aggrandizing their family, or rather their estate, which is the favourite object, they secure every purchase by an entail; and the same course will be followed, till no land be left to be purchased. Thus every entailed estate in Scotland becomes in effect a mortmain,[21] admitting additions without end, but absolutely barring alienation; and if the legislature interpose not, the period is not distant, when all the land in Scotland will be locked up by entails, and withdrawn from commerce. [...]

I begin with effects of a private or domestic nature. To the possessor, an entail is a constant source of discontent, by subverting that liberty and independence, which all men covet with respect to their goods as well as their persons. What can be more vexatious to a proprietor of a great land-estate, than to be barred from the most laudable acts, suitable provisions, for example, to a wife or children? Not to mention numberless acts of benevolence, that endear individuals to each other, and sweeten society. A great proportion of the land in Scotland is in such a state that, by laying out a thousand pounds or so, an intelligent proprietor may add a hundred pounds yearly to his rent-roll. But an entail effectually bars that improvement: it affords the proprietor no credit; and supposing him to have the command of money independent of the estate, he will be ill-fated if he have not means to employ it more profitably for his own interest. An entail, at the same time, is no better than a trap for an improvident possessor: to avoid altogether the contracting debt, is impracticable; and if a young man be guided more by pleasure than by prudence, which commonly is the case of young men, a vigilant and rapacious substitute,

---

[20] [The person who possesses, but does not own, an estate because of a liferent (right to use and enjoy the property of another for life).]

[21] [An estate of the 'dead hand', that is property which becomes permanently prevented from being transferred. Property given in mortmain or granted in mortification were donations to churches or monasteries.]

taking advantage of a forfeiting clause, turns him out of possession, and delivers him over to want and misery. [...]

But an entail is productive of consequences still more dismal, even with respect to heirs. A young man upon whom the family-estate is entailed without any power reserved to the father, is not commonly obsequious to advice, nor patiently submissive to the fatigues of education: he abandons himself to pleasure, and indulges his passions without control. In one word, there is no situation more subversive of morals, than that of a young man, bred up from infancy in the certainty of inheriting an opulent fortune.

The condition of the other children, daughters especially, is commonly deplorable. The proprietor of a large entailed estate leaves at his death children who have acquired a taste for sumptuous living. The sons drop off one by one, and a number of daughters remain, with a scanty provision, or perhaps with none at all. A collateral male heir[22] succeeds, who, after a painful search, is discovered in some remote corner, qualified to procure bread by the spade or the plough, but entirely unqualified for behaving as master of an opulent fortune. By such a metamorphosis, the poor man makes a ludicrous figure; while the daughters, reduced to indigence, are in a situation much more lamentable than are the brats of beggars. [...]

Few tenants in tail can command money for improvements, however profitable. Such discouragement to agriculture, hurtful to proprietors of entailed estates, is still more so to the public. It is now an established maxim, that a state is powerful in proportion to the product of its land: a nation that feeds its neighbours, can starve them. The quantity of land that is locked up in Scotland by entails, has damped the growing spirit of agriculture. There is not produced sufficiency of corn at home for our own consumption: and our condition will become worse and worse by new entails, till agriculture and industry be annihilated. Were the great entailed estates in Scotland split into small properties of fifty or a hundred pounds yearly rent, we should soon be

---

[22] [A male heir who is not in a direct line of descent.]

enabled, not only to supply our own markets, but to spare for our neighbours.

In the next place, our entails are no less subversive of commerce than of agriculture. There are numberless land estates in Scotland of one, two, or three hundred pounds yearly rent. Such an estate cannot afford bare necessaries to the proprietor, if he pretend to live like a gentleman. But he has an excellent resource: let him apply to any branch of trade, his estate will afford him credit for what money he wants. The profit he makes, pays the interest of the money borrowed, with a surplus; and this surplus, added to the rent of his estate, enables him to live comfortably. A number of land-proprietors in such circumstances, would advance commerce to a great height. But alas! There are not many who have that resource: such is the itch in Scotland for entailing, as even to descend lower than one hundred pounds yearly. Can one behold with patience, the countenance that is given to selfish wrong-headed people, acting in direct opposition to the prosperity of their country? Commerce is no less hurt in another respect: when our land is withdrawn from commerce by entails, every prosperous trader will desert a country where he can find no land to purchase; for to raise a family, by acquiring an estate in land, is the ultimate aim of every merchant, and of every man who accumulates money.

Consider [...] the influence that great and small estates have on manners. Gentlemen of a moderate fortune, connected with their superiors and inferiors, improve society, by spreading kindly affection through the whole members of the state. In such only resides the genuine spirit of liberty, abhorrent equally of servility to superiors, and of tyranny to inferiors. The nature of the British government creates a mutual dependence of the great and small on each other. The great have favours to bestow: the small have many more, by their privilege of electing parliament-men; which obliges men of high rank to affect popularity, however little feeling they may have for the good of their fellow creatures. This connection produces good manners at least, between different ranks, and perhaps some degree of cordiality. Accumulation of land into great estates, produces opposite manners: when all the land in Scotland is swallowed up by a number of grandees, and few gentlemen of the middle rank are left; even the appearance of popularity will vanish, leaving pride and insolence on the one hand, and abject servility on the other. In a word, the distribution of land into many shares, accords charmingly with the free spirit of the British constitution; but nothing is more repugnant to that spirit, than overgrown estates in land.

[...] Arts and sciences can never flourish in a country, where all the land is engrossed by a few. Science will never be cultivated by the dispirited tenant, who can scarce procure bread; and still less, if possible, by the insolent landlord, who is too self-sufficient for instruction. There will be no encouragement for arts: great and opulent proprietors, fostering ambitious views, will cling to the seat of government, which is far removed from Scotland; and if vanity make them sometimes display their grandeur at their country-seats, they will be too delicate for any articles of luxury but what are foreign. The arts and sciences being thus banished, Scotland will be deserted by every man of spirit who can find bread elsewhere.

[...] Such overgrown estates will produce an irregular and dangerous influence with respect to the House of Commons. The parliament-boroughs will be subdued by weight of money; and, with respect to county-elections, it is a chance if there be left in a county as many qualified landholders as to afford a free choice. In such circumstances, will our constitution be in no danger from the ambitious views of men elevated above others by their vast possessions? Is it unlikely, that such men, taking advantage of public discord, will become a united body of ambitious oppressors, overawing their sovereign as well as their fellow-subjects? Such was the miserable condition of Britain, while the feudal oligarchy subsisted: such at present is the miserable condition of Poland: and such will be the miserable condition of Scotland, if the legislature do not stretch out a saving hand.
[...]

3. Equity

From: *Principles of Equity*, 3rd ed. (1778), 'Introduction', pp. 1–40

Equity, scarce known to our forefathers, makes at present a great figure. It has, like a plant, been tending to maturity, slowly indeed, but constantly; and at what distance of time it shall arrive at perfection, is perhaps not easy to foretell. Courts of equity have already acquired such an extent of jurisdiction, as to obscure in a great measure courts of law.[23] A revolution so signal, will move every curious enquirer to attempt, or to wish at least, a discovery of the cause. But vain will be the attempt, till first a clear idea be formed of the difference between a court of law and a court of equity. The former we know follows precise rules: but does the latter act by conscience solely without any rule? This would be unsafe while men are the judges, liable no less to partiality than to error: nor could a court without rules ever have attained that height of favour, and extent of jurisdiction, which courts of equity enjoy. But if a court of equity be governed by rules, why are not these brought to light in a system? One would imagine, that such a system should not be useful only, but necessary; and yet writers, far from aiming at a system, have not even defined with any accuracy what equity is, nor what are its limits and extent. One operation of equity, universally acknowledged, is, to remedy imperfections in the common law, which sometimes is defective, and sometimes exceeds just bounds; and as equity is constantly opposed to common law, a just idea of the latter may probably lead to the former. In order to ascertain what is meant by common law, a historical deduction is necessary; which I the more cheerfully undertake, because the subject seems not to be put in a clear light by any writer.

After states were formed and government established, courts of law were invented to compel individuals to do their duty. This innovation, as commonly happens, was at first

---

[23] [This refers to the distinction in English law between the courts who have jurisdiction in matters of equity (providing discretionary remedies where the strict rules of the common law do not provide a right) and courts with jurisdiction as regards the common law. See also below in the main text.]

confined within narrow bounds. To these courts power was given to enforce duties essential to the existence of society; such as that of forbearing to do harm or mischief. Power was also given to enforce duties derived from covenants and promises, such of them at least as tend more peculiarly to the well-being of society: which was an improvement so great, as to leave no thought of proceeding farther; for to extend the authority of a court to natural duties of every sort, would, in a new experiment, have been reckoned too bold. Thus, among the Romans, many pactions were left upon conscience, without receiving any aid from courts of law: buying and selling only, with a few other covenants essential to commercial dealing, were regarded.[24] Our courts of law in Britain were originally confined within still narrower bounds: no covenant whatever was by our forefathers countenanced with an action: a contract of buying and selling was not; and as buying and selling is of all covenants the most useful in ordinary life, we are not at liberty to suppose that any other was more privileged.

But when the great advantages of a court of law were experienced, its jurisdiction was gradually extended, with universal approbation: it was extended, with very few exceptions, to every covenant and every promise: it was extended also to other matters, till it embraced every obvious duty arising in ordinary dealings between man and man. But it was extended no farther; experience having discovered limits, beyond which it was deemed hazardous to stretch this jurisdiction. Causes of an extraordinary nature, requiring some singular remedy, could not be safely trusted with the ordinary courts, because no rules were established to direct their proceedings in such matters; and upon that account, such causes were appropriated to the king and council, being the paramount court.[25] Of this nature were actions for proving the tenor or contents of a lost writ; extraordinary

---

[24] [This is a reference to the Roman law principle that informal agreements based on consent only were not enforceable, except, however, the sale (*emptio venditio*), hire (*locatio conductio*), partnership (*societas*), and agency (*mandatum*).]

[25] [Footnote by Kames] We find the same regulation among the Jews [...] Exodus, xviii, 25, 26.

removings against tenants possessing by lease; the causes of pupils, orphans, and foreigners; complaints against judges and officers of law, and the more atrocious crimes, termed, *Pleas of the crown*. Such extraordinary causes, multiplying greatly by complex and intricate connections among individuals, became a burden too great for the king and council. In order therefore to relieve this court, extraordinary causes of a civil nature, were in England devolved upon the court of chancery; a measure the more necessary, that the king, occupied with the momentous affairs of government, and with foreign as well as domestic transactions, had not leisure for private causes. In Scotland, more remote, and therefore less interested in foreign affairs, there was not the same necessity for this innovation: our kings, however, addicted to action more than to contemplation, neglected in a great measure their privilege of being judges, and suffered causes peculiar to the king and council to be gradually assumed by other sovereign courts. The establishment of the court of chancery in England, made it necessary to give a name to the more ordinary branch of law that is the province of the common or ordinary courts: it is termed, *the Common Law*: and in opposition to it, the extraordinary branch devolved on the court of chancery is termed *Equity*; the name being derived from the nature of the jurisdiction, directed less by precise rules, than *secundum aequum et bonum*,[26] or according to what the judge in conscience thinks right.[27] Thus equity, in its proper sense, comprehends every matter of law that by the common law is left without remedy; and supposing the boundaries of the common law to be ascertained, there can no longer remain any difficulty about the powers of a court of equity. But as these boundaries are not ascertained by any natural rule, the jurisdiction of common law must depend in a great measure upon accident and arbitrary practice; and accordingly the boundaries of common law and equity, vary in different countries, and at different times in the same country. We have seen, that the common law of Britain was

---

[26] ['According to what is just/equitable and good.']
[27] [Here Kames's footnote refers to Francis Bacon's *De Augmentis Scientiarum* lib. 8. cap. 3, aphor. 32.]

originally not so extensive as at present; and instances will be mentioned afterward, which evince, that the common law is in Scotland farther extended than in England. Its limits are perhaps not accurately ascertained in any country; which is to be regretted, because of the uncertainty that must follow in the practice of law. It is lucky, however, that the disease is not incurable: a good understanding between the judges of the different courts, with just notions of law, may, in time, ascertain these limits with sufficient accuracy.

Among a plain people, strangers to refinement and subtleties, lawsuits may be frequent, but never are intricate. Regulations to restrain individuals from doing mischief, and to enforce performance of covenants, composed originally the bulk of the common law; and these two branches, among our rude ancestors, seemed to comprehend every subject of law. The more refined duties of morality were, in that early period, little felt, and less regarded. But law, in this simple form, cannot long continue stationary: for in the social state under regular discipline, law ripens gradually with the human faculties; and by ripeness of discernment and delicacy of sentiment, many duties, formerly neglected, are found to be binding in conscience. Such duties can no longer be neglected by courts of justice; and as they made no part of the common law, they come naturally under the jurisdiction of a court of equity.

The chief objects of benevolence considered as a duty, are our relations, our benefactors, our masters, our servants, etc.; and these duties, or the most obvious of them, come under the cognizance of common law. But there are other connections, which, though more transitory, produce a sense of duty. Two persons shut up in the same prison, though no way connected but by contiguity and resemblance of condition, are sensible, however, that to aid and comfort each other is a duty incumbent on them. Two persons, shipwrecked upon the same desert island, are sensible of the like mutual duty. And there is even some sense of this kind, among a number of persons in the same ship, or under the same military command.

Thus mutual duties among individuals multiply by variety of connections; and in the progress of society, benevolence becomes a matter of conscience in a thousand instances, formerly disregarded. The duties that arise from connections so slender, are taken under the jurisdiction of a court of equity; which at first exercises its jurisdiction with great reserve, interposing in remarkable cases only, where the duty is palpable. But, gathering courage from success, it ventures to enforce this duty in more delicate circumstances: one case throws light upon another: men, by the reasoning of the judges, become gradually more acute in discerning their duty: the judges become more and more acute in distinguishing cases; and this branch of law is imperceptibly moulded into a system.[28] In rude ages, acts of benevolence, however peculiar the connection may be, are but faintly perceived to be our duty: such perceptions become gradually more firm and clear by custom and reflection; and when men are so far enlightened, it is the duty as well as honour of judges to interpose.

This branch of equitable jurisdiction shall be illustrated by various examples. When goods by labour, and perhaps with danger, are recovered from the sea after a shipwreck, every one perceives it to be the duty of the proprietor to pay salvage. A man ventures his life to save a house from fire, and is successful; no mortal can doubt that he is entitled to a recompense from the proprietor, who is benefited. If a man's affairs by his absence be in disorder, ought not the friend who undertakes the management to be kept *indemnis*,[29] though the subject upon which his money was usefully bestowed may have afterward perished casually? Who can doubt of the following proposition, that I am in the wrong to demand money from my debtor, while I withhold the sum I owe him, which perhaps may be his only resource for doing me justice? Such a proceeding must, in the common sense of mankind, appear partial and oppressive. By the common law, however, no remedy is afforded in this case, nor in the others mentioned. But equity affords a remedy, by enforcing what in such circumstances every man perceives to be his duty. I shall add but one example more: In a violent storm,

---

[28] [Here Kames's footnote refers to Francis Bacon's *De Augmentis Scientiarum* lib. 8. cap. 3, aphor. 38.]

[29] ['Free from loss or damage, indemnified.']

the heaviest goods are thrown overboard, in order to disburden the ship: the proprietors of the goods preserved by this means from the sea, must be sensible that it is their duty to repair the loss; for the man who has thus abandoned his goods for the common safety, ought to be in no worse condition than themselves. Equity dictates this to be their duty; and if they be refractory, a court of equity will interpose in behalf of the sufferer.

It appears now clearly, that a court of equity commences at the limits of the common law, and enforces benevolence where the law of nature makes it our duty. And thus a court of equity, accompanying the law of nature in its gradual refinements, enforces every natural duty that is not provided for at common law.

The duties hitherto mentioned arise from connections independent altogether of consent. Covenants and promises also, are the source of various duties. The most obvious of these duties, being commonly declared in words, belong to common law. But every incident that can possibly occur in fulfilling a covenant, is seldom foreseen; and yet a court of common law, in giving judgment upon covenants, considers nothing but declared will, neglecting incidents that would have been provided for, had they been foreseen. Further, the inductive motive for making a covenant, and its ultimate purpose and intendment, are circumstances disregarded at common law: these, however, are capital circumstances; and justice, where they are neglected, cannot be fulfilled. Hence the powers of a court of equity with respect to engagements. It supplies imperfections in common law, by taking under consideration every material circumstance, in order that justice may be distributed in the most perfect manner. It supplies a defect in words, where will is evidently more extensive: it rejects words that unwarily go beyond will; and it gives aid to will where it happens to be obscurely or imperfectly expressed. By taking such liberty, a covenant is made effectual according to the aim and purpose of the contractors; and without such liberty, seldom it happens that justice can be accurately distributed.

In handling this branch of the subject, it is not easy to suppress a thought that comes across the mind. The jurisdiction of a court of common law, with respect to covenants, appears to me odd and unaccountable. To find the jurisdiction of this court limited, as above mentioned, to certain duties of the law of nature, without comprehending the whole, is not singular nor anomalous. But with respect to the circumstances that occur in the same cause, it cannot fail to appear singular, that a court should be confined to a few of these circumstances, neglecting others no less material in point of justice. This reflection will be set in a clear light by a single example. Every one knows, that an English double bond[30] was a contrivance to evade the old law of this island, which prohibited the taking interest for money: the professed purpose of this bond is, to provide for interest and costs, beyond which the penal part ought not to be exacted; and yet a court of common law, confined strictly to the words or declared will, is necessitated knowingly to commit injustice. The moment the term of payment is past, when there cannot be either costs or interest, this court, instead of pronouncing sentence for what is really due, namely, the sum borrowed, must follow the words of the bond, and give judgment for the double. This defect in the constitution of a court, is too remarkable to have been overlooked: a remedy accordingly is provided, though far from being of the most perfect kind; and that is, a privilege to apply to the court of equity for redress. Far better had it been, either to withdraw covenants altogether from the common law, or to empower the judges of that law to determine according to the principles of justice. I need scarce observe, that the present reflection regards England only, where equity and common law are appropriated to different courts. In Scotland, and other countries where both belong to the same court, the inconvenience mentioned cannot happen. — But to return to the gradual extension of equity, which is our present theme:

A court of equity, by long and various practice, finding its own strength and utility, and impelled by the principle of justice, boldly undertakes a matter still more arduous; and that is, to correct or mitigate the rigour, and what even in a proper sense may be termed the *injustice* of common law. It

---

[30] [This is a conditional bond undertaken by a debtor obliging him to pay a penalty if he does not fulfil the condition set out in the bond.]

is not in human foresight to establish any general rule, that, however salutary in the main, may not be oppressive and unjust in its application to some singular cases. Every work of man must partake of the imperfection of its author; sometimes falling short of its purpose, and sometimes going beyond it. If with respect to the former a court of equity be useful, it may be pronounced necessary with respect to the latter; for, in society, it is certainly a greater object to prevent legal oppression, which alarms every individual, than to supply legal defects, scarce regarded but by those immediately concerned. The illustrious Bacon, upon this subject, expresses himself with great propriety: 'Habeant curiae praetoriae potestatem tam subveniendi contra rigorem legis, quam supplendi defectum legis. Si enim porregi debet remedium ei quem lex praeteriit, multo magis ei quem vulneravit.'[31]

All the variety of matter hitherto mentioned, is regulated by the principle of justice solely. It may, at first view, be thought, that this takes in the whole compass of law, and that there is no remaining field to be occupied by a court of equity. But, upon more narrow inspection, we find a number of law-cases into which justice enters not, but only utility. Expediency requires that these be brought under the cognizance of a court; and the court of equity, gaining daily more weight and authority, takes naturally such matters under its jurisdiction. I shall give a few examples. A lavish man submits to have his son made his interdictor:[32] this agreement is not unjust; but, tending to the corruption of manners, by reversing the order of nature, it is reprobated by a court of equity, as *contra bonos* mores.[33] This court goes farther: it discountenances many things in themselves indifferent, merely because of their bad tendency. A *pactum*

---

[31] [Kames's footnote refers to Francis Bacon's *De Augmentis Scientiarum* lib. 8. cap. 3, aphor. 35: 'Let the praetorian courts have power as well as to abate the rigour of the law as to make good its defects; for if a remedy be afforded to a person neglected by the law, much more to him who is hurt by the law.']

[32] [In Scots law someone could put himself under voluntary restraint (voluntary interdiction), exercised by the interdictor.]

[33] ['Against good morals.']

de quota litis[34] is in itself innocent, and may be beneficial to the client as well as to the advocate: but to remove the temptation that advocates are under to take advantage of their clients instead of serving them faithfully, this court declares against such pactions. A court of equity goes still farther, by consulting the public interest with relation to matters not otherwise bad but by occasioning unnecessary trouble and vexation to individuals. Hence the origin of regulations tending to abridge lawsuits.

A mischief that affects the whole community, figures in the imagination, and naturally moves judges to stretch out a preventive hand. But what shall we say of a mischief that affects one person only, or but a few? An estate, for example, real or personal, is left entirely without management, by the infancy of the proprietor, or by his absence in a remote country: he has no friends, or they are unwilling to interpose. It is natural, in this case, to apply for public authority. A court of common law, confined within certain precise limits, can give no aid; and therefore it is necessary that a court of equity should undertake cases of this kind; and the preventive remedy is easy, by naming an administrator, or, as termed in the Roman law, *curator bonorum*.[35] A similar example is, where a court of equity gives authority to sell the land of one under age, where the sale is necessary for payment of debt: to decline interposing, would be ruinous to the proprietor; for without authority of the court no man will venture to purchase from one under age. Here the motive is humanity to a single individual: but it would be an imperfection in law, to abandon an innocent person to ruin, when the remedy is so easy. In the cases governed by the motive of public utility, a court of equity interposes as court properly, giving or denying action, in order to answer the end purposed: but in the cases now mentioned, and in others similar, there is seldom occasion for a process; the court acts by magisterial powers.

---

[34] ['Agreement about a share in the amount litigated over': in such an arrangement the client agrees to pay his advocate for the advocate's services a portion of the sum he wants to recover in litigation.]

[35] [Administrator of an estate.]

The powers above set forth assumed by our courts of equity, are, in effect, the same that were assumed by the Roman Praetor,[36] from necessity, without any express authority. 'Jus praetorium est quod praetores introduxerunt, adjuvandi vel supplendi vel corrigendi juris Civilis gratia, propter utilitatem publicam.'[37]

Having given a historical view of a court of equity, from its origin to its present extent of power and jurisdiction, I proceed to some other matters, which must be premised before entering into particulars. The first I shall insist on is of the greatest moment, namely, whether a court of equity be, or ought to be, governed by any general rules? To determine every particular case according to what is just, equal, and salutary, taking in all circumstances, is undoubtedly the idea of a court of equity in its perfection; and had we angels for judges, such would be their method of proceeding, without regarding any rules: but men are liable to prejudice and error, and for that reason cannot safely be trusted with unlimited powers. Hence the necessity of establishing rules, to preserve uniformity of judgment in matters of equity as well as of common law: the necessity is perhaps greater in the former, because of the variety and intricacy of equitable circumstances. Thus, though a particular case may require the interposition of equity to correct a wrong or supply a defect; yet the judge ought not to interpose, unless he can found his decree upon some rule that is equally applicable to all cases of the kind. If he be under no limitation, his decrees will appear arbitrary, though substantially just: and, which is worse, will often be arbitrary, and substantially unjust; for such too frequently are human proceedings when subjected to no control. General rules, it is true, must often produce decrees that are materially unjust; for no rule can be equally just in its application to a whole class of cases that are far

---

[36] [In the Roman Republic the Praetor was an appointed magistrate (and deputy of the consuls) who was in charge of the formulary system of the Roman civil procedure, among other things.]

[37] [Footnote by Kames] l. 7. §1. De justitia et jure [*On justice and law*, Digest 1.1.7.1: 'Praetorian law is that which in the public interest the Praetors have introduced in aid or supplementation or correction of the *jus civile* (civil law)' (ed. Watson).]

from being the same in every circumstance: but this inconvenience must be tolerated, to avoid a greater, that of making judges arbitrary. A court of equity is a happy invention to remedy the errors of common law: but this remedy must stop somewhere; for courts cannot be established without end, to be checks one upon another. And hence it is, that, in the nature of things, there cannot be any other check upon a court of equity but general rules. [...]

In perusing the following treatise, it will be discovered, that the connections regarded by a court of equity seldom arise from personal circumstances, such as birth, resemblance of condition, or even blood, but generally from subjects that in common language are denominated *goods*. Why should a court, actuated by the spirit of refined justice, overlook more substantial ties, to apply itself solely to the grosser connections of interest? Does any connection founded on property make an impression equally strong with that of friendship, or blood-relation, or of country? Does not the law of nature form duties on the latter, more binding in conscience than on the former? Yet the more conscientious duties are left commonly to shift for themselves, while the duties founded on interest are supported and enforced by courts of equity. This, at first view, looks like a prevailing attachment to riches; but it is not so in reality. The duties arising from the connection last mentioned, are commonly ascertained and circumscribed, so as to be susceptible of a general rule to govern all cases of the kind. This is seldom the case of the other natural duties; which, for that reason, must be left upon conscience, without receiving any aid from a court of equity. There are, for example, not many duties more firmly rooted in our nature than that of charity; and, upon that account, a court of equity will naturally be tempted to interpose in its behalf. But the extent of this duty depends on such a variety of circumstances, that the wisest heads would in vain labour to bring it under general rules: to trust, therefore, with any court, a power to direct the charity of individuals, is a remedy which to society would be more hurtful than the disease; for instead of enforcing this duty in any regular manner, it would open a wide door to legal tyranny and oppression. Viewing the matter in this light, it will appear, that such duties are left upon conscience, not from neglect or insensibility, but from the difficulty of a proper remedy. And when such duties can be brought under a general rule, I except not even gratitude, though in the main little susceptible of circumscription, we shall see afterward, that a court of equity declines not to interpose.

In this work will be found several instances where equity and utility are in opposition; and when that happens, the question is, which of them ought to prevail? Equity, when it regards the interest of a few individuals only, ought to yield to utility when it regards the whole society. It is for that very reason, that a court of equity is bound to form its decrees upon general rules; for this measure regards the whole society by preventing arbitrary proceedings.

It is commonly observed, that equitable rights are less steady and permanent than those of common law: the reason will appear from what follows. A right is permanent or fluctuating according to the circumstances upon which it is founded. The circumstances that found a right at common law, being always few and weighty, are not variable: a bond of borrowed money, for example, must subsist till it be paid. A claim in equity, on the contrary, seldom arises without a multiplicity of circumstances; which make it less permanent, for if but a single circumstance be withdrawn, the claim is gone. Suppose, for example, that an infeftment of annualrent[38] is assigned to a creditor for his security: the creditor ought to draw his payment out of the interest before touching the capital; which is an equitable rule, because it is favourable to the assignor or cedent,[39] without hurting the assignee. But if the cedent have another creditor who arrests the interest,[40] the equitable rule now mentioned ceases, and gives place to another; which is, that the assignee ought to

---

[38] [In an infeftment of an annualrent under Scots law the creditor obtained a real burden, through a feudal obligation, being a kind of restricted property right which entitled the creditor to a certain sum of money from the land each year.]

[39] [The old, original, creditor or assignor (transferor) in the assignment of a debt.]

[40] [In Scots law this is the attaching or execution of a debtor's property in the hands of a third party in case of the debtor's non-payment of the debt.]

draw his payment out of the capital, leaving the interest to be drawn by the arrester. Let us next suppose, that the cedent has a third creditor, who after the arrestment adjudges[41] the capital. This new circumstance varies again the rule of equity: for though the cedent's interest weighs not in opposition to that of his creditor arresting, the adjudging creditor and the arrester are upon a level as to every equitable consideration; and upon that account, the assignee, who is the preferable creditor,[42] ought to deal impartially between them: if he be not willing to take payment out of both subjects proportionally, but only out of the capital, or out of the interest; he ought to make an assignment to the postponed creditor,[43] in order to redress the inequality; and if he refuse to do this act of justice, a court of equity will interpose.

This example shows the mutability of equitable claims: but there is a cause which makes them appear still more mutable than they are in reality. The strongest notion is entertained of the stability of a right of property; because no man can be deprived of his property but by his own deed. A claim of debt is understood to be stable, but in an inferior degree; because payment puts an end to it without the will of the creditor. But equitable rights, which commonly accrue to a man without any deed of his, are often lost in the same manner: and they will naturally be deemed transitory and fluctuating, when they depend so little on the will of the persons who are possessed of them.

In England, where the courts of equity and common law are different, the boundary between equity and common law, where the legislature does not interpose, will remain always the same. But in Scotland, and other countries where equity and common law are united in one court, the boundary varies imperceptibly; for what originally is a rule in equity, loses its character when it is fully established in practice; and then it is considered as common law: thus the *actio*

---

[41] [In Scots law this is the process of attachment (execution) to heritable property (immoveable property, land) to discharge an unpaid debt by the debtor.]

[42] [That creditor who has the priority when it comes to payment.]

[43] [That creditor who ranks after the preferable creditor in relation to payment.]

negotiorum gestorum,[44] retention, salvage,[45] etc. are in Scotland scarce now considered as depending on principles of equity. But by cultivation of society, and practice of law, nicer and nicer cases in equity being daily unfolded, our notions of equity are preserved alive; and the additions made to that fund, supply what is withdrawn from it by common law.

What is now said suggests a question, no less intricate than important, whether common law and equity ought to be committed to the same or to different courts. [...] Of all questions those which concern the constitution of a state, and its political interest, being the most involved in circumstances, are the most difficult to be brought under precise rules. I pretend not to deliver any opinion; and feeling in myself a bias against the great authority mentioned,[46] I scarce venture to form an opinion. It may be not improper, however, to hazard a few observations, preparatory to a more accurate discussion. [...] In the science of jurisprudence, it is undoubtedly of great importance, that the boundary between equity and common law be clearly ascertained; without which we shall in vain hope for just decisions: a judge, who is uncertain whether the case belong to equity or to common law, cannot have a clear conception what judgment ought to be pronounced. But a court that judges of both, being relieved from determining this preliminary point, will be apt to lose sight altogether of the distinction between common law and equity. On the other hand, may it not be urged, that the dividing among different courts things intimately connected, bears hard upon every one who has a claim to prosecute? Before bringing his action, he must at his peril determine an extreme nice point, whether the case be governed by common law, or by equity. An error in that

---

[44] [An action for the expenses of the voluntary intervener on behalf and exclusively for the benefit of somebody else, but without the latter's prior consent or knowledge.]

[45] [A right to reward and reimbursement of expenses by a volunteer for the recovery of someone else's ship or cargo after loss or danger at sea.]

[46] [Kames has quoted just before Francis Bacon, *De Augmentis Scientiarum* lib. 8. cap. 3, aphor. 45. Bacon advocates the separation of the courts of common law from the courts of equity.]

preliminary point, though not fatal to the cause because a remedy is provided, is, however, productive of much trouble and expense. Nor is the most profound knowledge of law sufficient always to prevent this evil; because it cannot always be foreseen what plea will be put in for the defendant, whether a plea in equity or at common law. In the next place, to us in Scotland it appears extremely uncouth, that a court should be so constituted, as to be tied down in many instances to pronounce an iniquitous judgment. This not only happens frequently with respect to covenants, as above mentioned, but will always happen where a claim founded on common law, which must be brought before a court of common law, is opposed by an equitable defence, which cannot be regarded by such a court. Weighing these different arguments with some attention, the preponderance seems to be on the side of a united jurisdiction; so far at least, as that the court before which a claim is regularly brought, should be empowered to judge of every defence that is laid against it. The sole inconvenience of a united jurisdiction, that it tends to blend common law with equity, may admit a remedy, by an institute distinguishing with accuracy their boundaries: but the inconvenience of a divided jurisdiction admits not any effectual remedy.[47] These hints are suggested with the greatest diffidence; for I cannot be ignorant of the bias that naturally is produced by custom and established practice.

In Scotland, as well as in other civilized countries the King's council was originally the only court that had power to remedy defects or redress injustice in common law. To this extraordinary power the court of session naturally succeeded, as being the supreme court in civil matters; for in every well-regulated society, some one court must be trusted with this power, and no court more properly than that which is supreme. It may at first sight appear surprising, that no mention is made of this extraordinary power in any of the

---

[47] [This refers to the fact that the English courts of equity (the Court of Chancery and the equitable side of the Court of Exchequer) and the English common law courts (the King's Bench, Common Pleas, and the Court of the Exchequer) were separate courts (until 1875).]

regulations concerning the court of session. It is probable, that this power was not intended, nor early thought of; and that it was introduced by necessity. [...] Now, for more than a century, the court of session has acted as a court of equity, as well as of common law. Nor is it rare to find powers unfolded in practice, that were not in view at the institution of a court. When the Roman Praetor was created to be the supreme judge, in place of the consuls, there is no appearance that any instructions were given him concerning matters of equity. And even as to the English court of chancery, though originally a court of equity, there was not at first the least notion entertained of that extensive jurisdiction to which in later times it has justly arrived.

In Scotland, the union of common law with equity in the supreme court, appears to have had an influence upon inferior courts, and to have regulated their powers with respect to equity. The rule in general is, that inferior courts are confined to common law: and hence it is that an action founded merely upon equity, such as a reduction upon minority and lesion,[48] upon fraud, etc. is not competent before an inferior court. But if against a process founded on common law an equitable defence be stated, it is the practice of inferior courts to judge of such defence. Imitation of the supreme court, which judges both of law and equity, and the inconvenience of removing to another court a process that has perhaps long depended, paved the way to this enlargement of power. Another thing already taken notice of, tends to enlarge the powers of our inferior courts more and more; which is, that many actions, founded originally on equity, have by long practice obtained an establishment so firm as to be reckoned branches of the common law. This is the case of the *actio negotiorum gestorum,* of recompense, and many others, which, for that reason, are now commonly sustained in inferior courts.

Our courts of equity have advanced far in seconding the laws of nature, but have not perfected their course. Every clear and palpable duty is countenanced with an action; but

---

[48] [The setting aside of a deed granted by a minor on the ground that it is to his detriment or damage ('to his lesion').]

many of the more refined duties, as will be seen afterward, are left still without remedy. Until men, thoroughly humanized, be generally agreed about these more refined duties, it is perhaps the more prudent measure for a court of equity to leave them upon conscience. Neither does this court profess to take under its protection every covenant and agreement. Many engagements of various sorts, the fruits of idleness, are too trifling, or too ludicrous, to merit the countenance of law: a court, whether of common law or of equity, cannot preserve its dignity if it descend to such matters. Wagers of all sorts, whether upon horses, cocks, or accidental events, are of this sort. People may amuse themselves, and men of easy fortunes may pass their whole time in that manner, because there is no law against it; but pastime, contrary to its nature, ought not to be converted into a serious matter, by bringing the fruits of it into a court of justice. [...]

Having thus given a general view of my subject, I shall finish with explaining my motive for appearing in print. Practising lawyers, to whom the subject must already be familiar, require no instruction. This treatise is dedicated to the studious in general, such as are fond to improve their minds by every exercise of the rational faculties. Writers upon law are too much confined in their views: their works, calculated for lawyers only, are involved in a cloud of obscure words and terms of art, a language perfectly unknown except to those of the profession. Thus it happens, that the knowledge of law, like the hidden mysteries of some Pagan deity, is confined to its votaries; as if others were in duty bound to blind and implicit submission. But such superstition, whatever unhappy progress it may have made in religion, never can prevail in law: men who have life or fortune at stake, take the liberty to think for themselves; and are no less ready to accuse judges for legal oppression, than others for private violence or wrong. Ignorance of law has in this respect a most unhappy effect: we all regard with partiality our own interest; and it requires knowledge no less than candour, to resist the thought of being treated unjustly when a court pronounces against us. Thus peevishness and discontent arise, and are vented against the judges of the land. This, in a free government, is a dangerous and infectious spirit, to remedy which we cannot be too solicitous. Knowledge of those rational principles upon which law is founded I venture to suggest, as a remedy no less efficacious than palatable. Were such knowledge universally spread, judges who adhere to rational principles, and who, with superior understanding can reconcile law to common sense, would be revered by the whole society. The fame of their integrity, supported by men of parts and reading, would descend to the lowest of the people; a thing devoutly to be wished! Nothing tends more to sweeten the temper, than a conviction of impartiality in judges; by which we hold ourselves secure against every insult or wrong. By that means, peace and concord in society are promoted; and individuals are finely disciplined to submit with the like deference to all other acts of legal authority. Integrity is not the only duty required in a judge: to behave so as to make every one rely upon his integrity, is a duty no less essential. Deeply impressed with these notions, I dedicate my work to every lover of science; having endeavoured to explain the subject in a manner that requires in the reader no particular knowledge of municipal law. In that view I have avoided terms of art; not indeed with a scrupulous nicety, which might look like affectation; but so as that with the help of a law-dictionary, what I say may easily be apprehended.

Order, a beauty in every composition, is essential in a treatise of equity, which comprehends an endless variety of matter. To avoid obscurity and confusion, we must, with the strictest accuracy, bring under one view things intimately connected, and handle separately things unconnected, or but slightly connected. Two great principles, justice and utility, govern the proceedings of a court of equity; and every matter that belongs to that court, is regulated by one or other of these principles. Hence a division of the present work into two books, the first appropriated to justice, the second to utility; in which I have endeavoured to ascertain all the principles of equity that occurred to me. I thought it would benefit the reader to have these principles illustrated in a third book, where certain important subjects are selected to be regularly discussed from beginning to end; such as furnish the most frequent opportunities for applying the principles ascertained in the former part of the work.

Five

Enlightened Improvement of Society

1. Progress of Commerce

From: *Sketches of the History of Man*, 3rd ed. (1788), book 1, sketch 3, pp. 127–161

The few wants of men in the first stage of society, are supplied by barter in its rudest form. In barter, the rational consideration is, what is wanted by the one, and what can be spared by the other. But savages are not always so clear-sighted: a savage who wants a knife, will give for it any thing that is less useful to him at the time, without considering either the present wants of the person he is dealing with, or his own future wants. An inhabitant of Guiana will for a fish-hook give more at one time, than at another he will give for a hatchet, or for a gun. Kempfer[1] reports, that an inhabitant of Puli Timor, an island adjacent to Malacca, will, for a bit of coarse linen not worth three-halfpence, give provisions worth three or four shillings. But people improve by degrees, attending to what is wanted on the one side, and to what can be spared on the other; and in that lesson, the American savages in our neighbourhood are not a little expert.

---

[1] [Engelbert Kaempfer (1651–1716), natural scientist and physician. The passage Kames refers to and paraphrases comes from Kaempfer, *History of Japan*, vol. 1.]

Barter or permutation, in its original form, proved miserably deficient when men and their wants multiplied. That sort of commerce cannot be carried on at a distance; and, even among neighbours, it does not always happen that the one can spare what the other wants. Barter is somewhat enlarged by covenants: a bushel of wheat is delivered to me, upon my promising an equivalent at a future time. But what if I have nothing that my neighbour may have occasion for? Or what if my promise be not relied on? Thus barter, even with the aid of covenants, proves still defective. The numberless wants of men cannot readily be supplied, without some commodity in general estimation, which will be gladly accepted in exchange for every other. That commodity ought not to be bulky, nor be expensive in keeping, nor be consumable by time. Gold and silver are metals that possess these properties in an eminent degree. They are at the same time perfectly homogeneous in whatever country produced: two masses of pure gold or of pure silver are always equal in value, provided they be of the same weight. These metals are also divisible into small parts, convenient to be given for goods of small value.[2]

Gold and silver, when introduced into commerce, were probably bartered, like other commodities, by bulk merely. Rock-salt in Ethiopia, white as snow, and hard as stone, is to this day bartered in that manner with other goods. It is dug out of the mountain Lafta, formed into plates a foot long, and three inches broad and thick; and a portion is broken off equivalent in value to the thing wanted. But more accuracy came to be introduced into the commerce of gold and silver: instead of being given loosely by bulk, every portion was weighed in scales: and this method of barter is practised in China, in Ethiopia, and in many other countries. Even weight was at length discovered to be an imperfect standard. Ethiopian salt may be proof against adulteration; but weight is no security against mixing gold and silver with base metals. To prevent that fraud, pieces of gold and silver are

---

[2] [Kames cites here from the Digest, book 18, title 1 (Paulus, *On the Edict*), 'De contrahenda emptione' (On the contract of purchase/sale).]

impressed with a public stamp, vouching both the purity and quantity; and such pieces are termed *coin*. This was a notable improvement in commerce; and was probably at first thought complete. It was not foreseen, that these metals wear by much handling in the course of circulation; and consequently, that in time the public stamp is reduced to be a voucher of the purity only, not of the quantity. Hence proceed manifold inconveniences; for which no other remedy occurs, but to restore the former method of weighing, trusting to the stamp for the purity only. This proves an embarrassment in commerce, which is remedied by the use of paper-money. And paper-money is attended with another advantage, that of preventing the loss of much gold and silver by wearing. Formerly in China, gold and silver were coined as among us; but the wearing of coin by handling obliged them to recur to scales; and now weight alone is relied on for determining the quantity. Copper is the only metal that is circulated among them without weighing; and it is with it that small debts are paid, and small purchases made.

When gold or silver in bullion is exchanged with other commodities, such commerce passes under the common name of *barter* or *permutation*: when current coin is exchanged, such commerce is termed *buying* and *selling*; and the money exchanged is termed *the price of the goods*.

As commerce cannot be carried on to any extent without a standard for comparing goods of different kinds, and as every commercial country is possessed of such a standard, it seems difficult to say by what means the standard has been established. It is plainly not founded on nature; for the different kinds of goods have naturally no common measure by which they can be valued: two quarters of wheat can be compared with twenty; but what rule have we for comparing wheat with broad cloth, or either of them with gold, or gold with silver or copper? Several ingenious writers have endeavoured to account for the comparative value of commodities, by reducing them all to the labour employed in raising food; which labour is said to be a standard for measuring the value of all other labour, and consequently of all things produced by labour. 'If, for example, a bushel of wheat and an ounce of silver be produced by the same quantity of labour, will they not be equal in value?' This standard is imperfect in many respects. I observe, first, that to give it a plausible appearance, there is a necessity to maintain, contrary to fact, that all materials on which labour is employed are of equal value. It requires as much labour to make a brass candlestick as one of silver, though far from being of the same value. A bushel of wheat may sometimes equal in value an ounce of silver; but an ounce of gold does not always require more labour than a bushel of wheat; and yet they differ widely in value. The value of labour, it is true, enters into the value of every thing produced by it; but is far from making the whole value. If an ounce of silver were of no greater value than the labour of procuring it, that ounce would go for payment of the labour, and nothing be left to the proprietor of the mine: such a doctrine will not relish with the King of Spain; and as little with the Kings of Golconda and Portugal, proprietors of diamond-mines. Secondly, the standard under review supposes every sort of labour to be of equal value, which however will not be maintained. A useful art in great request may not be generally known: the few who are skilful will justly demand more for their labour than the common rate. An expert husbandman bestows no more labour in raising a hundred bushels of wheat, than his ignorant neighbour in raising fifty: if labour be the only standard, the two crops ought to afford the same price. Was not Raphael entitled to a higher price for one of his fine pictures, than a dunce is for a tavern-sign, supposing the labour to have been equal? Lastly, as this standard is applicable to things only that require labour, what rule is to be followed with respect to natural fruits and other things that require no labour?

Where a pound of one commodity gives the same price with a pound of another, these commodities are said to be of equal value; and therefore, whatever rule can be given for the price of commodities, that rule determines also their comparative values. Montesquieu[3] attempts to account for the price as follows. He begins with supposing, that there is

---

[3] [Footnote by Kames] [Montesquieu, *De l'esprit des lois*], book 22, chapter 7.

but one commodity in commerce, divisible like gold and silver into parts, the parts like those of gold and silver uniform and equally perfect. Upon that supposition, the price, says he, of the whole commodity collected into a mass, will be the whole current gold and silver; and the price of any particular quantity of the former, will be the corresponding quantity of the latter, the tenth or twentieth part of the one corresponding to the tenth or twentieth part of the other. He goes on to apply the same computation to all the variety of goods in commerce; and concludes in general, that as the whole mass of goods in commerce corresponds to the whole mass of gold and silver in commerce as its price, so the price of the tenth or twentieth part of the former will be the tenth or twentieth part of the latter. According to this computation, all different goods must give the same price, or, which is the same, be of equal value, provided their weight or measure be the same. Our author certainly did not intend such an absurdity; and yet I can draw no other inference from his reasoning. In the very next chapter he admits the negroes on the coast of Africa to be an exception from the general rule, who, says he, value commodities according to the use they have for them. But, do not all nations value commodities in the same manner?

Rejecting, then, the foregoing attempts to account for the comparative value of commodities, I take a hint from what was last said to maintain, that it is the demand chiefly which fixes the value of every commodity. Quantity beyond the demand renders even necessaries of no value; of which water is an instance. It may be held accordingly as a general rule, that the value of goods in commerce depends on a demand beyond what their quantity can satisfy; and rises in proportion to the excess of the demand above the quantity. Even water becomes valuable in countries where the demand exceeds the quantity: in arid regions, springs of water are highly valued; and, in old times, were frequently the occasion of broils and bloodshed. Comparing next different commodities with respect to value, that commodity of which the excess of the demand above the quantity is the greater, will be of the greater value. Were utility or intrinsic value only to be considered, a pound of iron would be worth ten pounds of gold; but as the excess of the demand for gold above its quantity is much greater than that of iron, the latter is of less value in the market. A pound of opium, or of Jesuits bark, is, for its salutary effects, more valuable than gold; and yet, for the reason given, a pound of gold will purchase many pounds of these drugs. Thus, in general, the excess of the demand above the quantity is the standard that chiefly fixes the mercantile value of commodities. Interest is the price or premium given for the loan of money; and the rate of interest, like the price of other commodities, is regulated by the demand. Many borrowers and few lenders produce high interest: many lenders and few borrowers produce low interest.

The causes that make a demand seem not so easily ascertained. One thing is evident, that the demand for necessaries in any country, must depend on the number of its inhabitants. This rule holds not so strictly in articles of convenience; because some people are more greedy of conveniences than others. As to articles of taste and luxury, the demand appears so arbitrary as not to be reducible to any rule. A taste for beauty is general, but so different in different persons, as to make the demand extremely variable: the faint representation of any plant in an agate, is valued by some for its rarity; but the demand is far from being universal. Savages are despised for being fond of glass beads; but were such toys equally rare among us, they would be coveted by many: a copper coin of the Emperor Otho is of no intrinsic value, and yet, for its rarity, would draw a great price.

The value of gold and silver in commerce, like that of other commodities, was at first, we may believe, both arbitrary and fluctuating; and, like other commodities, they found in time their value in the market. With respect to value, however, there is a great difference between money and other commodities. Goods that are expensive in keeping, such as cattle, or that are impaired by time, such as corn, will always be first offered in exchange for what is wanted; and when such goods are offered to sale, the vender must be contented with the current price: in making the bargain, the purchaser has the advantage; for he suffers not by reserving his money to a better market. And thus commodities are brought down by money, to the lowest value that can afford any profit. At the same time, gold and silver sooner find their value than other commodities. The value of the latter depends both on the quantity and on the demand; the value of the former depends on the quantity only, the demand being unbounded: and even with respect to quantity, these precious metals are less variable than other commodities.

Gold and silver, being thus sooner fixed in their value than other commodities, become a standard for valuing every other commodity, and consequently for comparative values. A bushel of wheat, for example, being valued at five shillings, a yard of broad cloth at fifteen, their comparative values are as one to three.

A standard of values is essential to commerce; and therefore where gold and silver are unknown, other standards are established in practice. The only standard among the savages of North America is the skin of a beaver. Ten of these are given for a gun, two for a pound of gunpowder, one for four pounds of lead, one for six knives, one for a hatchet, six for a coat of woollen cloth, five for a petticoat, and one for a pound of tobacco. Some nations in Africa employ shells, termed *couries*, for a standard.

As my chief view in this sketch is, to examine how far industry and commerce are affected by the quantity of circulating coin, I premise the following plain propositions. Supposing, first, the quantity of money in circulation, and the quantity of goods in the market, to continue the same, the price will rise and fall with the demand. For when more goods are demanded than the market affords, those who offer the highest price will be preferred: as, on the other hand, when the goods brought to market exceed the demand, the venders have no resource but to entice purchasers by a low price. The price of fish, flesh, butter, and cheese, is much higher than formerly; for these being now the daily food even of the lowest people, the demand for them is greatly increased.

Supposing a fluctuation in the quantity of goods only, the price falls as the quantity increases, and rises as the quantity decreases. The farmer whose quantity of corn is doubled by a favourable season, must sell at half the usual price; because the purchaser, who sees a superfluity, will pay no more for it. The contrary happens upon a scanty crop: those who want corn must starve, or give the market-price, however high.

The manufactures of wool, flax, and metals, are much cheaper than formerly; for though the demand has increased, yet by skill and industry the quantities produced have increased in a greater proportion. More pot-herbs are consumed than formerly: and yet by skilful culture the quantity is so much greater in proportion, as to have lowered the price to less than one half of what it was eighty years ago.

It is easy to combine the quantity and demand, supposing a fluctuation in both. Where the quantity exceeds the usual demand, more people will be tempted to purchase by the low price; and where the demand rises considerably above the quantity, the price will rise in proportion. In mathematical language, these propositions may be thus expressed, that the price is *directly* as the demand, and *inversely* as the quantity.

A variation in the quantity of circulating coin is the most intricate circumstance; because it never happens without making a variation in the demand for goods, and frequently in the quantity. I take the liberty, however, to suppose that there is no variation but in the quantity of circulating coin; for though that cannot happen in reality, yet the result of the supposition will throw light upon what really happens: the subject is involved, and I wish to make it plain. I put a simple case, that the half of our current coin is at once swept away by some extraordinary accident. This at first will embarrass our internal commerce, as the vender will insist for the usual price, which now cannot be afforded. But the error of such demand will soon be discovered; and the price of commodities, after some fluctuation, will settle at the one half of what it was formerly. At the same time, there is here no downfall in the value of commodities, which cannot happen while the quantity and demand continue unvaried. The purchasing for a sixpence what formerly cost a shilling, makes no alteration in the value of the thing purchased; because a sixpence is equal in value to what a shilling was formerly. In a word, when money is scarce, it must bear a high value: it must in particular go far in the purchase of goods; which we express by saying, that goods are cheap. Put next the case, that by some accident our coin is instantly doubled: the result must be, not instantaneous indeed, to double the price of commodities. Upon the former supposition, a sixpence is in effect advanced to be a shilling: upon the present supposition, a shilling has in effect sunk down to a sixpence. And here again it ought to be observed, that though the price is augmented, there is no real alteration in the value of commodities. A bullock that, some years ago, could have been purchased for ten pounds, will at present yield fifteen. The vulgar ignorantly think, that the value of horned cattle has arisen in that proportion. The advanced price may, in some degree, be occasioned by a greater consumption; but it is chiefly occasioned by a greater quantity of money in circulation.

Combining all the circumstances, the result is, that if the quantity of goods and of money continue the same, the price will be in proportion to the demand. If the demand and quantity of goods continue the same, the price will be in proportion to the quantity of money. And if the demand and quantity of money continue the same, the price will fall as the quantity increases, and rise as the quantity diminishes.

These speculative notions will enable us with accuracy to examine, how industry and commerce are affected by variations in the quantity of circulating coin. It is evident, that arts and manufactures cannot be carried on to any extent without coin. Persons totally employed in any art or manufacture require wages daily or weekly, because they must go to market for every necessary of life. The clothier, the tailor, the shoemaker, the gardener, the farmer, must employ servants to prepare their goods for the market; to whom, for that reason, wages ought to be regularly paid. In a word, commerce among an endless number of individuals, who depend on each other even for necessaries, would be inextricable without a quantity of circulating coin. Money may be justly conceived to be the oil, that lubricates all the springs and wheels of a great machine, and preserves it in motion.[4] Supposing us now to be provided with no more of

---

[4] [Footnote by Kames] Money cannot be justly said to be deficient where there is sufficiency to purchase every commodity, and to pay for every kind of labour that is wanted. Any greater quantity is hurtful to commerce, as will be seen afterward. But to be forced to contract debt even when one deals prudently and profitably, and consequently to be subjected to legal execution, is a proof, by no means

that precious oil than is barely sufficient for the easy motion of our industry and manufactures, a diminution of the necessary quantity must retard them: our industry and manufactures must decay; and if we do not confine the expense of living to our present circumstances, which seldom happens, the balance of trade with foreign nations will turn against us, and leave us no resource for making the balance equal but to export our gold and silver. And when we are drained of these metals, farewell to arts and manufactures: we shall be reduced to the condition of savages, which is, that each individual must depend entirely on his own labour for procuring every necessary of life. The consequences of the balance turning for us, are at first directly opposite: but at the long-run come to be the same: they are sweet in the mouth, but bitter in the stomach. An influx of riches by this balance, rouses our activity. Plenty of money elevates our spirits, and inspires an appetite for pleasure: we indulge a taste for show and embellishment, become hospitable, and refine upon the arts of luxury. Plenty of money is a prevailing motive even with the most sedate, to exert themselves in building, in husbandry, in manufactures, and in other solid improvements. Such articles require both hands and materials, the prices of which are raised by the additional demand. The labourer now whose wages are thus raised, is not satisfied with mere necessaries, but insists for conveniences, the price of which also is raised by the new demand. In short, increase of money raises the price of every commodity; partly from the greater quantity of money, and partly from the additional demand for supplying artificial wants. Hitherto a delightful view of prosperous commerce: but behold the remote consequences. High wages at first promote industry, and double the quantity of labour: but the utmost exertion of labour is limited within certain bounds; and a perpetual influx of gold and silver will not for ever be attended with a proportional quantity of work: The price of labour will rise in proportion to the quantity of money; but

---

ambiguous, of scarcity of money, which till of late was remarkably the case in Scotland.

the produce will not rise in the same proportion; and for that reason our manufactures will be dearer than formerly. Hence a dismal scene. The high price at home of our manufactures will exclude us from foreign markets; for if the merchant cannot draw there for his goods what he paid at home, with some profit, he must abandon foreign commerce altogether. And, what is still more dismal, we shall be deprived even of our own markets; for in spite of the utmost vigilance, foreign commodities, cheaper than our own, will be poured in upon us. The last scene is to be deprived of our gold and silver, and reduced to the same miserable state as if the balance had been against us from the beginning.

However certain it may be, that an addition to the quantity of money must raise the price of labour and of manufactures, yet there is a fact that seems to contradict the proposition, which is, that in no other country are labour and manufactures so cheap as in the two peninsulas on the right and left of the Ganges, though in no other country is there such plenty of money. To account for this singular fact, political writers say, that money is there amassed by the nabobs, and withdrawn from circulation. This is not satisfactory: the chief exportation from these peninsulas is their manufactures, the price of which comes first to the merchant and manufacturer; and how can that happen without raising the price of labour? Rice, it is true, is the food of their labouring poor; and an acre of rice yields more food than five acres of wheat: but the cheapness of necessaries, though it has a considerable influence in keeping down the price of labour, cannot keep it constantly down, in opposition to an overflowing current of money. The populousness of these two countries is a circumstance totally overlooked. Every traveller is amazed how such swarms of people can find bread, however fertile the soil may be. Let us examine that circumstance. One thing is evident, that, were the people fully employed, there would not be a demand for the tenth part of their manufactures. Here, then, is a country where hand-labour is a drug for want of employment. The people, at the same time, sober and inclining to industry, are glad to be employed at any rate; and whatever pittance is gained by labour, makes always some addition. Hence it is, that in these peninsulas, superfluity of hands overbalancing both the quantity of money and the demand for their manufactures, serves to keep the price extremely low.

What is now said discovers an exception to the proposition above laid down. It holds undoubtedly in Europe, and in every country where there is work for all the people, that an addition to the circulating coin raises the price of labour and of manufactures: but such addition has no sensible effect in a country where there is a superfluity of hands, who are always disposed to work when they find employment.

From these premises it is evident, that, unless there is a superfluity of hands, manufactures can never flourish in a country abounding with mines of gold and silver. This in effect is the case of Spain: a constant influx of these metals, raising the price of labour and manufactures, has deprived the Spaniards of foreign markets, and also of their own: they are reduced to purchase from strangers even the necessaries of life. What a dismal condition will they be reduced to, when their mines come to be exhausted! The Gold coast in Guinea has its name from the plenty of gold that is found there. As it is washed from the hills with the soil in small quantities, every one is on the watch for it; and the people, like gamesters, despise every other occupation. They are accordingly lazy and poor. The kingdom of Fidah,[5] in the neighbourhood, where there is no gold, is populous: the people are industrious, deal in many branches of manufacture, and are all in easy circumstances.

To illustrate this observation, which is of great importance, I enter more minutely into the condition of Spain. The rough materials of silk, wool, and iron, are produced there more perfect than in any other country; and yet flourishing manufactures of these, would be ruinous to it in its present state. Let us only suppose, that Spain itself could furnish all the commodities that are demanded in its American territories, what would be the consequence? The gold and silver produced by that trade would circulate in Spain: money would become a drug: labour and manufactures would rise to a high price; and every necessary of life, not excepting

---

[5] [Formerly Kingdom of Whydah, 'Slave Coast', today in the state of Benin.]

manufactures of silk, wool, and iron, would be smuggled into Spain, the high price there being sufficient to overbalance every risk: Spain would be left without industry, and without people. Spain was actually in the flourishing state here supposed when America was discovered: the American gold and silver mines enflamed the disease, and consequently was the greatest misfortune that ever befell that once potent kingdom. The exportation of our silver coin to the East Indies, so loudly exclaimed against by shallow politicians, is to us, on the contrary, a most substantial blessing: it keeps up the value of silver, and consequently lessens the value of labour and of goods, which enable us to maintain our place in foreign markets. Were there no drain for our silver, its quantity in our continent would sink its value so much as to render the American mines unprofitable. Notwithstanding the great flow of money to the East Indies, many mines in the West Indies are given up, because they afford not the expense of working; and were the value of silver in Europe brought much lower, the whole silver mines in the West Indies would be abandoned. Thus our East-India commerce, which is thought ruinous by many, because it is a drain to much of our silver, is for that very reason profitable to all. The Spaniards profit by importing it into Europe; and other nations profit, by receiving it for their manufactures.

How ignorantly do people struggle against the necessary chain of causes and effects! If money do not overflow, a commerce in which the imports exceed in value the exports, will soon drain a nation of money, and put an end to its industry. Commercial nations for that reason struggle hard for the balance of trade; and they fondly imagine, that it cannot be too advantageous. If greatly advantageous to them, it must in the same proportion be disadvantageous to those they deal with; which proves equally ruinous to both. They foresee indeed, but without concern, immediate ruin to those they deal with; but they have no inclination to foresee, that ultimately it must prove equally ruinous to themselves. It appears the intention of Providence that all nations should benefit by commerce as by sun-shine; and it is so ordered, that an unequal balance is prejudicial to the gainers as well as to the losers: the latter are immediate sufferers; but no less so, ultimately, are the former. This is one remarkable instance, among many, of providential wisdom in conducting human affairs, independent of the will of man, and frequently against his will. An ambitious nation, placed advantageously for trade, would willingly engross all to themselves, and reduce their neighbours to be hewers of wood and drawers of water. But an invincible bar is opposed to such ambition, making an overgrown commerce the means of its own destruction. The commercial balance held by the hand of Providence, is never permitted to preponderate much to one side; and every nation partakes, or may partake, of all the comforts of life. Engrossing is bad policy: men are prompted, both by interest and duty, to second the plan of Providence; and to preserve, as near as possible, equality in the balance of trade.

Upon these principles, a wise people, having acquired a stock of money sufficient for an extensive commerce, will tremble at a balance too advantageous: they will rest satisfied with an equal balance, which is the golden mean. A hurtful balance may be guarded against by industry and frugality: but by what means is a balance too favourable to be guarded against? With respect to that question, it is not the quantity of gold and silver in a country that raises the price of labour and manufactures, but the quantity in circulation; and may not that quantity be regulated by the state, permitting coinage as far only as is beneficial to its manufactures? Let the registers of foreign mints be carefully watched, in order that our current coin may not exceed that of our industrious neighbours. There will always be a demand for the surplus of our bullion, either to be exported as a commodity, or to be purchased at home for plate; which cannot be too much encouraged, being ready at every crisis to be coined for public service. The senate of Genoa has wisely burdened porcelain with a heavy tax, being a foreign luxury; but it has no less wisely left gold and silver plate free; which we most unwisely have loaded with a duty.

The accumulating money in the public treasury, anciently the practice of every prudent monarch, prevents superfluity. Lies there any good objection against that practice, in a trading nation where gold and silver flow in with impetuosity? A great sum locked up by a frugal King, Henry VII of England for example, lessens the quantity of money in circulation: profusion in a successor, which was the case with Henry VIII, is a spur to industry, similar to the influx of gold and silver from the new world. The canton of Bern, by locking up money in its treasury, possesses the miraculous art of reconciling immense wealth with frugality and cheap labour. A climate not kindly, and a soil not naturally fertile, enured the inhabitants to temperance and to virtue. Patriotism is their ruling passion; they consider themselves as children of the republic; are fond of serving their mother; and hold themselves sufficiently recompensed by the privilege of serving her. The public revenue greatly exceeds the expense of government: they carefully lock up the surplus for purchasing land when a proper opportunity offers; which is a shining proof of their disinterestedness as well as of their wisdom. By that politic measure, much more than by war, the canton of Bern, from a very slender origin, is now far superior to any of the other cantons in extent of territory. But in what other part of the globe are there to be found ministers of state, moderate and disinterested like the citizens of Bern! In the hands of a British ministry, the greatest treasure would vanish in the twinkling of an eye; and do more mischief by augmenting money in circulation above what is salutary, than formerly it did good by confining it within moderate bounds. But against such a measure there lies an objection still more weighty than its being an ineffectual remedy: in the hands of an ambitious prince it would prove dangerous to liberty.

If the foregoing measures be not relished, I can discover no other means for preserving our station in foreign markets, but a bounty on exportation. The sum would be great: but the preserving our industry and manufactures, and the preventing an influx of foreign manufactures, cannot be purchased too dear. At the same time, a bounty on exportation would not be an unsupportable load: on the contrary, superfluity of wealth, procured by a balance constantly favourable, would make the load abundantly easy. A proper bounty would balance the growing price of labour and materials at home, and keep open the foreign market. By neglecting that salutary measure, the Dutch have lost all their manufactures, a neglect that has greatly benefited both England and France. The Dutch indeed act prudently in with-holding that benefit as much as possible from their powerful neighbours: to prevent purchasing from them, they consume the manufactures of India.

The manufactures of Spain, once extensive, have been extirpated by their gold and silver mines. Authors ascribe to the same cause the decline of their agriculture; but erroneously: on the contrary, superfluity of gold and silver is favourable to agriculture, by raising the price of its productions. It raises also, it is true, the price of labour; but that additional expense is far from balancing the profit made by high prices of whatever the ground produces. Too much wealth indeed is apt to make the tenant press into a higher rank: but that is easily prevented by a proper heightening of the rent, so as always to confine the tenant within his own sphere.

As gold and silver are essential to commerce, foreign and domestic, several commercial nations have endeavoured most absurdly to bar the exportation by penal laws; forgetting that gold and silver will never be exported while the balance of trade is on their side, and that they must necessarily be exported when the balance is against them. Neither do they consider, that if a people continue industrious, they cannot be long afflicted with an unfavourable balance; for the value of money, rising in proportion to its scarcity, will lower the price of their manufactures, and promote exportation: the balance will turn in their favour; and money will flow in, till by plenty its value be reduced to a par with that of neighbouring nations.

It is an important question, whether a bank, upon the whole, be friendly to commerce. It is undoubtedly a spur to industry, like a new influx of money: but then, like such influx, it raises the price of labour and of manufactures. Weighing these two facts in a just balance, the result seems to be, that in a country where money is scarce, a bank properly constituted is a great blessing, as it in effect increases the quantity of money, and promotes industry and manufactures; but that in a country which possesses money sufficient for extensive commerce, the only bank that will not injure foreign commerce, is what is erected for supplying the merchant with ready money by discounting bills. At the same time, much caution and circumspection is necessary with respect to banks of both kinds. A bank erected for discounting bills, ought to be confined to bills really granted in the course of commerce; rejecting fictitious bills drawn merely for procuring a loan of money. And with respect to a bank purposely erected for lending money, there is great danger of extending credit too far; not only with respect to the bank itself, but with respect to the nation in general, by raising the price of labour and of manufactures, which is the never failing result of too great plenty of money, whether coin or paper.

The different effects of plenty and scarcity of money, have not escaped that penetrating genius, the sovereign of Prussia.[6] Money is not so plentiful in his dominions as to make it necessary to withdraw a quantity by heaping up treasure. He indeed always retains in his treasury six or seven millions Sterling for answering unforeseen demands: but being sensible that the withdrawing from circulation any larger sum would be prejudicial to commerce, every farthing saved from the necessary expense of government, is laid out upon buildings, upon operas, upon any thing rather than cramp circulation. In that kingdom, a bank established for lending money would promote industry and manufactures.

2. Progress of Flax-Husbandry in Scotland

From: *Progress of Flax-Husbandry in Scotland* (1766), pp. 3–31

As the power of a state consists chiefly in the number and industry of its people, everything must be of importance that contributes to these ends. This observation puts the linen manufacture in a conspicuous light; for it employs many hands, and requires the most painful industry. In Scotland, this manufacture, which, within the memory of man, scarce deserved the name, has of late years made a progress so rapid, as to become our chief manufacture, circulating more money than all our other manufactures in conjunction. Nor is there any symptom of its being stationary: on the contrary, it is every year boldly advancing with wider and wider steps.

---

[6] [Frederic II of Prussia.]

This prospect must be agreeable to every well-hearted Briton; and to gratify the laudable curiosity of such persons, the following brief account of the progress of the manufacture is presented. The board of Trustees was established *anno* 1727; the value of the linen stamped from November 1727 to November 1728, not including what was made for private use, was:

Anno	£.	Anno	£.
[1728]	103,312	1747	262,866
1729	114,383	1748	293,846
1730	131,262	1749	322,045
1731	145,656	1750	361,736
1732	168,322	1751	367,167
1733	182,766	1752	409,047
1734	185,224	1753	445,321
1735	177,466	1754	406,816
1736	168,177	1755	345,349
1737	183,620	1756	367,721
1738	185,026	1757	401,511
1739	198,068	1758	424,141
1740	188,777	1759	451,390
1741	187,658	1760	523,153
1742	191,689	1761	516,354
1743	215,927	1762	474,807
1744	229,364	1763	552,281
1745	224,252	1764	573,243
1746	222,870	1765	579,227

Though the progress of the linen manufacture in general is not the professed purpose of this paper, yet I shall endeavour to account for it, as a proper introduction to a historical narrative of the measures taken by the Trustees for promoting our flax-husbandry.

The union of the two crowns of England and Scotland, was a fatal event for the latter. The great increase of power which our kings thereby acquired, reduced the Scotch nobility to a state of humble dependence. From being petty monarchs, they became slaves to the crown, and had nothing left to support their accustomed dignity, but, under protection of the crown, to enslave their inferiors. The national spirit, bold and brave, subsided by degrees; and a general torpor succeeded, the never-failing effect of slavery. Though restored to liberty and independence, by the union of the two nations, yet mutual jealousy and enmity obstructed long the advantages of our new situation. At length the blessings of liberty and independence became conspicuous, and the invigorated multitudes to exert themselves in laudable undertakings. And hence that spirit for improvement in Scotland, displayed upon husbandry, upon manufactures, upon commerce, and upon literature.

The establishing a board of Trustees for directing this national spirit, upon fisheries, and upon the manufactures of linen and woollen, was a measure wise and political, zealously promoted by a worthy patriot, who was rewarded, by the opportunity he long had of serving his country, as an eminent member of that board. His statue was erected in the senate-house, by those of his own profession, in token of their veneration for him, as a judge above all corruption. From his fellow-citizens in general a statue was not less due, as a token of their gratitude for his patriotism.

But whatever was his zeal for the public good, and whatever zeal he inspired into others, yet the operations of that board were not at first attended with great success. The indolence and ignorance of the low people, and their want of honesty, could not be cured but by perseverance and artful management. But unluckily we were at that time ill provided with political physicians, skilled in the cure: which is always the case in a country where industry is dead, and no person thinks of it. The Trustees were forced for some time to grope in the twilight of knowledge: they frequently mistook their road, and adopted measures that were not always adequate to the ends proposed. But, as the intendment of this paper is neither to make a satire nor encomium upon the Trustees, it shall only be observed in passing, that the ignorance of this nation with respect to manufactures, and with respect to the means of promoting them, may well excuse the few errors committed by the Trustees at the commencement of their management; and that these errors ought not to derogate from their merit, in serving their country without the slightest motive of private interest.

The Trustees, having with great assiduity surmounted endless difficulties and obstructions, were encouraged to redouble their diligence. The people are in a measure of reclaimed from idleness and dishonesty: industry is gaining ground, and is spreading even to distant corners: spinners and weavers, greatly multiplied, are daily acquiring more and more skill: many bleach-fields are perfected, and the colour of our linens is much improved: nor have water-mills been neglected for dressing flax on our own growth; though these, after much expense bestowed, do not now give general satisfaction.

These expensive articles drew great sums from the Trustees; so great, that little was left for promoting other branches. But these articles being now far advanced, so as not to require much further support, it is the intention of the Trustees to promote the growth of our own flax with their utmost assiduity. This appears the proper time for encouraging that capital article, because a market is now provided for it, *viz.* a home market, which of all is the best; and no person can doubt of this market when he is informed, that foreign flax to the amount of £110,000 is yearly imported into Scotland.

The saving this annual sum to the nation, is not the only, nor indeed the greatest benefit that will accrue by promoting flax-husbandry. A manufacture cannot but be upon a precarious footing, when recourse must be had to a foreign market for the crude materials; and a nation must be upon a precarious footing, when it is in the power of foreigners, with a single *Fiat*, to starve a great proportion of its people, by withdrawing from them the means of labour. This observation is in part unhappily verified by the present state of our flax-commerce; for foreign flax has, within these seven years, been gradually so much raised upon us, that we pay now for it fifty *per cent* more than formerly. 2*dly*, for further encouragement to raise flax, the farmer may be assured, that our own flax, when skilfully managed, and the ground well prepared, is tough, compact, and smooth; and consequently, for thread, lace, gauze, cambric, and lawn, is better fitted than that of Holland, which generally is spongy and cottony. Scotch flax, when brought to its utmost perfection, may probably rival even that of Flanders. It is too good for Osnaburgs, which require coarse Russian flax.[7] The Dutch flax is only preferable for thick hollands. 3*dly*, all the labour bestowed upon foreign flax purchased by us, in preparing the ground, in sowing and pulling, in watering, grazing, and dressing for the heckle, is paid for by us. What a benefit to this nation must it be, to give bread to numbers of our own people, by employing them in that work? 4*thly*, as a considerable proportion of the flax we use is of foreign growth, and as the heckler and the spinner must pay money for it, the one is disposed to over-heckle it, and the other to draw it out into too fine yarn, in order to make the most of their money. This evil would be in a good measure prevented by having flax in plenty of our own growth; for the heckler and spinner would in that case use it freely, without labouring to draw it beyond its grist.

The Trustees, for these reasons, cannot direct their management to a more important object than to that of flax-raising. This indeed they had early in view, though they did not always hit upon the most effectual means. They brought flax-raisers and flax-dressers from Holland, Flanders, and England: they published directions for raising flax: they laid out money for breeding apprentices to flax-raising and flax-dressing: they encouraged the erection of lint-mills; gave salaries to stationed raisers and dressers of flax, and distributed heckles. The article last mentioned did good, and continues to do good: but most of the other articles were less

---

[7] [A coarse type of linen, woven in Scotland from flax as an imitation of Osnaburgs, a coarse German cloth, originally from Osnabrück.]

successful than was expected; because the Trustees, inflamed with the spirit of patriotism, made a more rapid progress than was consistent with the circumstances of the country. For one instance, it seldom happens that the best artists are moved by the hope of greater gain to desert their native country; and therefore to send some hopeful young men abroad to be thoroughly perfected in the art, is a measure more slow indeed, but always more successful. And had this method been followed, the superior skill of the men thus educated would have procured them good bread, without burdening the public fund with salaries. By neglecting this safe measure, there were few or no skilful persons that could be employed as stationary raisers and dressers of flax; and the Trustees were forced to take up with such persons as could procure the best recommendations; which generally proceeded from interested motives. The negligence, accordingly, and unskilfulness of their persons, ruined all.

One of the encouragements for flax-raising, was a premium of fifteen shillings upon every acre prepared for flax-seed according to a method prescribed. This premium was in effect putting the plough before the horses. It indeed excited many to sow lint-seed; but it was soon discovered, and might have been foreseen, that it was no sufficient encouragement, without providing a market for the flax when separated from the ground. The premium was not the half of the price of the seed: the product lay upon the farmer's hand, who had neither skill nor people for dressing it with stock and hand, lint-mills being at that time extremely rare; and, by their means, he was upon the whole a great loser by this premium.

Lint-boors[8] came next in play, by a hint taken from Holland and Flanders. The lint-boors there purchase all the green lint in the neighbourhood, water and graze it, and, if a word, prepare it for the spinner. This measure had a fair appearance; the Trustees were fond of it, and gave great encouragement for carrying it into execution. But this measure provided abortive; and it could not happen otherwise. It was not adverted to, that the culture of flax had

---

[8] [(Scot.) buyers of flax.]

subsisted in Holland and Flanders for centuries; and that considerable stocks were acquired by dealing in the different branches of the manufacture; part of which could not be better employed than in the lucrative trade of a lint-boor, surrounded with lint-fields, that save the expense of carriage. In Scotland every article was opposite. The manufacture was still in its infancy: no provision of skilful hands: lint-fields were thinly scattered; and it was a great burden upon the lint-boor to carry so weighty a crop from a great distance: no person had a stock for building houses, preparing canals, etc.; and had there been such persons, they would not have stooped to an inferior branch, while the higher branches lay open to employ their money upon.

The water-mills mentioned above, having a specious appearance, met with vigorous encouragement, and exhausted a great deal of public money. They were favourites of the country-people, by saving labour in dressing the flax; of which those were the most sensible who were acquainted with the slowness and fatigue of the stock and hand. It was not doubted but that these mills would incline every farmer to raise flax; and the Trustees were intent to accelerate that effect. A premium was notified of eighteen pence *per* stone for dressed flax of our own growth; which was confined to the three great linen counties of Perth, Fife, and Angus, because the public fund was not adequate to a more general premium. The success of this measure has been considerable; and would have been still more considerable, had a sufficient number of skilful flax-raisers been provided to instruct the country-people. The demand for foreign flax has greatly subsided in these counties; and in a few years will probably vanish altogether. This premium is now transferred to the counties of Lanark, Air, Renfrew, Dumbarton, and Stirling, where it will certainly produce the same beneficial effects; and the intention is, to carry it progressively through the kingdom.

For the same purpose of promoting flax-raising, quantities of lint-seed have been distributed, mostly in the Highlands, at first *gratis*, and afterward under prime cost. This measure had a good effect; but not equivalent to the sums bestowed upon it. For the farmers were not sufficiently skilled in preparing the ground: and they were not sufficiently anxious to be instructed, because they put little value upon seed which they got for nothing, or at a low price.

To remedy this evil, and to excite a spirit of cultivation, large premiums were given for the greatest quantities of flax produced upon an acre. This inflamed the industry of the farmer, and had the effect of procuring very rich crops. Some farmers became expert in dressing for flax-seed, and every one was fond to receive instruction; which was the great object of the premium. And yet the Trustees were forced to drop this premium, though with great reluctance, before the effect was completed. Industry was not so far advanced as to have reclaimed entirely the labouring poor from trick and deceit. The premiums were considerable; and if, upon the one hand, they promoted good husbandry, they, on the other, were a temptation to practise fraudulent methods for obtaining false reports of the quantities of flax produced. Such frauds are infectious; and the Trustees saw no other means to prevent the infection, but to withdraw the bounty altogether. There is no reason however to repent of having set this measure on foot; for though it may not have had the complete effect intended, it has undoubtedly promoted skill in flax-husbandry, and has also given sufficient evidence to the flax-farmer, that plentiful corps can be produced by high cultivation.

To proceed in the history of water-mills, experience discovered that they were attended with many inconveniences. The labour of carrying rough lint to these mills from a distance, came to be felt; as also the delay of getting the lint dressed, when the mill happens to be much employed. At the same time, the ordinary yield of this mill in dressed flax, is so much inferior in quantity to that of stock and hand, as to overbalance fully what is saved upon labour; not to mention the hurt that is done to the flax by the violent and ill-directed action of the mill. But the worst of all is, that the lint-miller, being under no check nor control, is tempted to defraud his customers of part of their dressed flax: and there are instances where the whole has been withheld from poor people, who it was thought would not have courage to bring a lawsuit. In many places there is not sufficient house-room provided for the flax that is brought to the mill; which, in a throng time, is often exposed to the air for months together before the miller can reach it. By these means, many lint-millers, I am far from saying the whole, are so sunk in their credit, that the farmers in their neighbourhood, rather than submit to the foregoing hardships, choose to abandon flax-raising altogether.

It is peculiarly lucky for Scotland, that, during this distressing situation, a flax-machine has been invented, that promises not only to remedy the said inconveniences, but also to advance flax-dressing to its perfection, with no less frugality than expedition. It is wrought by a single hand, takes up little room, is portable in a cart, and so little expensive, that three or four neighbouring farmers may have one in common for a mere trifle contributed by each. Its motion, at the same time, is so easy, and so much under command, that it is equal to stock and hand with respect to the yield of dressed flax, and also with respect to the gentleness of its motions. And taking into the account the expedition of this machine, which performs at least thrice the work of stock and hand, it must be pronounced a happy invention.

But we have not exhausted all that can be said in its favour, nor indeed the greater part. It is a capital advantage, that by it the farmer can superintend the dressing his flax without hazard of being cheated; and, what is still more, to get his flax dressed without a farthing of charge; which may be done by the following method. The flax is generally watered and grazed before the corn-harvest, or at least before it turn throng; and therefore may be done by the farm-servants, without interrupting other work. The flax may be housed at the end of a barn or other convenient place till winter, when the farm-servants, for want of light, are laid idle for some hours in the afternoon. During this time, the farmer and his servants cannot be more profitably employed than in dressing their flax; and the long nights afford more than sufficient time for dressing all that will be raised by a knot of neighbouring farmers. And even supposing the swiftest progress of lint-husbandry, every farmer may afford to purchase a machine for his own use solely, which may be employed but only during the dark hours of the afternoon, but frequently in day-light, when bad weather forbids all field-operations.

It is difficult, I am sensible, to entice people to employ in labour their accustomed idle hours; but address and perseverance will conquer many difficulties. And to operate this conversion of idleness into labour, there is one means among many that cannot fail of success. An article is commonly stipulated by farm-servants as part of their wages, which is, to have ground allotted them for sowing some lint-seed. They are generally put off with the worst soil, ill prepared: their crops are scanty: the expanse of dressing unconscionable: and stating every article by a just calcul, lint purchased at a market would come cheaper to them than what they thus procure. To engage them to work at the machine, no more is necessary but that the farmer take them in as partners. He has, for example, one hogshead of lint-seed; they another among them. Let it be all sown promiscuously in the same field; upon which, for his own sake, the farmer will bestow the highest dressing. It is watered in common, grazed in common, and dressed in common. When a division is made in proportion to the quantities sown, the poor labourers will rejoice in a double increase, purchased with a little additional labour, without any expense. Far from grudging this labour, their convening together in one place, with a fire for drying the flax, will afford them high amusement. Their labour will be easy, being divided among many hands, and it is fit that the farmer encourage them by taking part in the labour. A little care, at the same time, with proper lanterns, such as are used in heckling, will remove all hazard of fire; especially if the farmer himself take a narrow survey every evening when the servants leave off work.

Though the dressing of flax by this machine requires not more skill than by stock and hand, yet to show the management of it, particularly the dexterous handling of the flax, and to instruct the country-people in the preceding articles of choosing and preparing ground, weeding, pulling, watering, and grazing, it must be of consequence that the Trustees educate and employ in different parts a number of itinerants. This method of having the flax dressed by the country-servants in their otherwise idle hours, is far superior to that of lint-boors, even supposing we were ripe for these artists;

because by no other means is it possible to get flax dressed without expense, and indeed without any labour that can be reckoned upon. The expense of dressing has hitherto been a bulky article; and, considering the waste occasioned by water-mills, is perhaps not under 40 *per cent* of the flax; all of which may be saved by the machine under consideration.

Though few of the measures laid down by the Trustees for promoting flax-husbandry, have corresponded to the sanguine hopes at first conceived of them; yet these measures, imperfect as they were, contributed considerably to the flax-husbandry, which is farther advanced than is commonly thought. The value of flax annually produced in Scotland, after it is heckled, and ready for the spinner, may be pretty nearly ascertained as follows. The linen cloth now made in a year amounts to about £700,000; the value of the thread manufactured in a year cannot be less than £100,000; we are more uncertain about the quantity of the linen yarn exported; but we cannot be far wrong in stating it at another £100,000: and these articles amount in whole to £900,000. The next point is, to ascertain the value of heckled flax used in these different articles. Taking all the different kinds of linen cloth at an average, the value of the heckled flax may be about a third; and the proportion is rather more in thread. Of the yarn exported, the value of the flax cannot be much below the half. Joining these particulars together, the value of the heckled flax annually manufactured in Scotland amounts to £316,666. Subtract the value of the flax imported, and the price of heckling it, which is performed at home, computed to £125,000, the remainder, £191,666, or £190,000 in round numbers, is the value of the heckled flax from our own growth.

The purpose of this paper is, to encourage land-holders and farmers to apply vigorously to flax-raising, which, from what is said above, will appear equally beneficial to themselves and to their country. The Trustees struggled at first with many difficulties; the ignorance, the idleness, the indocility of the people. But happily these difficulties are in a measure surmounted. There are not wanting hands expert in raising and dressing flax; and the Trustees are bent upon increasing their number. To deal in this article, the encouragement must be great, when there is a market at home; and there must always be such a market while importation continues. The late premiums for the greatest quantity of flax upon an acre, have spread the art of preparing land for flax-seed; and reiterated experiments of the great produce of flax from high dressing, must rouse every farmer. The bounty of eighteen pence *per* stone for dressed flax, though limited to a few counties, will in time make its progress through every county; and farmers, if they regard their interest, will early prepare for receiving the benefit of this bounty when it reaches them. But of all encouragements for flax-raising, that of the new machine is in reality the greatest; by preventing a great waste of flax, by rescuing farmers out of the fraudulent hands of lint-millers, and by saving an endless expense formerly laid out for bringing lint to the heckle. In using this machine, a farmer superintends the dressing his own flax; it is done by his own servants when they cannot be otherwise employed; and it is done without expense. A crop of flax, of all the most lucrative, will by these means pay a considerable part of the rent, and make quicker returns of money than most other crops. Nor ought it to be overlooked, that the finding employment for servants when they would otherwise be idle, comes to the same with lessening their wages. The Trustees will scatter a few of these machines *gratis* in different quarters to serve as models. The machine is of easy construction, and can be correctly copied by any good workman.

It is zealously to be wished, and may reasonably be expected, that flax-raising will be greatly promoted by this machine, and will creep into every corner. But there is something still wanting to complete the encouragement; and that is, a ready market for the flax when it is prepared for the heckle. To that end the Trustees will consider whether it may not be proper to appoint lint-markets in certain counties, where buyers and sellers may resort; and to proclaim premiums for the greatest quantities of flax brought by individuals to these markets; and we cannot copy a better model than the premiums given for improving the staple of our wool, a regulation that has a fine effect. It is submitted, whether it may not be proper to begin with appointing three or four markets within the five western counties, which at present enjoy the bounty of eighteen pence *per* stone for home flax; because frauds that may be committed in claiming the proposed premiums, will be easily checked by the itinerant raisers and dressers of flax appointed for instructing the people in these counties. The Trustees will also consider, whether it may not be useful to proclaim at the same time flax-fairs in the central places of other counties, assuring the inhabitants of the premium in their course.

Having discussed flax-raising, we shall subjoin an appendix regarding the linen manufacture in general. As this manufacture is now advanced much beyond what is necessary for our own consumption, it is the duty of the Trustees to attend to the commerce of that commodity, and to use their endeavours to put it upon the best footing. To form a solid judgment upon this important subject, one must be previously acquainted with the manner in which that commerce is carried on at present; a brief view of which is as follows. London is our capital market: our linens are consigned to factors who fell upon time: to them it is of little consequence what the price be, or whether punctual payment be made, because they remit only what money they receive: commission and other charges are subtracted; which, with flow payments, is a grievous burden upon the dealers in this country. Of a commerce carried on in this manner, the natural and necessary effect with respect to the dealers here, is to confine it to those who have large stocks, and can afford to lie out of their money. This state of our linen-commerce must cramp the manufacture exceedingly: it is in effect a monopoly, and a monopoly of the very strictest kind, confining manufacturers to the wholesale-dealer who lives among them, or in their neighbourhood; for to try all the dealers where a single web only is to be sold, would be a great waste of time, with little prospect of a better price. There are, it is true, some petty dealers engaged in this commerce, known by the name of *hawkers*, who afford to the weaver some slight relief against this slavish dependence. These men lay out their small stocks in picking up linen cloth as it comes from the loom; which they also must sell to the wholesale-man, for they cannot afford to deal directly with London. But being better able than a weaver with a single web, to cope with the wholesale-dealers, and having more knowledge of the trade they generally obtain a more equal price, because they can change about if they be ill treated. Hence it is, that these hawkers are no favourites of the wholesale-men; which remarkably appeared in an application to the board of Trustees, inveighing bitterly against hawkers, and calling forth the vengeance of the board upon them, as destructive to the manufacture. It was possibly imagined, that the Trustees might have overlooked a maxim of which none are ignorant, viz. that the more numerous purchasers are, the better for the manufacture. But this incident may justly give reason to apprehend a combination among the wholesale-dealers to destroy hawkers: an agreement not to purchase from them, or to keep down the price, will produce that effect; and, by this simple means, the whole trade may be monopolized by the great dealers without a competitor.

The plan that bids the fairest for putting this commerce upon its most advantageous footing, is, that there be four linen fairs held annually at Edinburgh, as the most central place, each of them to continue four or five days; which will naturally produce a considerable circulation of ready money, and consequently afford the poor manufacturer some instant relief for carrying on his business. We indeed can scarce hope for commissions from wholesale-merchants in London, who have linen-drapers at hand to furnish them goods for completing their assortments. But an instance somewhat similar, gives encouragement to hope that other English dealers may resort to our fairs. When the commerce of black cattle was laid open by the union, our people carried their droves to England: but expense of travelling, and fluctuation of markets, made this a precarious and hazardous commerce, and reduced to bankruptcy many of our drovers. At length the prospect of choice and cheapness at a public market, drew down to this country the English dealers; and now the greater part of our cattle are sold at home for ready money. What reason have we to doubt, but that the English dealers will resort to our fairs for linen, as they do for cattle? There is no reason to doubt, provided we perform our part; which is, to be industrious in advancing our linens to their perfection. Our situation for such fairs is undoubtedly better than that of Ireland: for, supposing other articles equal, an English dealer, unaccustomed and averse to sea-voyages, will never prefer a perilous navigation before a safe and snug journey upon *terra firma.*

The trouble and expense of carrying home goods that remain unsold at a fair, have suggested a linen-hall, as a repository for such goods, where dealers may be provided during the interval between two fairs. But as it is difficult to foresee the fate of any new project, the Trustees, sensible of former disappointments, will probably be disinclined to adopt any expensive plan for a linen-hall. It is the safest course to be frugal in making the experiment: success may encourage them hereafter to be more bold.

One capital view of the plan proposed, which can scare fail of success, is, to rescue the poor weavers from the oppression of the wholesale-dealer, by affording them a choice of markets. If the price offered by their neighbour, the wholesale-man, be not thought sufficient, a number of them clubbing together may send their goods to an Edinburgh fair, under the care of one of themselves, or of any trusty person. This plan will be a signal blessing to the hawkers in particular: it will enlarge their field of action: it will make them independent: and it will augment their number; than which nothing can be more beneficial to the manufacturer. Every web is picked up as it comes from the loom, with a view to some little profit at an approaching fair; and in so swift a circulation, a very slender profit will content a hawker. This plan will be equally convenient for peddlers, who, instead of painful journeys through the country to make up their assortments, find at hand in a fair, every sort they have occasion for. Nor need we be diffident of commissions from Glasgow, Liverpool, and other trading towns on the west coast; because the dealers in these towns will find themselves cheaper served here than at London.

These effects of the plan are obvious at first view. But there appear other good effects, some more, some less extensive, that cast up upon further consideration. In the *first* place, frugal persons, who purchase for their own use, will undoubtedly resort to the public market, because ready money will afford them both choice and cheapness. *2dly*, buyers and sellers coming to be mutually acquainted, the reputation of the best artists will procure them private commissions for all the linen they make. *3dly*, these fairs will be a great means for improving the fabric of our linens. At present there is little opportunity for a comparative trial; but here manufacturers will soon be made sensible that they have little chance to vend their goods if the fabric be in any degree imperfect. *Lastly*, the quick circulation of money produced by these fairs, will enable the manufacturer to vend his goods at the lowest price; and the current price for ready money being thus fixed, must have the effect to regulate in some measure the bargains that are made upon time.

Every one who gives attention to what is passing in the world, must perceive the importance of the linen manufacture to Scotland. Like a stone rolled half-way up-hill, it must be pushed to the summit, or it will fall to the bottom, and involve all in ruin. Honest labour and unrelenting industry will push this manufacture to the summit, and produce a moderate degree of opulence, with its never-failing attendants, plenty and population. Opulence so acquired, being distributed through every vein of the politic body, serves to animate every member. May heaven avert from our thoughts the ambition of acquiring wealth independent of labour and industry; for profuse wealth, being always unequally distributed, never fails to sap the foundations of virtue, to erect a throne for luxury, and for depraved selfishness, which reduce a nation to an abject state of degeneracy, and terminate in a total corruption of manners.

Index of Names

Adams, John, 5
Aristotle, 103, 104, 107, 109

Bacon, Francis, 193, 195, 198, 204
Boswell, James, 1
Buffon, George Louis Leclerc, 93

Cicero, Marcus Tullius, 21, 78, 104, 105, 115
Clarke, Samuel, 145
Corneille, Pierre, 34, 35, 37
Craig, Thomas, 68
Cujas, Jacques (Cujacius), 184
Curtius, Quintus Rufus, 35

David I (Scottish king), 70
Descartes, René, 110, 176
Dubos, Jean-Baptiste (Abbé du Bos), 52

Euclid, 109

Ferguson, Adam, 98
Fleury, Claude, 105
Frederick II of Prussia, 225

Grotius, Hugo, 90, 180

Henry III (English king), 72
Herder, Johann Gottfried, 5
Homer, 48, 133
Horace (Quintus Horatius Flaccus), 44, 47, 49

Hume, David, 3, 116, 136, 157, 158
Hutcheson, Francis, 6, 20, 135, 136

Irenaeus (St. Irenaeus), 106

James I (Scottish king), 72, 74
James II (Scottish king), 73
James VI (Scottish/English king), 73, 74
Jefferson, Thomas, 5
John, King John of England (Johan sanz Terre), 67, 72

Kaempfer, Engelbert, 209
Kant, Immanuel, 5

Locke, John, 27, 122
Longinus (usual name for the unknown author of *On the Sublime*), 42, 44
Lucretius, 112

Malcolm II (Scottish king), 66, 69
Malcolm III Canmore (Scottish king), 70, 71
Mendelssohn, Moses, 5
Millar, John, 3, 175
Milton, John, 23, 39, 46, 47
Montesquieu, Charles-Louis de Secondat, 99, 212

Paulus (Roman jurist), 210
Petronius Arbiter, 112
Plato, 104, 105, 107, 110, 115
Plautus, Titus Maccius, 46
Pliny the Elder, 115
Plutarch, 117
Pufendorf, Samuel, 180

Quintilian (Marcus Fabius Quintilianus), 43, 49

Reid, Thomas, 3
Rubens, Peter Paul, 53

Shaftesbury, Earl of (Anthony Ashley Cooper), 6, 135, 153

Shakespeare, William, 33, 34, 36, 38, 39, 44, 47, 49, 50, 51, 52
Smith, Adam, 3
Spelman, Sir Henry, 68
Stair, Viscount of (James Dalrymple), 183

Tasso, Torquato, 36

Virgil (Publius Vergilius Maro), 41, 42, 43, 51, 52
Voltaire (François-Marie Arouet), 5, 105

William the Conqueror, 69

Zeno, 105

www.ingramcontent.com/pod-product-compliance
Lightning Source LLC
Chambersburg PA
CBHW070940230426
43666CB00011B/2500